GERRY ADAMS

Malachi O'Doherty is a writer and broadcaster based in Belfast. He is a regular contributor to the *Belfast Telegraph* and to several BBC radio programmes. He covered the Troubles and the peace process as a journalist and has written for several Irish and British newspapers and magazines, including the *Irish Times*, the *New Statesman*, the *Scotsman* and the *Guardian*. This is his seventh book.

Praise for *Gerry Adams: An Unauthorised Life*:
'A new comprehensive biography of the Sinn Féin president that is instructive, illuminating and well written. It provides an insight into one of the most controversial and enduring figures in Irish politics. Visionary to some, brutal warmonger to others, what cannot be disputed is his pivotal role in the peace process. This book makes an important contribution to understanding the man who embodies many of the contradictions of his era and country. A welcome change from the usual one-sided affair!' Professor Deirdre Heenan, University of Ulster

'O'Doherty provides fascinating insights into the life and times of one of the Troubles' most iconic figures. He offers unique perspectives on the growth of the Provisional IRA and its ideological struggles.' Martin Dillon, author of *The Dirty War*

'O'Doherty tackles his controversial subject with gusto. He seeks to shed light on the Sinn Féin president's remarkable career by interviewing political opponents, IRA victims, and old comrades about "the Big Lad". A feast of intriguing anecdotes peppers this book. O'Doherty adopts the innovative approach of psychoanalysing, in layperson's language, the enigma that is Gerry Adams.' Suzanne Breen

Gerry Adams

An Unauthorised Life

MALACHI O'DOHERTY

FABER & FABER

First published in 2017
by Faber & Faber Ltd
Bloomsbury House
74–77 Great Russell Street
London WC1B 3DA

Typeset by Faber & Faber Ltd
Printed and bound in the UK by CPI Group (UK), Croydon CR0 4YY

The author wishes to thank the Arts Council of Northern Ireland
for grant support received during the writing of this book

LOTTERY FUNDED

A CIP record for this book
is available from the British Library

ISBN 978–0–571–31595–6

FSC
www.fsc.org
MIX
Paper from
responsible sources
FSC® C020471

4 6 8 10 9 7 5 3

For Maureen

Contents

Illustrations

All plates © Malachi O'Doherty.

A shop on the site of the demolished Adams family house in Ballymurphy.

Gerry Adams addresses an Easter Rising commemoration in Roslea with uniformed IRA men in attendance.

Ann Travers, whose sister Mary was shot dead by the IRA, is now a campaigner for justice for victims.

Anthony McIntyre was a teenage scout for Joe McCann on the day he was killed. He later joined the Provisional IRA and served a life sentence for murder. He is now a critic of Gerry Adams.

Old republicans and members of D Company, the IRA unit once led by Brendan 'Darkie' Hughes, conduct a flag-lowering ceremony on the Falls Road, to remember their dead.

An Orange band honours a loyalist brigadier killed by the IRA. The parades have often been the focus of unrest.

Austin Stack's father was a prison officer, murdered by the IRA. Gerry Adams brought him to meet a senior IRA man, who read him a statement accepting responsibility for the killing. Stack is still critical of Adams and accuses him of withholding the name of the IRA contact from police investigating the killing.

A wreath to Gerry Adams's old friend Joe McCann is hung every year at the corner of Joy Street in Belfast on the anniversary of the day he was shot dead by British paratroopers in April 1972. A bullet strike is still clear in the brickwork below it.

Mairia Cahill worked with Sinn Féin in her teens and was raped by an IRA man. She claims that the IRA terrorised her.

Mairia Cahill crosses the Upper Springfield Road, past graffiti which appeared after reports that the IRA had investigated her rape by one of their members.

Michael Donnelly was a senior IRA man in Derry and knew Gerry Adams in Long Kesh during internment.

Richard O'Rawe was the press officer for the IRA hunger strikers in the Maze prison and accuses Gerry Adams of prolonging the protest.

Tommy McKearney was an IRA hunger striker.

Gerard Hodgins was the last of the IRA hunger strikers. He now accuses Gerry Adams of prolonging the hunger strike for political advantage.

A mural dedicated to Gerry Adams, erected on the Falls Road when he was arrested in May 2014. When he was released he asked for it to be removed.

Graffiti on the Falls Road on the day after Gerry Adams appeared on television reflecting on the life of Jesus.

Introduction

'Since I was little I have seen how you battle with your tears for me, and with a proud glad look, although your heart was breaking.'

This is the most tender language used by Gerry Adams in public. It is addressed to his mother, after her death in 1992, contained in a death notice in a daily Belfast newspaper, the *Irish News*. The words are not his own; they are taken from a poem by Patrick Pearse, the leader of the 1916 Easter Rising, written in Kilmainham Gaol as he awaited his execution. In choosing them, Adams appears to compare himself to Pearse, who believed that his own mother was 'proud' of him as an armed revolutionary and 'glad' that he had had the courage to lead the Irish Volunteers into battle.

Adams has made a slight change to the line. In the original, the phrase 'since I was little' is the concluding part of an earlier line and is followed by a colon. In his version, the battling with tears and the 'proud glad look' date back to his early childhood.

But the parallel between the two men fails on Gerry Adams's own insistence that he was never a member of the IRA. What was it that his mother had to be proud and glad of yet which would also fill her eyes with tears that she would have to battle against?

It was, perhaps, the danger he had put himself in, as a committed republican political activist, pursued by the police who took him for more and by loyalist paramilitaries who, believing him to be what he said he was not, plotted several times to kill him.

The parallel succeeds on one level that Adams would not have wanted to acknowledge back in 1992, before the Irish peace process was properly under way. Both he and Pearse redirected the republican movement against its deeper instincts. Pearse took the Irish Volunteers in Dublin to war against the orders of the national leadership; hence the Easter Rising. Adams coaxed republicans slowly into democratic politics against a fundamental principle that a reformed Northern Ireland was a trap to be avoided.

Adams was the Anti-Pearse.

The *Irish News* is where all the death notices of the Catholic community appear. The esteem in which clans and their widening circles of in-laws and friends are held can be measured by the number of tributes. Annie Adams got several columns over two days when she died, three days after a stroke at her own front door in Oakman Street on the Falls Road. Many of those tributes were expressions of support for Gerry Adams himself and for his four brothers and five sisters in their grief.

Gerry Adams had been at war for more than twenty years. He had been imprisoned for part of that time, had shaped a political party, Sinn Féin, out of the wider republican movement, and moved from being a committed supporter of revolution to challenging for power through democratic party politics.

Any mother might have worried about such a son, and about her four other sons who had all been active republicans and all spent time in jail. When the Adams family sang rebel songs together they changed the words of the famous 'Four Green Fields'. Instead of the mother in the song singing that she had 'fine strong sons', in their version she had 'five strong sons', Gerry, Paddy, Dominic, Sean and Liam.

Gerry was the one the world knew about.

At least three of them, including Gerry, had bullet wounds now. Dominic, the youngest, wrote in his prison memoir, *Faoi Ghlas*, that when he was arrested in possession of a pistol while targeting a policeman, his mother visited him in Crumlin Road Gaol to assure him that she and the whole family were behind him and that he had to worry about nothing. 'My mother had been a republican all her life and had never once attempted to dissuade her children from being the same. With great dignity she visited each of her imprisoned sons, as well as numerous other relations and friends who were held captive."[1]

As a child, Dominic had so much taken for granted that he would one day go to jail like his big brothers, that, helping his mother put together a food package for one of them, he had asked her to be sure to send him the same biscuits when his turn came. He was eight years old at the time.

And danger had come to the mother too, her home raided many times by British soldiers.

Her first stroke in the year she died followed a horrific shooting incident at the Sinn Féin offices when a rogue policeman killed three people. Annie Adams had visited the office that very day, to leave parcels for republican prisoners in Long Kesh (the internment camp that later became the Maze Prison). But for timing she might have been the target herself, as any of her children might; she might have seen the bloodied bodies in the reception area and on the stairs.

Her head reeled with the horror. She had had enough of it. Her heart was breaking.

The 'proud glad look' was taken away from her.

Gerry Adams says in one of his books[2] that her first stroke was actually triggered by the stress of what he calls an 'altercation' with police at her home, of which he claims 'they charged into the house shouting and yelling abuse' at her grandson, Patrick Mulvenna. In his account she 'ordered them from her home, but it was some minutes and further verbal abuse later before they left'.

That stroke was not a warning but a precursor. Annie Adams recovered in the following months, regained her speech, but then was felled again in September.

She was barely conscious in the ambulance with her daughter Margaret and her distraught husband, Gerry Adams senior.

Her son Sean was in the ward above her, under guard, a prisoner. Adams says Sean was allowed to visit her, handcuffed to a prison officer. He himself did not visit her and writes that he is sure that she would have understood that his presence would just have endangered her other visitors. She did not recover consciousness anyway.

She died in a routinely murderous week. On the same day, eighteen-year-old Peter McBride was gunned down by soldiers while running from them after they stopped him in Spamount Street. Two Scots Guards would be jailed for his murder and released in 1998.

Two days before Annie Adams was buried, loyalist gunmen murdered Charlie and Tess Fox at their home near the Moy, County Tyrone, for want of being able to get at members of the IRA in their extended family.

Annie was buried in Milltown Cemetery after a bilingual Irish and English mass in a packed Falls Road church, St Paul's. Sean was then given a twenty-four-hour parole to attend. A grandson, on remand in Crumlin Road Gaol on charges that would later be dropped, was released for six hours. These were people for whom the Troubles were family history. This was a tight religious Catholic culture in which, paradoxically, neighbours trusted each other not to steal from them yet one might be respected for having served time in prison, for having killed or tried to kill in the name of Irish freedom.

Annie Hannaway had married Gerry Adams senior just a year after he had come out of jail himself for shooting a policeman in the foot in a hapless ambush. Annie, like her young husband, was from a republican family with a history behind her of generations who had armed themselves, learnt to make bombs and been imprisoned for their cause. Adams senior, at sixteen, was hit by three bullets while trying to flee with a gun that had jammed. He served five years of an eight-year sentence, in the same jail where two of his older brothers were interned at the time. That was during the Second World War and the IRA was trying to win the support of Nazi Germany. They were all held in the grim old Crumlin Road Gaol in north Belfast, behind a wall of grey stone blocks. Another brother was in jail in Dublin.

The police had seen no harm in young Adams despite the fact that he had tried to shoot one of them. They were perhaps amused by his incompetence. They even gave him a character reference. The charge could have been attempted murder but they kept it to possession of explosives; that is, of the bullets in his gun, most of which had failed to fire. He was put to work in prison making shoes, a skill that might have earned him a living if he'd applied himself, but he was a troublesome prisoner. When he refused to wear prison clothes, insisting that he wasn't a criminal, the prison authorities registered him not as a protester but as a nudist.[3]

His son, also called Gerry Adams, was forty-four years old when Annie died and had spent his whole adult life in the republican movement. He supported and endorsed a street militia that grew from organising riots in the streets around their home in Ballymurphy to bombing the Conservative Party Conference and firing missiles at Downing Street and Heathrow Airport. Gerry Adams junior's whole life was about to be transformed.

Had he died himself in 1992, he would have gone down in history as a cheerleader for fanatical terrorism. Instead, his work since then establishes him in the minds of many as a creative peacemaker. He was fifty-five when his father died and in the intervening years he had taken the IRA into a peace process and ended its campaign. He had also learnt things about his father that appalled him. By the time the old man died, in 2003, having outlived Annie by eleven years, Gerry Adams and his siblings had come to accept that their father was not such a hero after all. Yes, he had been in the IRA. He had taken his place in history not just for botching an attempt to kill a policeman but also for founding a drinking club, The Felons, where you could only be a full member if you had served a prison sentence.

What Gerry Adams discovered about his father when he was fifty was that the old man had sexually abused children in the family. He says he confronted his father with that. By then he had also learnt that his brother Liam had raped his own daughter, which must have made him fear there was a contagion in the family.

So he was not tender in writing his tribute to his father, yet he carried his coffin, draped with an Irish tricolour, behind a lone piper, to St Michael's Church for a mass with three priests officiating. The old bastard went to his grave with IRA military honours.

And the tributes for Gerry senior came from a similarly wide circle to that which had honoured Annie. There were even condolences from the Workers' Party, the political outgrowth of a rival IRA that had feuded with the Provisionals. These mainly addressed their sympathies to Margaret Adams, one of Gerry's five sisters, who, alone among the Adamses, had stayed loyal to the original IRA movement, the Official IRA, 'the Stickies'. (The nickname was derived from the adhesive paper Easter lilies they were issued, to be worn on the lapel in commemoration of the Easter Rising of 1916; those issued by the Provisionals were worn with a pin.)

'Deepest sympathy to our friend and comrade, Margaret on the death of her father. Deeply regretted by the Turf Lodge branch of the Workers' Party.'

There were messages from the Clonard Monastery Youth Centre for Liam, who worked there. The Ardoyne and Ligoniel Ex-Republican Prisoners' Group, Amach agus Isteach ('Outside and Inside'), sent its sympathies and asked all ex-prisoners to attend. The message expressed sympathies to 'Gerry, Paddy, Dominic, Sean and the entire Adams family circle'. Liam, alone among the brothers, was unnamed, which suggests that he was out of favour.

In the years between his mother's heart being broken by the

violence and the danger, and his later accepting that his father was a paedophile, Gerry Adams changed and everything he touched changed.

He took the republican movement in the reverse direction to that in which Pearse, whom he'd likened himself to, had taken it. He had become a republican heretic and yet carried almost the whole movement with him. He had opted for the primacy of party politics over armed revolution.

Adams brought the IRA campaign to an end, entered protracted and faltering negotiations with the British government and other political parties, and he conceded constitutional arrangements that he had dedicated his life to opposing.

He overturned the republican project, reconfigured its vision and argued that peace was possible on political terms, without the need to kill and destroy.

And from being a fanatical revolutionary street politician in perpetual danger of arrest and assassination, he became a political leader with access to the British and Irish Prime Ministers and the US President, as well as a writer and a millionaire. He had become a statesman admired around the world, though still reviled by many at home who believed that thousands might have been spared horrible deaths if he had come to these ideas earlier.

Part One

Street Warrior

Chapter 1

With one child in the pram, the little girl Margaret, and her oldest, a boy called Gerard, on foot beside her, Annie Adams walked down the Shore Road but had little sense of being close to the sea. What gulls she heard were city scavengers more used to rifling through bins and feeding on chips thrown to them from wrapped newspaper by men in drab gabardines and cloth caps. She could smell kelp but it was mixed with oil and traces of sewage off the Lough, which received the effluence of the whole of Belfast.

The two other children, Paddy and Ann, were at home with their father. He had little to do but look after them but it wasn't certain he could even do that right.

Much of this area they passed through was Protestant. There were new estates going up where she would have scant chance of a house, even if she wanted one here. But the front of the road was commercial, little closely packed shops, newsagents and grocers, mechanics and hardware stores that sold coal scuttles, garden tools and hooks. There were drapers where she could buy furnishings and curtain fabric, perhaps material for a dress. The chemists sold nappies and Dettol; the sweetshop sold lollipops, the grocer candy apples.

She walked, often having to lift the boy and appease him. He was that awkward age, too old for a pram, too young for walking any distance, too heavy to be carried.

She crossed North Queen Street and under the railway bridge where the train for Derry thundered and rattled in one long scare that the children would find exciting when they were older. Past the top of Donegall Street and St Patrick's stone-built chapel, she was in more familiar, homely territory. Down that street was where the morning newspapers were written and printed. Up there, towards the mountain, was the Shankill Road. That was all Protestants too, but good for shopping.

Soon she was in Smithfield market among the pawn shops and the second-hand bookshops and chemists that sold things you wouldn't know what to do with. A fascinating place. There was a joke shop that sold stink bombs and messy puppy, and balloons a child could put under the cushion to make a sound like a fart when daddy sat down. Smithfield had always excited her.

Then there was another big church, St Mary's, and the holy shops that sold luminous statues and pictures of the Sacred Heart and a hundred different kinds of rosary beads, some dainty for a little girl's Holy Communion, to hang from her wrists, white to match her dress and the mother-of-pearl cover on her prayer book.

'Where do people find the money?' she wondered.

Up Divis Street past the hostel for the homeless and the police station, she was into the narrow and familiar Falls Road where she had grown up, played skips on the streets, met her husband.

Redbrick terraces fronted the main road and the even narrower side streets. Here the long low drone of the factory horn told hundreds of men that lunchtime was over. She crossed the road carefully at the top of Leeson Street as big double-decker trolley buses hummed past her. A child would be amazed at the sight of these, the long shafts from the roof of the bus that connected with the parallel overhead cables, the electrical sparks at the point of contact, the occasional accident of one of the shafts breaking away and the bus conductor having to raise it on a long pole and connect it again with more sparks, even flames.

They would go first to Granny Adams's house in Abercorn Street where her husband's mother lived. The house was small, two bedrooms upstairs and a toilet in the back yard where some of the neighbours kept a pig to fatten and kill. She would have been glad of a house like this instead of the flat the nuns rented to her up the Shore Road. She would be closer to her own family too.

The children, Gerard and Margaret, had both been babies here.

Annie told her mother-in-law that she had come over to the Falls to meet Councillor McKearney.

'We're hoping he can get us a house.'

'Where would that be?'

'On the new estate, up the Whiterock. Ballymurphy.'

'Dear God, you'll be as far away again in the other direction.'

'Not quite. And at least we won't be sharing a toilet with strangers.'

Ballymurphy was growing on the side of the same range of Belfast hills that overlooked the Shore Road. A fit walker like Annie could have hiked the eight miles between the two on her own. The houses were bigger than those in the little terraces of the Falls Road side streets, but the Adams family was already large enough to fill one and would get even bigger. Their white frontage was unlike the traditional bare redbrick; they had a third bedroom and they had gardens.

On Annie's first acquaintance with her new home it was a corner of a building site, beyond the farthest point to which the bus would then go. She could look back down the hill and see the whole city below her, the Castlereagh hills beyond it, and relaxed and solitary among them the grandiose Stormont parliament, looking like an ornament fit for a cake.

The estate was on the edge of the countryside and at the foot of Black Mountain, which looms over Belfast and casts an evening shadow over the streets below. In another city, Ballymurphy might have been selected for more middle-class development with its attractive elevation and scenery but it also had the drawback of being colder than the valley floor. It was the part of the city that the rains and chill winds from the north reached first. It would differ from the Falls in that it would be mixed at first, with Protestant and Catholic families living side by side.

On the day, months later, when Annie and Gerry moved the family in, they picked their way over mud to get to the front door. There was no path or demarcated garden. Many of the houses around them were still unfinished shells.

She and Gerry would have the box room, the boys, Paddy and Gerard, could go in one of the larger bedrooms and the wee girls, Margaret and Ann, in the other. They'd be fine at least until more children came along. In time there would be ten children arranged in bunk beds and double beds, in one room for the girls and one for the boys, with not enough blankets for winter, and their overcoats over them too. Ballymurphy was on the border between town and countryside. It was planned as a mixed estate and a British soldier lived next door to them. There, a child of the city might walk up the street to see green fields and gorse on the side of Black Mountain and the scar of the gully that divided it from Divis. That mountain is an escarpment that stretches like an arm guarding the whole city. It extends from the furthest estates in the west to the Lough shore. There were overgrown scars from Neolithic quarrying in front of them and further out the active quarry from which, occasionally, explosions of commercial gelignite were audible on the breeze from the west.

More used to playing the games of narrow streets, like swinging on lamp posts or handball against a gable, wee Gerard and his brothers and sisters now had access to a vast open terrain, slanting to the sky from just up the street. The mountain seemed to billow out towards them. There were fields to be played in, hedges to be scrambled over, ditches to get dirty in and trees to climb, all sitting like a huge picture before them.

Behind them were the closer confines of the estate. Ballymurphy was built to look good from the main Springfield Road and to hide its tight closeness in the interior. The family said the rosary most nights together when the children were young, in English. And on Sunday mornings Gerry Adams walked his wife and children down the Springfield Road to mass at Clonard Monastery, and afterwards to visit Annie's mother, Granny Hannaway.

Ballymurphy, with its few shops, was serviced by McKee's Van and the rag man with his horse and cart, and the Cantrell & Cochrane's lemonade man who would bring sarsaparilla in bottles to the doorstep the way the milkman did. A child could make a few pennies for sweets like the penny chew and the ha'penny chic by running messages. But long summer days might be spent just sitting bored on the kerb stone, looking for someone to play games with in the narrow streets, fantasising about the long tails of smoke that drifted across the face of the mountain from fires that came with the dry weather, lit perhaps by farmers, by vandals, by accident, by red Indians, the smoke sometimes coming down into the street like a subtle signal from another world.

Margaret and the girls on the street played skips, singing, 'On a hillside, stands a lady, who she is, I do not know. All she wants is gold and silver, all she wants is a nice young man.'

Gerard Adams, or little Gerry, was blighted by a terrible stammer that Margaret taunted him over. He was moved out of the house when he was eight years old, as more children arrived, and he later wrote that he was relieved to be away from her. Gerry and Annie sent him back to stay with Granny Adams in the little house where he had lived as a baby. He stayed there until he was twelve, when Granny Adams moved to Canada to join her son Sean who had settled in Toronto in 1953 with his young bride Rita Miskimmin. Sean and Rita then started a branch of the family across the Atlantic, which maintained a sentimental reverence for the republican culture too.

Gerry Adams went to St Finian's School on the Falls Road, which was run by the De La Salle Brothers. Margaret went to St Peter's School in Raglan Street, nearby, just as far from the family home in Ballymurphy, and she had her lunch every day with Granny Hannaway.

In those days a boy at primary school wore short trousers of standard grey cotton as part of the uniform. Wee Gerard walked to school with his legs bare even on icy mornings and often spent the first hour in class just warming up. The long trousers were saved until his legs were hairy, but an equally important concern was that small boys fell when they ran and played on the tarmac of the school playground and an expensive pair of trousers might be ruined by tears and scuffs. Nearly all small boys had a kneecapped look in those days, a dark scab healing on one knee, a fresh cut on the other. These were as routine as the runny nose, the home-done haircut and the tie that could never sit straight.

If he cried himself to sleep some nights, missing his mother, he doesn't say. His own account of this period presents his life as idyllic. He was slapped on his first day at the new school but says he remembers only the injustice, not the pain. He says in his autobiography *Before the Dawn* that Granny Adams was an important influence over him, and taught him never to trust a man who wouldn't take a bottle of stout. She also had 'an innate sense of dignity and respect for people'.[1]

He says also that his granny discouraged him from thinking politically. At that time association with the IRA was often regarded as an embarrassment and a threat to any chance of getting a good job.

There were shocks in his young life. The death of baby Brendan, one of twins; the deaths of Seamus and David just after they were born, buried in unmarked graves because they died before they could be baptised. But he presents a picture of innocence, completed by his own account of his first confession, perhaps inspired by one of Frank O'Connor's famous short stories on the same theme. Gerry's sin was cheating at marbles, however that was done.

School wasn't easy for him. He failed but was able to resit the eleven-plus and secure a grammar school place at St Mary's Christian Brothers' School further down the Falls Road in Barrack Street. This was a horrid, squat building closer to the city centre with no sports fields but another tarmac playground. Most of the teachers were Brothers, members of another celibate religious order who wore black soutanes and thin clerical collars that signified that they were not fully ordained priests. The school promoted Gaelic language and sports. Each teacher was issued with a leather strap. Slaps were applied to the palm of the hand, usually in twos, fours and sixes, depending on the gravity of the child's offence.

Others who were there remember young Adams as a poor mixer, a boy who during lunch break would stand aside from the boisterous melee.

Many of the Brothers at that time were republican-minded like Adams senior but they were southerners who were proud of the republican tradition that had secured independence for their part of Ireland and contemptuous of the survival of militancy in the North, which threatened instability. For them, the war was over. It had ended more than forty years earlier. For most southerners then, an IRA man had to have been part of the old campaign from 1916 to 1921 to be revered in memory. Those who preserved the militant tradition had been defeated in the civil war that followed a treaty and the partition of Ireland. Few wanted the resurrection of a defeated rump.

But beyond these arguments, the mission of the Christian Brothers, as they saw it, was to prepare boys for work in Northern Irish institutions like local government or the Post Office. Their response to the discrimination they expected against Catholics was to encourage boys to fit in and to thrive, not to stand ostentatiously over religious and political principles that would get them branded as troublemakers.

The order was also keen to recruit new members.

The second- and third-year classes were given routine lectures on the work of the order in the foreign missions, usually in Africa. They were encouraged to pray for guidance on whether God was calling them to this work and every year several boys would leave the school to continue their education in Dublin at seminaries in Baldoyle and Cabra.

One day, at the age of fifteen, young Gerry, back home in Ballymurphy, confronted his father, upstairs in the house in Divismore Park, with the news that he believed he had such a vocation. He felt called to join the Christian Brothers. This was close to the end of his father's authority over him but the man was furious and was heard shouting at him that it would suit him better to join the IRA and fight for his country.

Chapter 2

Jimmy Steele's reputation as an IRA man stemmed from his leading a raid on Campbell College in his twenties. That was in 1935. He and his men planned to steal guns from the school's armoury but the first part of the operation entailed a takeover of the gate lodge; the woman who answered the door to them screamed and armed police came running. There was an exchange of fire and the IRA men scattered.

Thirty years later, in the mid-1960s, Steele was still a member of the IRA on the Falls Road in Belfast and the organisation was facing the same problem it had faced in his youth, a shortage of weapons. It was now essentially communist, dreaming grandiose dreams of a future revolution in Ireland and fruitlessly asking China and the Soviet Union for arms. Steele didn't know it, but the Campbell guns would have been a lot easier to take now. Neither Campbell College nor anyone else in Belfast was worrying about the IRA any more. Two years earlier a campaign against country police stations along the Irish border had been abandoned for lack of interest. So those who guarded the guns in the Campbell armoury trusted to the peaceful character of the times and signed out the guns for boys to take for target practice above west Belfast. Will Glendinning was one of those boys. He was a cadet at Campbell College then. The school was the nearest Belfast had to a proper British public school. And he and his classmates would travel with the guns by bus up the Falls Road, past Jimmy Steele's home, past Gerry Adams's school, to a firing range on Black Mountain, each of them with a .303 Lee-Enfield rifle propped between his knees and with a large box of ammunition sitting in the aisle of the bus.

They didn't even know that there were IRA men who would have wanted those guns and the IRA men didn't know that those guns were there to be taken. They had only two .303s of their own. The police, who patrolled the area on bicycles, would have been little help, if Jimmy Steele himself had simply stepped onto that bus with a revolver, when it stopped at traffic lights, and finished the job he had taken on in his youth. The Adams and Hannaway families would have been interested in those guns. At fourteen, Margaret Adams had joined Cumann na mBan, a republican women's militia formed in 1914 to support the fighting men.

She and other young republicans expected the struggle for Irish unity to be revived some day and they wanted to be ready. For the present, the movement was social and cultural. Young militants met others from families like their own in which the tradition of fighting for Ireland was preserved and revered.

They were aware of the failure of the last campaign. Republicans of the time sang a ballad to commemorate Sean South, an IRA man killed while attacking the police station at Brookeborough in County Fermanagh in January 1957. The organisers of that campaign sought to avoid fighting in Belfast, conscious of the danger of triggering a sectarian civil war. After the partition of Ireland in 1921 the majority of people in the North, the Protestants, regarded themselves as British. The whole point of partition had been to preserve territory for these people. The republicans were part of the minority Irish Catholic population there, a minority of that minority.

The southern leaders of the 1950s campaign had seemed to imagine that a few hundred men with rifles could drive Britain out of the North and prompt northern Protestants to realise that they were not British after all but Irish. It was a foolishly conceived effort, though some republicans were happy to keep the tradition of armed resistance alive. So long as an IRA was in place, with command structures and a few weapons, a new generation of militants would have leaders to turn to and a framework to build on.

Through the republican movement, Margaret met a young activist called Micky McCorry when she was selling lemonade at a concert in St Mary's Hall to raise money for the National Graves Association, which preserved the graves of the republican dead. She would later marry him. Her republicanism was more cultural at first, just something you did if you came from a family like hers that had republicanism in its bloodstream. She went to Bodenstown and Edentubber, the places of republican pilgrimage, and joined the Easter parade each year to graves at Milltown Cemetery. She evolved from that into a political activist.

The young Adamses were aware of sectarian tension between the Catholic and Protestant working-class communities. The Falls Road, which was almost entirely Catholic, ran parallel with the Shankill Road, which was as solidly Protestant. In the mid-1960s there was free movement between the communities, essential because Catholics liked shopping on the Shankill and Protestants needed access to the hospital and the city cemetery on the Falls.

But this wasn't a stable peace.

In the spring of 1964 Protestant football supporters ran amok on the Falls Road near Granny Adams's house. Young Gerry was sixteen at the time and living back in Ballymurphy. Supporters of Linfield, a team that then recruited members only from the Protestant community, routinely crossed the Falls Road on their way to their ground at Windsor Park in the south of the city. On Easter Tuesday that year, after beating a Catholic team, Distillery, hundreds of men returning to the Protestant Shankill Road spilled over into side streets off the Falls Road and clashed with the police and attacked and taunted Catholic residents.

The Royal Ulster Constabulary City Commissioner, Graham Shillington, witnessed the eruption of the riot and told his men later that he would not have believed it could have flared up so quickly had he not seen it himself.[1]

Margaret Adams was working then to help the election campaign of Billy McMillen, more commonly known in print as Liam McMillen, or McMillan on his election posters. She folded leaflets into envelopes in the campaign office. Sinn Féin had been banned that year, so McMillen ran as an Independent Republican. He had no hope of winning the Belfast West seat and wouldn't have taken it anyway, for republicans had no wish to be part of a British parliament governing a part of Ireland. But electioneering provided opportunities for spreading the message. The office was a small house on the lower Falls Road, facing St Comgall's School, with a tiny kitchen and one large square room. Margaret Adams liked McMillen. He was intelligent and self-educated. He was also the leader of the IRA in Belfast.

The election was due in October 1964. Harold Wilson would take over from Alec Douglas-Home as Prime Minister. Kosygin would take over from Khrushchev in the Soviet Union. Left-wing politics was animated globally but the chief opposition to McMillen was not focused on his ideology, more Soviet than Labour, but on the Irish flag, which could not legally be displayed in Northern Ireland. The flag was positioned in his office window, beside his photograph and the traditional flag of Irish socialism, the Starry Plough, modelled on the constellation. Even the Head Constable at nearby Hastings Street police station, later Chief Constable Jack Hermon, said the flag was set back from the window and only visible to passers-by 'in a wholly Catholic area',[2] therefore, by implication, unlikely to cause offence. If it had been the Soviet Hammer and Sickle, there would probably have been no protest mounted against it, unless by Catholics in the neighbourhood.

Free Presbyterian pastor Ian Paisley was a performer with a voice like thunder, ever eager for a platform. Groomed like a film star and delivering his impassioned oratory in a slightly Americanised accent, he emphasised the most fundamentalist kind of evangelical theology in support of British unionism. The basis of his rejection of Irish republicanism was religious. Ireland, he reasoned, was under the control of the Catholic Church and the border that divided the island was the best protection against its insidious 'satanic' ways.

So Paisley threatened to lead a parade of his followers from the City Hall in Belfast to Divis Street to remove the flag from the Sinn Féin office himself if the police did not uphold the law and confiscate it. To avoid trouble the police upheld the law. The flag had invited the state to demonstrate its intolerance of republicanism and, as republicans saw it, the state obliged.

In one of the ironies of the Troubles, the man who smashed the window to take out the flag was a Catholic, District Inspector Frank Lagan.

The IRA would now take the opportunity granted to it, to prove that trying to avoid a clash with Paisley, by doing his bidding, was not always the safest route to a quiet life for a police chief.

Jack Hermon describes how the police were almost overwhelmed in several nights of street fighting around the Hastings Street police station near the McMillen campaign office. On the second night of trouble he was ordered to prepare for a republican parade along the Falls Road but to stay out of the side streets, though he could hear the preparations for a riot, the breaking of concrete slabs and cast-iron drain covers for ammunition. Republicans smashed the street lights and attacked the police from the cover of the early evening October darkness.

The police were dressed in raincoats and helmets and fought back only with drawn batons. Confronted with shards of glass from broken windows thrown at them, Hermon ordered his men to pick up the stones littering the street and throw them back in concentrated volleys.

It was a riot so fierce that some might die.

One constable got a foot caught in a drain from which the metal grating had been removed and was attacked by the mob but was rescued by a group of older residents in Percy Street. When Hermon visited one of the residents to thank her a few days later, he discovered that her family was republican and that her husband had served time for possessing ammunition. Hermon appears not to have been briefed on her republican links before visiting her. Concern among the police about republicans, even after days of rioting, was low.

Gerry Adams claims that the removal of the flag from the window of the campaign office during the 1964 election prompted him towards an interest in republican politics, so he followed his sister into the movement. He says the removal of the flag demonstrated to him that the Northern Irish state was 'based upon the violent suppression of political opposition'.[3] In his book *Falls Memories* he hints that he actively joined the rioting. People were getting arrested for merely watching and 'some of us', he says, learnt that it was 'as well to be hanged for a stone as a stare'.[4]

A year earlier he had wanted to join a religious order; now he wanted to fight for Ireland.

He might have heard his teachers in St Mary's urging boys to stay off the streets during the riots but he was already rejecting their type of accommodation with the state. He first joined the IRA scout movement, Fianna Éireann, at sixteen and was part of a wider excitement of interest in the IRA after the riots. Some of the boys around him were keen on trouble. Teenage members of the IRA attacked a British army recruitment meeting in St Gabriel's Secondary School in north Belfast, in 1965, smashing a film projector with hurley sticks. One of them was Joe McCann, then a close friend of Gerry's in the republican movement.

McCann was sentenced to twelve months' imprisonment that same year, with four others, when caught in possession of bayonets and information about police movements. Another of the five was Sean Murphy. Gerry Adams says in his memoir that he knew them all.

Conscious of how the flag in the window had riled unionists and the police and generated a fillip in support, republicans looked to the next opportunity to put it on display.

The IRA was preparing for a major celebration, the fiftieth anniversary of the 1916 Easter Rising, and wanted to remind the whole country of its existence. Its most high-profile stunt that year was the bombing of Nelson's Column in O'Connell Street in Dublin, though the IRA leadership disowned the action and threatened to discipline errant members who carried out attacks.[5]

The government in the North was receiving intelligence reports on IRA arms training across the country and feared that the street celebrations might be used as cover for an armed insurrection. The IRA had about three hundred guns of different types around Ireland, and ran regular training camps in counties Louth and Monaghan, near the border.

It wasn't only republicans who were gearing up for trouble as the anniversary approached. There were also groups of Protestant working-class men plotting to contend with the anticipated insurgency. Augustus (Gusty) Andrew Spence, a former paratrooper who had served in Cyprus, had become the leader of a revived and minuscule Ulster Volunteer Force. The original UVF had been formed to resist Home Rule for Ireland and had had its own baptism of blood in 1916, having formed into a division of the British army and suffered huge casualties at the Battle of the Somme.

Spence and his comrades were not up to the job of seeking out actual IRA members in the alien territory of Catholic west Belfast, so they murdered two random Catholics.

On the day of the celebrations in Belfast the train from Dublin was cancelled for fear that it would bring hordes of armed militants north. But there was no trouble. The parade stretched the full length of the Falls Road, with people still at the starting point, ready to move off, when those at the front reached the rallying point at Casement Park Gaelic sports ground. The illegal Irish flag was flown boldly, not just on the parade but from hundreds, perhaps thousands, of windows on the Falls Road and the surrounding housing estates like Riverdale and Andersonstown, though not so much in Ballymurphy where there were only about half a dozen flags on display.

Gerry Adams helped steward the parade up the Falls Road.

But his education as a republican in the movement clashed with the teaching at school. And political work wasn't making him any money so he dropped out of school and became an apprentice barman. His sister Margaret also left school early, at fifteen, to work in a stitching factory, though her parents wanted her to stay on. Neither perhaps felt they had serious career prospects in a Belfast where Catholics were discriminated against in employment. The schools' solution to that problem was to help young Catholics get a better education than the average Protestant was getting. The young Adamses were not convinced.

The first bar Gerry Adams worked in was run by Catholics in a Protestant area but he says he got sacked on the eve of the Twelfth of July, the biggest parading day for the Protestant Orange Order. He had asked for the trade union rate for working through a public holiday. Then he moved to a bar that was also one of the most exciting hubs of political and cultural debate in Belfast at that time, The Duke of York in Commercial Court. This pub was in a narrow alley off Donegall Street, close to the three daily newspapers in Belfast, the *News Letter*, the *Belfast Telegraph* and the *Irish News*. Adams mixed with journalists and others, and perhaps first acquired an early cynicism about reporters, watching them phone copy through on the bar telephone. He was impressed by some of the personalities of the time, especially Ralph (Bud) Bossence, one of the great humourists. Bossence was a daily columnist on the *News Letter*, a rotund and verbose man who enjoyed dramatic flourishes and wrote philosophical whimsy about life in the streets and pubs. He questioned why the rounds system applied to buying drink but not to buying dinner courses. He wrote about being a single man who enjoyed his solitude. Among his favourite subjects were his coal fire and his daily intake of Guinness. He wrote, 'I have a certain flair for a bottle of stout and I have persevered with it.'

Another journalist who was a regular in The Duke of York remembers exchanges between Gerry Adams and Bud Bossence. 'Bud would come in at about a quarter to five for his first pint of Guinness, which had to be poured with due solemnity. Often you would see him then in the snug in heated discussions about politics with Gerry Adams.'

Those journalists didn't know that this lanky young barman was now a republican well acquainted with the IRA leadership; some, had they known, would have been more intrigued than wary.

One of them says, 'You would never have seen him as someone who would be pissing up against the wall of the establishment. There were barristers who came in, like Basil Kelly, with his cashmere coat and satin lapels, and Gerry was always civil; he always gave people their place.'

Michael McDowell, son of Hamilton McDowell, one of Bossence's contemporaries on the paper, remembers Adams slipping him a free glass of orange juice when he came into the bar with his father. These stories describe the young Adams as well mannered, respectful and considerate. His own account makes claim to his having been mischievous.

When the Stormont minister Robert Porter came to the bar he sneaked out to stuff a potato up the politician's exhaust pipe, or says he did. And he stole a greatcoat left behind by a police constable. He appears to be wearing such a coat in old footage of a republican parade at Bodenstown commemorating the anniversary of the death of the founder of the United Irishmen, Wolfe Tone, where he was either oblivious to, or mischievously indulging, his looking like the enemy.

It is from these stories that we begin to get a sense of Gerry

Adams as a personality, someone who combined a sense of fun with deadly serious politics, someone who could mingle with the intellectuals of his day yet not feel remotely tempted by ideas that contradicted those which he had assimilated already.

Old Mr Keaveney who owned the pub told friends in later years that he had never liked Gerry Adams, 'because he never smiled'.

But the IRA organisation that Adams knew then was so sluggish and ill-informed that it didn't notice that all it had to do to arm every member and more with his own rifle was to stop the regular bus from Campbell College to the rifle range, step on to it and take guns and ammunition from schoolchildren.

Chapter 3

Two young men are strolling through the Falls Park on a spring evening, when the daylight lasts longer in the north. They are alike, both tall and lean; both wearing tweed jackets over woollen pullovers; both smoking. They are serious young men. You might mistake them for student teachers from the training college at Trench House further up the road. You would take them for respectable lads, not like the teddy boys who hang around the Palm Grove coffee bar, playing Marty Wilde or Tommy Steele on the juke box. Nor are they like hard-working men who have oil stains and callouses on their hands and take pride in their physical work. You might guess that they are into Joni Mitchell. They're not. Nor are they swearing like layabouts, 'fucking this and fucking that'. They are not talking about girls and what they would do to them. Joe McCann and Gerry Adams are friends bonded by politics and conspiracy. They are on their ways, together at first, to being the most dangerous men in the city, but they look bookish, as far from being beatniks as from being hippies or rockers. There is a cultural revolution happening for other young people; not for them.

At that time, they were activists in a campaign focusing on housing conditions in Belfast. Adams had a motorbike. It was a Honda 50. When he rode it to The Duke of York, with his brother Paddy behind him after he got a job there too, it looked like a child's toy underneath them, not like the big bikes of Elvis and James Dean. When the Crystals sang 'He's a Rebel', they weren't singing about Gerry Adams or Joe McCann. Some have traced the heady revolutionary spirit of Belfast at that time to the example of the Paris students and the many university-centred campaigns and anti-Vietnam War protests in the USA, Germany and Britain, but McCann and Adams had been organising squats and pickets before the protest wave hit Europe and London. Adams's idea of dressing daringly was wearing the stolen RUC raincoat. Both were still practising Catholics. McCann was a member of the Third Order of St Francis, a lay order attached to the Franciscans, and committed himself to daily prayer and submitted to a spiritual director or mentor. He spent weekends at their monastery in Newry, and actually dressed in the robe and sandals of the order and was cruelly teased by others in the IRA for being a 'weekend monk'.

So they were not bucking against their parents or the Church. Dylan's sons and daughters 'beyond your command' did not include them. They were entering a tradition of republicanism that had been held dear in their families for generations. That republican tradition was tilting to the left, and they were both happy with that, but when they went to Bodenstown to honour Wolfe Tone, they wore their Sunday best like nearly everyone else. And though they would have been among many people of their own age, they would have seen that republicanism was not a youth movement. They knelt on the grass and said the rosary and discussed a proposal before the IRA that a Presbyterian minister be invited to officiate at the commemoration of Wolfe Tone, missing the point that the leader of the United Irishmen had been an Anglican; that is, theologically closer to Rome than to Knox or Calvin.

Their tradition had its own music. At parades and rallies, accordion bands played marching tunes, but in the bars and clubs, when republicans drank together, and on their gramophone record players at home, they listened to rebel songs like 'Roddy McCorley', 'Kelly the Boy from Killane', 'Slievenamon' and 'Boolavogue', songs that recalled the United Irishmen and the Fenians. There were songs of the more recent revolutionary periods too: 'Kevin Barry' ('just a lad of eighteen summers, yet there's no one can deny, as he walked to death that morning, proud he held his head up high') in honour of a young IRA man hanged by the British during the war of independence, and 'Sean South of Garryowen', commemorating the death of an IRA man while attacking Brookeborough police station in 1957 during the border campaign. And there was a spate of militantly nationalist memoirs for the young rebel to read, reissued to coincide with the anniversary of 1916, including Dan Breen's *My Fight for Irish Freedom*, Tom Barry's *Guerrilla Days in Ireland*, Ernie O'Malley's *On Another Man's Wound* and many others. Older IRA men whose war was over could write frankly about their campaigns without the risk of being charged and imprisoned. Some, like Breen and Barry, emerged from their stories as gruff simple-minded men who lived with few if any doubts about what they had done; O'Malley was the one who could reflect intelligently on how the experience of war had shaped him. He was conscious of the hurt he had caused others.

The young republicans could celebrate past wars and hope for a future one, but they could have had little real sense that such a war was imminent. Their more pressing concerns were the campaigns against Ireland's entry into the Common Market and on housing. The republicans were part of the coalition of groups that formed the Northern Ireland Civil Rights Association (NICRA) in 1967. Adams's agitation over housing centred on the largest housing development in Belfast at that time, in the heart of the lower Falls Road, around St Peter's Pro-Cathedral. The housing stock there was poor and overcrowded and Belfast Corporation's plan was to demolish and build a twenty-storey tower block and several eight-storey rows of flats or 'maisonettes', Divis Flats. The Church was in favour of this plan because it retained the population within St Peter's parish, which subscribed to the upkeep of the bishop.

The IRA was one strand flowing into the Civil Rights movement. The Communist Party and the trade union movement also contributed significantly to the new organisation, as did political activists like Ivan Cooper, a liberal Protestant, and Austin Currie and others who would later form the Social Democratic and Labour Party (SDLP). The Civil Rights movement extended its appeal beyond republican interest to many who argued that what they were fighting for was British rights for British citizens in Northern Ireland. The central demand was for the reform of housing, employment and the local government franchise. Republicans, while campaigning for these demands, had different expectations to many of those they marched beside. They believed that the unionist state could not concede to their demands and that, in refusing to, it would expose itself as colonial and undemocratic.

Marches were planned by NICRA and by a student protest movement called People's Democracy. PD was a more ad hoc movement, without a formal membership system. It was started in Queen's University by left-wing students Michael Farrell and Bernadette Devlin and others. Younger and more confrontational than NICRA, it came out of the generation that had most to lose by discrimination, those who, in a fair society, would have expected their education to open better opportunities for them.

The marches planned by both groups were promptly banned by William Craig, the paranoid Unionist Party Minister for Home Affairs, confirming young republicans like Gerry Adams and Joe McCann in their vision of the state as inherently dictatorial.

Many of the marches attracted young professionals and middle-class people concerned for their rights and prospects. They were not natural street fighters. People often turned out for marches in the rain or wintry wind in the high streets of busy towns, for gatherings that had an air of carnival to them, earnest in their insistence that Northern Ireland should be fairly run and should include them. A favourite slogan of the time was 'One Man One Vote'. They might be singing 'We Shall Overcome' or chanting calls for the Home Affairs Minister to resign, 'Craig Out!'

They did not see themselves either as the cutting edge of an insurrection or as dupes being toyed with by slicker revolutionary forces. They were often led by people who had futures in centre left political parties opposed to violence, who thought that capitalism would function better if Catholics were not discriminated against.

And in time, each march would predictably come to a barrier erected by the police, a line of men in black raincoats, with shining helmets and visors, ready to beat them back with their batons and round shields. The police themselves were ill-prepared for this. They did not have crowd-control training. They were not wearing flameproof clothing. And when the young activists and republicans opted for a fight, there was never enough of them to cope.

Usually the protesters would split before the challenge from the police, some content that they had made their point but not wanting violence, others going forward to berate the stolid and disciplined constables, push at their barrier and start a tussle that would often escalate into stoning and baton charges. Once, in Newry, protesters managed to pitch a police vehicle into the canal.

Sometimes the standoff between police and protesters would be observed by loyalists led by the rabble-rousing preacher Ian Paisley. These were often older people, men and women.

In Donegall Street in Belfast one Saturday afternoon at just such a standoff, some women with Paisley, behind the police line, flung racist taunts at the students of People's Democracy about their absent leader. Bernadette Devlin had recently given birth. 'Why have we not seen the baby?' they shrieked. 'It's because it's black, that's why.'

Unionism fractured under the strain of protest between slow reformers like the Premier Terence O'Neill and others like William Craig, his Home Affairs Minister, who feared that the Civil Rights movement was an insurrection in disguise.

In the first few days of 1969 a long march headed off from

Belfast to Derry, organised by the students of People's Democracy. Loyalists and members of the B Special Constabulary attacked them at Burntollet Bridge just south of Derry. Momentum was building towards a calamity.

Craig believed that the Civil Rights movement was the IRA in disguise. It being, therefore, the expression of the Catholic community, it had no right seeking to walk in areas that were predominantly Protestant. The Civil Rights counter-argument to this was that they were neither nationalist nor Catholic, but essentially secular and interested in rights for all. In essence, the Civil Rights movement concentrated on a Social Contract idea of citizenship rather than a patriotic one and called on the state to meet its responsibilities, to treat all citizens equally.

Some voices in unionism tried to correct Craig in his assumptions. The *Belfast Telegraph*, in an editorial, said that the government was not defending the Britishness of Northern Ireland by denying demands for the law there to be brought into line with that of the rest of the UK on local government elections and housing allocation.[1] It wasn't just the liberal unionist press that thought Craig should relax his opposition to the Civil Rights movement. Some senior police officers argued that banning the parades risked escalating street violence to a level they couldn't cope with.

Craig was right to observe that the IRA was involving itself in the Civil Rights movement but wrong to suppose it was wholly directing it.

A man who prefers to be called JL (not his actual initials), a Belfast republican who was in the IRA at the time, says that the IRA leadership actually instructed volunteers to vote non-republicans onto the NICRA executive and other bodies. 'When we arrived at a meeting we would be issued with a list of the people we were to vote for and some of our people weren't happy to be voting for communists, for instance, but we would do it. Because it was important to the IRA that NICRA should have a broad base.'

Civil Rights campaigners were not the only ones who wanted to parade on the roads to declare their politics. A popular opposition to them organised by Ian Paisley, the Paisleyites, set up rival marches to challenge them. And the traditional Protestant loyal orders, like the Orange Order, had thousands of parades every summer commemorating past battles, which Catholics often saw as triumphal irritants.

The loyalist parading tradition in Northern Ireland is routine and goes back more than two centuries. Drum and flute bands triumphantly celebrate Protestant victories in the seventeenth century and the sacrifice of the Ulster Division in the First World War. Lodges of stern men in bowler hats and orange collarettes march behind ornate banners. There is an air of drunken celebration and carnival, but with an underlying note of threat to enemies of the Union. Usually the parades are peaceful, but their season comes in like a tide every summer that lifts the passions around any other sectarian disputes that happen to be active at the time. In Derry in August 1969, republicans clashed with police when protesting against a parade of a loyal order called The Apprentice Boys, established in commemoration of apprentices who shut the gates of the besieged city in 1689. Once the riot was under way, huge numbers of local people from the mainly Catholic housing estates of Bogside and Creggan turned on the police too, ready for battle, and engaged them for days with petrol bombs and stones.

That riot had a festive atmosphere. The police had little prospect of achieving anything, either of making arrests or protecting the people and property any more effectively than they would have done simply by turning round and going away.

Gerry Adams says in *Before the Dawn* that he attended a meeting at the Wellington Park Hotel in Belfast on 13 August at which a tape-recorded message was played from the riot leaders in Derry. His sister Margaret and her boyfriend Micky McCorry were there too. The voice on the tape suggested a plan. Parades should be organised all over Northern Ireland to overstretch the resources of the police so that they would have to withdraw from Derry. Some accounts say that the Civil Rights movement was averse to protests being organised in Belfast, given the greater danger of sectarian clashes there, where much larger populations of Protestants and Catholics lived in neighbouring working-class communities. Others disagreed.

Gerry Adams says that he left the Wellington Park to make petrol bombs[2] and to organise protests on the Falls Road that would set much of the city alight. JL, the IRA volunteer, who was also on the Falls Road that night, says the IRA leadership summoned all units in Belfast to Divis Street, which extends from the Falls Road towards the city centre. His estimate is that about twenty-five IRA volunteers were under orders on the ground. Some of the IRA members brought guns from their local dumps and handed these to the leadership, who allocated them to men in designated positions.

They were preparing for serious trouble but within limits. Their young quartermaster in charge of the weapons was ordered to leave behind in the dump the only two .303 rifles the IRA had in Belfast.

Billy McMillen, who was directing the IRA's riot plan, appeared to expect a clash on a scale similar to the riots that they had fought five years earlier, after the police attack on his office to remove the Irish tricolour.

The republicans staged a march to Hastings Street police station where Joe McCann and another man tried to hand in a letter protesting against the heavy policing in Derry. The police station was a low redbrick structure. The front door opened onto Divis Street. When McCann and the protesters behind him were refused admission they marched from Hastings Street to Springfield Road station, about a mile further out from the city centre. It was a northern summer night and bright as day until after ten o'clock. The police officers in the station bolted the door and fired two shots, wounding two people in the crowd.

Gerry Adams says in his memoir that the RUC did not engage with the protesters on the first night of rioting and that he confronted a member of the IRA when he discovered that some of them were armed. The IRA man argued with Adams that he was there to defend the crowd if the police opened fire. Adams says he argued that in the crowd they wouldn't know who was firing, whether the police or themselves, and that they would only get people killed.

The IRA man said that he could not withdraw unless he had orders from 'Batt Staff' so Adams left to remonstrate with the IRA command to stand down the gunmen, given that none of them could possibly have experience of combat. There was no further shooting that night.

Next morning, Gerry Adams went to work at The Duke of York, though he'd had little sleep. While there a messenger from Billy McMillen called to say he was needed on the Falls Road. That was the end of his career as a barman. He never finished his apprenticeship. Adams says he went straight to a planning meeting with the IRA's Belfast leadership in Leeson Street but that he argued there against 'any attempt to militarise the situation'.[3]

That evening, 14 August, McMillen ordered a concerted petrol bomb attack on Hastings Street police station. He was fired by two ideas; one was that the IRA could prevent Belfast police from travelling to Derry by keeping them busy on their home patch. The other was the belief that if pressure was maintained at a pitch of intensity, the Irish army would intervene, and rumours spread that it was indeed ready to do so. If Irish soldiers crossed the border, invading British territory, that would have initiated a war between the Irish Republic and the United Kingdom, a desirable outcome for the IRA and the effective revival of the war for independence that had ended nearly fifty years earlier.

That night the rioting was heavier. The IRA men, supported by other young people who wanted to join in, gathered at Hastings

Street police station and battled with the police, each side more tactically engaged this time. The rioters threw stones at the police lines to tempt snatch squads to rush at them. Then they would fall back and lure the police into the range of petrol bombers on the roof of the 200-foot-high Divis Flats tower block, whose erection republicans had opposed but which they now used to stark tactical advantage. The petrol bombers dropped whole crates of petrol onto the roads to create pools that could be ignited with a single petrol bomb when the police charged into range.

The police were, in many ways, fighting the last war they had planned for. They used Shorland armoured cars, nicknamed 'whippets'. These were built on a Land Rover body and had been devised for pursuing IRA gangs through country roads. With the heavy machine guns mounted on their turrets they could fire across open fields. The RUC had been issued with these to address the particular problems of the IRA's 1950s campaign. They improvised with them in Belfast to try to break up the rioting groups by attacking them from side streets, to fragment the body of rioters and facilitate arrests by snatch squads on foot.

McMillen had few guns under his control. In D Company on the lower Falls he had twelve pistols, an m/45 submachine gun, two Thompson submachine guns and a Sten gun. These were weapons for close-quarter fighting and good for scattering a crowd. His decision to leave the two .303 Lee-Enfield rifles in the dump probably saved lives. He ordered men to other areas that he thought were in danger of attack from loyalists. He asked Gerry Adams to return to Ballymurphy with his brother Paddy to look out for a possible ambush from neighbouring Protestant estates on the other side of the Springfield Road.

Down on the Falls, after hours of attacking Hastings Street police station, and rioters trying to coax the snatch squads back into range of the petrol bombs from the flats, a senior officer came out to speak to a watching crowd on the city side of the station. He told them that their safety could not be guaranteed and urged the people to go home. As members of that small audience dispersed down Durham Street and up the Grosvenor Road to avoid the battle, the first shots were fired, including probably the one that killed little Patrick Rooney, aged nine, hiding behind a door in his family home in Divis Flats. The police had mounted a machine gun on the roof of Hastings Street station, firing tracer bullets. And though hell seemed to have broken out all over the city, the miracle, for those who heard it, was that so few died that night.

One IRA man who was there says that he was in a group that confronted twenty policemen advancing up Leeson Street to the Falls, to challenge the rioters from behind. The IRA threw one grenade and emptied a revolver at the police lines and scattered them. He says he was shocked that they had panicked and run away when they were much more heavily armed than the IRA men.

The IRA men in the crowd seem to have thought they were having another riot like the one they'd had in 1964 when they could humiliate the police, crack a few skulls and then go home to their beds. They torched several buildings on the Falls Road, including Isaac Agnew car showrooms. Some of the mills were set alight. JL, who participated in this, says, 'It wasn't a big plan. Our blood was up. Nobody told us to go and burn the showrooms, we just did.'

A crowd of Protestants on the Shankill Road came down through the adjoining streets behind the police. They fought with young rioters on the Falls, many of whom were not under McMillen's control. He was still clinging to the hope that he could have a battle with the police without a major sectarian riot. Some of the Protestants attacked Catholic homes and reached the Falls Road itself.

Brendan Hughes, who gave his account of that night to Boston College researcher and former IRA prisoner Anthony McIntyre, suggested that the death toll would have been much higher if he had had his way. He had brought an IRA man with the Thompson submachine gun onto the roof of his old school, St Comgall's in Divis Street, where the IRA man had orders from McMillen to fire over the heads of a loyalist crowd invading the Falls Road.

Hughes said he was urging the gunman to shoot into the crowd.

JL says, 'You have never seen a crowd scatter the way it will when shots are fired over it.' But he says some of the loyalists were persistent and McMillen gave orders to fire at specific individuals. Herbert Roy, a Protestant who had come down from the Shankill with the mob, was hit and killed.

Margaret Adams was on the Falls Road that night while her brother was in Ballymurphy. She was providing support and she helped an IRA gunman in St Comgall's who had some kind of seizure, perhaps a panic attack.

Her brother, from his position up in Ballymurphy, on that clear August night, though in the shadow of the mountain to the immediate north of them, heard the shooting and saw the tracer fire over the city. He also heard the commotion and the echo of gunfire from Ardoyne, seeming to come from the mountain itself. He had a view of the fires from the burning mills and the car showroom, the light of flames, the flares of petrol bombs, the sparks of bullets from Browning machine guns, and heard the rattle of the Thompson gun doing more to scare the loyalists than to actually harm them.

He had never heard or seen anything like this in his life before.

The police misread the situation, bad enough as it was. They believed that they were confronting an IRA insurrection. The loyalists swarming onto the Falls perhaps really did fear that the police had been overwhelmed and that the Shankill was exposed to an invasion by the IRA. The prevailing reality was chaos and confusion. Authors Eamonn Mallie and Patrick Bishop[4] say that there must have been many occasions when the police and loyalists heard their own side's guns from neighbouring streets and thought they were under attack. The tragedy was that the ill-equipped IRA had over-reached itself sufficiently to panic the forces of the state without having the resources to contend with them or the channels of communication that would be needed to reassure them. The Republican Labour MP for Belfast Central, Paddy Kennedy, phoned Robert Porter, the Home Affairs Minister, the one whose exhaust pipe Gerry Adams had jammed with a potato, and was told by him that an IRA uprising was under way and that Donegall Pass police station was under attack. There was actually no trouble on Donegall Pass, but men inside the station were listening to gunfire from the Falls, echoing off the mountain, and never having heard so much firing before believed they were a target.[5]

Next day on television, Porter was on the brink of tears, acknowledging that the police had lost the moment at which they might have resorted to tear gas and contained the rioting.

The republicans in action that night came away with a sense that they had protected the Falls against an appalling onslaught, a vision untainted by much doubt about whether they were right to start the riot in the first place.

Asked what would have happened if the IRA plan had worked and the police had simply crumpled and left the twenty-five IRA men and their rioting supporters to face the loyalist mob, JL says that undoubtedly many more people would have been killed. 'That's not to say that a lot of people weren't up for that; they were.'

On the following day British soldiers arrived in Belfast to keep the peace. They marched up Durham Street to the Falls with their helmets on and bayonets fixed as if they were going into battle. Their first job was to relieve the embattled and overstretched police but they failed to prevent a further loyalist attack on streets between the Shankill and the Falls, the burning of Bombay Street and the further escalation of a refugee crisis.

Gerry Adams wrote that the first sight of British soldiers angered him 'in a way which I couldn't fully comprehend',[6] suggesting that some atavistic revulsion had stirred in his folk memory. He wrote that one 'defender', enraged by the sight of

British soldiers, opened fire on them and wounded one of them.

Republicans who regarded the army as an enemy may have been angered by their arrival, but other images and reports from the time suggest that many Catholics on the Falls Road were relieved that soldiers had come in and stopped the rioting.

Chapter 4

Adams and McCann, with so much in common, went different ways after the shock of August 1969. Belfast was seething with apprehension that the violence would return and the republicans split in two between those who wanted to push for a full revolt against British rule and those who wanted to stick with the socialist vision and avoid sectarian warfare. Adams and McCann supported different factions, both of which were rearming and hostile to the other.

Adams insists still that he was never an IRA member but he was at least so closely acquainted with leadership figures that he was sharing some of their risks.

Hundreds of people fled their homes in riot-torn areas and took shelter in schools and with relatives until they could be resettled. Adams describes a pattern of chaos in a city in which all order has broken down. His father 'liberated' or looted a bread delivery lorry from Hughes Bakery to feed refugees. This will only have saved him the trouble of going to the corner shop and buying it, for normal life functioned around the riot-stricken areas. The only actual shortage at the time was of alcohol, for the Stormont government ordered the closure of pubs, paradoxically now blaming drunkenness for the trouble where previously it had seen conspiracy.

There was a prospect of Belfast returning to normality and calm in the days and weeks after August 1969 but the city had suffered a trauma that would not subside. The IRA was re-energised and hundreds of young men and women now wanted to join and acquire weapons training. They turned to the IRA for that opportunity and aligned themselves with a republican analysis.

But there were two analyses to choose from, and McCann chose one of them while Adams chose the other. McCann would stay with Billy McMillen, who wanted to avoid a sectarian war and unite the working classes into a revolution against capitalism. Others accused McMillen of having failed to defend the Catholics against the Protestant hordes and wanted to fight to bring down the government at Stormont and get rid of the Irish border. Gerry Adams was part of a new urgency within the republican movement. He was among those who wanted to shift the centre of decision-making away from the IRA leadership in Dublin to Belfast. This was the beginning of a split that would be formalised in an IRA Convention and a Sinn Féin Ard Fheis (conference; pronounced 'ard esh') at the turn of the new year.

In the autumn of 1969 the IRA moved 150 weapons from dumps in the Republic into the North.

The IRA in Belfast had difficulty with errant members who wanted weapons practice and, on at least one occasion, a group of men borrowed guns from its dump to practise with. One of the men was Liam McParland, an inactive member of the IRA's B Company in Ballymurphy. He was more than twenty years older than Adams and had been interned during the 1950s border campaign. Adams was sidelined by the leadership at the time,[1] perhaps in anticipation that he would go with the breakaway faction, but also because of his links to McParland.

McParland was believed to have taken an m/45 submachine gun or 'grease gun' and two pistols with him to teach younger IRA members how to fire them. Returning to Belfast one evening, his car ran off the motorway and crashed. He was badly injured. Adams has said, 'I was with him that fateful day. In fact, we changed seats not long before the car plunged off the M1 motorway just up from Kennedy Way at the entrance to Belfast.'[2]

McParland died of his injuries but the IRA refused to sanction a traditional volley of shots over his grave because of his involvement in borrowing guns without permission. The Provisional IRA's list of its dead in the tribute book *Tírghrá*, however, describes McParland as a member, though he died before the split, and records that he was 'on active service' at the time.

Around this time, Adams was suspended from his leadership role in Ballymurphy Sinn Féin. By his own account, he was being sidelined by 'the Belfast leadership' who wanted to impose their authority on Ballymurphy.[3]

But he was disliked by some of the senior IRA members in Belfast. A former member from that time remembers that even in 1968 one of the senior men, Malachy McGurran, had expressed suspicion that Gerry Adams was more interested in himself than in the movement.

Billy McMillen, on the other hand, had huge respect for Adams and saw him as a politically talented man who would lead the republican movement in the future. Despite all this political activity, Adams had to make a living and before Christmas he took a job with a bottling company, delivering beer and spirits to rural pubs. Political activism was still a part-time responsibility and a man had to earn a wage. It was hard physical work in the cold winter weather, stopping at pubs and stacking crates of beer and soft drinks onto hand trolleys and wheeling them to the pub storerooms. The draught beer barrels were awkward, too heavy to lift and hard to roll ahead of you, especially for a tall man having to bend to them.

He doesn't say much about this in his memoir but he has included a short story based on that period in his collection *The Street and Other Stories*.[4] Although presented as a piece of fiction it is a revealing story.

The first-person narrator recounts how he was paired with a Shankill Road Protestant, Geordie, to make pub deliveries first around Belfast and unnervingly onto the Shankill Road and later around the Mountains of Mourne, which provide the title for the story. The two men are wary of each other, conscious of the sectarian difference between them. Both of them know the sectarian character of Belfast pubs, the increasing tendency at that time for Catholics and Protestants to drink in their own communities and neighbourhoods. Too many pubs had been burnt out during the riots. Catholics who had worked for years in pubs in Protestant areas had been rejected by their own customers and had returned to the home patch for safety. This was a sensitive time for anyone to be crossing boundaries. The working-class pub was a place where men felt free to express their sectarian contempt, and a stranger walking into that argumentative space had to look out for himself and expect no mannered or contrived civility.

The story brings the two men into a quarrel. The narrator, like Adams, is a political activist who is taking a break. He is discovering that both he and the struggle 'appear to be surviving without each other . . . a big admission for me to make, even to myself.' When they have to go to the Protestant Shankill, the narrator is unwilling and apprehensive. From the Shankill side he is able to see the burnt buildings on the Falls Road from a different angle. Geordie takes him home. A soldier catches his eye and tries to be friendly.

But the crux of the story comes when they meet a drunk man in a pub and give him a lift home along the coast, round the Mourne Mountains. The man is a republican. The narrator and this man annoy Geordie by exchanging pleasantries in Irish. The man jokes that from part of the Mournes you can see long distances but you cannot see a border. He relishes the fact that even the 'Orange holes' have Irish names. Geordie is quiet but uncomfortable with this easy amity between republicans in his company. When the man has left them the two delivery men have a stand-up shouting match. Geordie sneers at their having spoken Irish. The narrator gives him a blast of his own republican ardour. Geordie rants that 'you', meaning the Catholics, may have the music and the names and even the mountains but 'we', meaning the Protestants, have everything else.

The narrator says Geordie has nothing and gets him to agree

that the people are entitled to their rights. And the sum of his case is that 'we can do better ourselves without the British', if only the Protestants would see that they are Irish too and that no one is denying them the language and the music but themselves.

In those days, at the beginning of his war, Adams appears to have believed that Protestants could be persuaded to change their minds about being British and to enjoy Irish music and learn the Irish language, that only some self-limiting obstinacy prevented them from accepting their Irishness.

Adams was in a tricky position now. Most of the young men like JL and Joe McCann who had come into the IRA around Billy McMillen after the riots of 1964 stayed with him in the Official IRA. And the McMillen faction would have been, in many ways, a more natural place for Gerry Adams too, alongside his friends, pursuing the socialist politics they had committed themselves to.

But even after McMillen's wing of the movement in Belfast accepted that they had lost the support of Adams he surprised them by continuing to turn up at political meetings. As formalisation of the split approached, McMillen's republicans met to plan their strategy. There would be an IRA Convention and a Sinn Féin Ard Fheis. The IRA would make the first decision and Sinn Féin, as customary, would endorse it.

Malachy McGurran was chairing a meeting called by the old guard to determine a strategy for the Ard Fheis, at which the split in the IRA would formally divide the party too. Joe McCann and Seamus Lynch were there and they were surprised to see Gerry Adams. McGurran even affected not to recognise him when he spoke to offer proposals. Adams claims that many of his former friends at the meeting supported his ideas but that McGurran's casting vote defeated it. But Adams had shown that he had the nerve to face those who would attack him, as blithely as if business was continuing on a normal basis.

The split was formally around questions of whether the movement should continue a policy of abstaining from the

British and Irish parliaments when it won seats and whether it should be part of a National Liberation Front, aligning itself with other political causes and trying to interest other groups in the republican analysis. Both of these projects were later advanced by Adams himself in later years, as crucial steps towards a peace process, yet he went with the faction that opposed them then.

There were concerns other than the ideological. In Dublin, Charles Haughey and Neil Blaney, members of the government, were offering money and guns to the IRA on the condition that it stop all armed activities south of the border and give up its socialist ambitions.[5]

The deciding factor in Gerry Adams's decision to go with the breakaway Provisional movement may have been family. The Hannaways and Gerry's father had sided with the defectors. Yet his sister Margaret continued to support McMillen. She was the only one in the family who did.

The mood in the Catholic communities, even as described by Adams in that story, 'The Mountains of Mourne', was now quiet, 'normal'. There was no apparent momentum towards warfare. Secretly guns were imported, groups were training; there were occasional riots and petrol bombings. The worst trouble was on the Shankill when loyalists protested against the reform of the police. Without insurrectionaries devising their own schemes and rallying their energies, the ordinary disinclination of people to storm out of their homes and clash on the streets, and jeopardise everything they have, would probably have stabilised society and even allowed time for political ideas to emerge on how to reform Northern Ireland.

The Provisionals were going to have none of that.

Chapter 5

Adams had a problem. He was a young and energetic politically minded republican with a vision. The very presence of British soldiers on the street, patrolling past his home, confirmed that vision. The old enemy was back. He had heard the story on his mother's knee as a child. That story had motivated his father and all his uncles, on both his mother's and his father's sides of the family. Ireland was not yet free. All of our problems stemmed from the unfinished business of the war for independence, which had left six Irish counties as part of Britain.

He passed the soldiers when he went for cigarettes, lines of them patrolling with long Belgian Self-Loading Rifles propped by the butt on a hip. That long rifle imposed a dainty swagger on a man. In their berets, khaki uniforms and big boots the soldiers looked incongruous and absurd. They didn't look fit for war. Some of them were weedy little men with specs. One in every line had a heavy radio pack on his back. He wouldn't be able to run far if there was trouble. Adams was contemptuous of them but some neighbours were civil to them. Some might say hello or stop and chat to them. Children would gather round them on the corner and ask questions about their guns, ask to see the bullets.

There was little chance of getting a revolution going against the soldiers if people didn't see them for what they were, a foreign invading force. And many did not see them that way.

Many Catholics in Belfast felt little animosity towards the army. But there would be occasional difficulties in the relationship for republicans to exploit. Bombay Street had been burnt by loyalists on 15 August and Catholic families had been driven from their homes on the very day that soldiers came into Belfast, unsure how to conduct themselves. Later other loyalist attempts to attack Catholic areas were robustly challenged by the army and the police.

The republican vision of the army as the enemy was not going to be credible if Catholics were content with the protection they were receiving. Two ingredients were needed for any formula for ending that confidence: a republican challenge to the army and a tactlessly heavy-handed response. The new Provisionals would provide one, the army the other.

Gerry Adams had an established republican grouping in Ballymurphy and he used it to organise protests against the British army base there. He has written about how he first encouraged a group of republican women to picket the local army base with a protest against the behaviour of soldiers towards them. Some in the IRA were later critical of the approach Adams took in Ballymurphy. Tommy Gorman (not to be confused with Tommie Gorman, a famous broadcaster) was later interned alongside him and noticed that those who knew him virtually revered him. 'They talk about him being a great strategist, exposing the people to the brutality of the British army. He told the IRA to leave.'

Gorman's criticism is essentially that Adams was more politically than militarily engaged. He says, 'He wanted to educate the people of Ballymurphy on British imperialism and they were going to get fucking gassed and their bollocks beat in because the IRA wasn't there to confront them. And people say it was all very strategic and all, fucking genius, how did he do this?'

So the question of whether Gerry Adams was an IRA leader is answered in part by some of his contemporaries in the IRA saying that he was not militaristic. He did not measure up to their idea of an armed republican taking the war to the British.

Gorman says, 'This idea that this was a strategy is a joke. I would rather have seen people out there hitting the Brits with Garands and submachine guns.' He claims that it was Gerry

Adams who prevented him doing that.

And what Gorman can't explain is how taking on the army in gun battles would have made life easier for the people of Ballymurphy.

Instead of attacking the British as the invaders of the area, as an imperial army with no legitimate right to be in Ireland, which is how he actually saw them, Adams organised protests over the way they conducted themselves. He challenged their hearts and minds approach and their management of disputes around Orange parades. He appears to have understood that the core republican analysis would not be enough to bring people onto the streets.

He met his future wife, Colette McArdle, while organising a defence of the virtue of the local women. He got the women to organise a picket of the Henry Taggart Memorial Hall where soldiers were based and where they ran a disco, inviting in local girls to meet the soldiers. He says this protest stopped the disco being held and started a period of 'low-intensity agitation through the spring of 1970'. It signalled to the soldiers that they were not going to have an easy, comfortable relationship with the community.

The local Provisionals staged a confrontation with loyalists over a parade of junior Orangemen from a neighbouring Protestant estate, New Barnsley. From the Orange perspective, this was a routine parade by a body of righteous and religious Protestants preserving tradition. Republicans viewed it as a cultural insult, a triumphalist reminder of past humiliations, particularly insensitive so soon after the sectarian riots of the previous August.

The Junior Orange Order Parade came out of New Barnsley onto the main Springfield Road that led south into the city across the Falls Road. Uniformed bandsmen marching in martial order led the lodges, groups of men in their smartest clothes and bowler hats, under big square colourful banners that billowed in the wind. But while this was a celebration of past wars it was not an assemblage of fighting men, though some carried ceremonial silver swords. The Orangemen were going to the seaside resort of Bangor in County Down to join the major Easter event. They could have boarded buses to take them to the railway station but they wanted to parade to the station along the main road, which would take them past Ballymurphy and other nationalist areas and across the Falls Road.

Young men from Ballymurphy assembled to attack the Orangemen. Adams says, 'Many who had been ambivalent in their attitudes to British troops until now became unambiguously hostile.' He reasons that this was because they had 'taken over the RUC's role as protectors of triumphalist marchers'. He acknowledges also that passions were raised by the manner in which the army had confronted the attackers, jeopardising the elderly and the unwell with their 'stupid' use of CS gas.

The Springfield Road would be a battlefield for weeks. The pattern of fighting was established on that first night. Soldiers would line up across the road with shields and batons. Men from the area would stone them. The stones would bounce off the Perspex shields and the soldiers would fire CS gas canisters back at them. On a night when the air was still, the gas would hang over the houses of Ballymurphy. The rioters worked out how to counter the effects of the gas using bandanas soaked in vinegar. Buckets of vinegar solution were set at the side of the road for people to use. The ones who were going to suffer most were the residents who were not rioting, who were sitting at home watching the riots on television as the gas seeped under their doors and into their living rooms.

These riots on the side of the mountain could be heard across the city and boys and men from neighbouring estates would travel to watch or join in. The army and the rioters met almost by appointment each night of that spring, though even Gerry Adams must have wondered about the commitment of those local fighters when they took a break to watch Glasgow Celtic play in the final of the European Cup on 6 May and lose to Feyenoord, 2–1 in extra time.

Gerry Adams describes how young rioters would lure snatch squads into traps, drawing them towards a cul-de-sac, enabling Adams senior and others to draw barbed wire across their only available exit. He says that when soldiers were stranded like this 'they encountered their greatest difficulties'.[2]

The local people, he says, organised against the army 'out of their own feelings of self-respect, outrage and resistance'. By his account, his own family suffered, though he takes no responsibility for that. Soldiers, he said, aware that he was a 'subversive', would taunt the family and shout his name in the street when passing the house. They fired gas into the house, making it uninhabitable for days and children had to be rescued by neighbours. He says his brother Dominic developed a stammer because of the trauma. His own stammer pre-dated this period.

The rioting was unpopular among many who did not want to see the estate ruined and the violence escalate. One night a group of women lined up across the Springfield Road between the rioters and the soldiers and forced an end to the fighting. Though the rioting was extensive and dangerous, no one on either side killed anyone on the other. The only death attributed to rioting in that period was that of the baby Francis McGuigan, who inhaled CS gas.

These were heady days in which rioting could almost be regarded as recreational, the outcome of a surfeit of energy in young men as spring settled in. Riots against the army were given the added potential for growth by the then custom on BBC television of announcing them through newsflashes. This practice was later dropped because it helped inform adventurous young people of the best places to go for a night's excitement throwing stones and petrol bombs at a line of soldiers crouching behind Perspex shields, and dodging the gas canisters fired back at them. Ballymurphy was setting a model for rioting that would be adopted across the nationalist areas of Belfast, but the IRA had not yet deployed explosives other than petrol bombs nor brought out its guns. Then, on 27 June 1970, after a day of Orange parades, in the worst violence since the army had come in, four Protestants and one Catholic man were shot dead by the Provisionals. Another Protestant was killed by a missile thrown during a riot on the Springfield Road. Describing the killings in west Belfast, Gerry Adams wrote, 'In this instance the IRA were ready and waiting and in the ensuing gun-battle, three loyalists were killed.'[3]

Far from being defensively 'ready', the IRA had attacked another Orange parade coming up the Springfield Road and had fought with loyalists for an hour before the army intervened. The one person killed there was hit on the head by a brick. The shootings were elsewhere, in north and east Belfast. The north Belfast shootings were described by Crown counsel in a later trial as a planned attack on a quiet area. Three men were each killed with a single shot to the chest. These were straightforward sectarian ambushes by the Provisional IRA. There are witness accounts of the other killings in east Belfast that describe sniper attacks by the IRA on Protestant civilians.

That evening loyalists from the Newtownards Road and the IRA in Short Strand in east Belfast, close to the River Lagan, fought with each other. Short Strand was a Catholic area backing onto the river, while most of the population along the Newtownards Road east of the city was Protestant. This was the area close to the heavy industry of the shipyard, the ropeworks and an aircraft factory, all of which employed mostly Protestants living in the rows of redbrick terraces off the main road. Closer to the river and the Albert Bridge were a few streets around Short Strand, and the Catholic church, St Matthew's. The violence of that night in Short Strand has become part of Provisional IRA folklore, which holds that a few armed men held back a rampaging mob set on burning St Matthew's. That version is contradicted by the fact that court hearings compensated the families of the Protestant victims on the basis that none of them were armed activists.

Gerry Adams believed when he wrote *Before the Dawn* that the Catholic who died in the church grounds was an IRA volunteer and his name does appear on a roll of honour. But he was not in fact a member. In their book *The Lost Revolution*, Brian Hanley and Scott Millar say he was a Catholic vigilante who was shot in error by the IRA itself.[4] So the supposed Protestant hordes had killed no one and the IRA defenders had only shot innocent unarmed Protestants.

The Provos were now killing, but it is safe to assume that most of those who did kill someone on that day had done so for the first time. The paramilitaries were gathering vital experience.

The McMillen faction was about to use its new guns too.

The Stickies, as the Official IRA was commonly called, had been as energetic in gathering weapons but had not yet had a serious confrontation with the army. Then troops, urged on by a new Conservative government in Westminster, raided homes in the lower Falls Road area for weapons and were rebuffed by gunfire.

This was another densely packed area of small redbrick terrace houses, around where Gerry Adams had walked to school as a boy. This was the territory on which the August 1969 riots had been fought, and though the Provisionals had split the IRA in protest against the management of that night's fighting and the perceived failure to defend the area against 'pogroms', the Officials were still the larger organisation there.

Fighting here was much more confined than it was in Ballymurphy. The rioters on the Springfield Road had space to retreat into, whether into the streets of Ballymurphy estate, into the fields at the edge of the mountain or just further back up the wide main Springfield Road and out of reach. They could hurl bricks and petrol bombs at the army lines with little danger to themselves and their neighbours. Down on the Falls Road, the side streets were short and narrow. Living-room windows of the little houses faced directly onto the footpaths with no intervening garden. This area was unsuitable for a gun battle, though there were wider spaces at Albert Street and Leeson Street where a sniper might have a better chance of hitting a target without killing a neighbour.

On Friday, 3 July, it was a glorious summer evening. People who lived in such small houses would often be on the street anyway, chatting with friends. A better time for a raid would have been when it was raining or later at night when it was dark, though in July it doesn't get dark in Belfast until well after 10 p.m. And in these early days of the Troubles people were excited by the prospects of a riot, even a little thrilled by the sound of gunfire.

Young men attacked the first army raiding parties with stones and bottles, then Official IRA snipers fired on them from several positions. The army drew back to reassess its strategy and, in the lull, members of the Officials positioned their snipers for battle. Army reinforcements arrived and waited outside the immediate area, in side streets off the Grosvenor Road. One awesome augur of the gravity of the crisis was the look of apprehension on the faces of those soldiers, crouching by their guns, waiting for the order to go in.

Then overhead a helicopter with a loudhailer announced that the lower Falls was under curfew. Those who could leave left, passed through the British army lines, and went home to listen to the gunfire from their beds. And the soldiers closed in and started to search every house.

The British army was now invading a residential area in a British city. Most people could only wait inside for the soldiers to come to them. Some had to move frantically and quietly to hide ms. Billy McMillen decided to use women to move guns in

f the team says she was told which house to go to and ns into the pram until it was so heavy that it was almost unmanageable. Her job was to walk the pram through the army lines and down the Falls Road to deliver the guns to Official IRA members in the Markets area by the river. She would have served about ten years in jail if she had been caught and her struggle with the unwieldy pram attracted the attention of a soldier. Perhaps as new to this as she was, he misread the problem and went to her aid and struggled with her to get the pram over a kerb and help her on her way.

On Sunday morning the army allowed people out to go to church and on Sunday afternoon a parade of women from Andersonstown, led by Provisional Sinn Féin leader Máire Drumm, approached the army barricade with food in prams for the besieged people and the army let them through.

The army had, by then, scooped thirty-five rifles, six machine guns and dozens of pistols. But things were looking good for the Provos. They wanted war and they were on their way. The Provo leadership, taking stock of their achievements that week, might have listed: a war commenced; the Stickies having been drawn into it; a general sense of escalation including increased pressure for the banning of Orange parades as likely irritants; a rift between the army and the Catholic community; and a sense that the Provos were forcing others to adapt to circumstances they had created. In addition, they had blooded new killers.

The Stormont government would, after the big parade of the Twelfth of July, ban all other parades that summer, a move that was unprecedented and has not been matched since. It also introduced a mandatory six-month prison sentence for disorderly behaviour, which would further alienate Catholics from the state when it was widely accepted that innocent people were being arrested and convicted, those watching riots being more vulnerable to arrest than those taking part in them.

The army General Officer Commanding, Lieutenant General Ian Freeland, announced on television that his soldiers regarded a petrol bomb as a lethal weapon and would shoot dead anyone seen preparing to throw one. Inevitably, when soldiers acting on this guidance claimed their first hit, killing nineteen-year-old Danny O'Hagan at the end of July, their account of the shooting was disputed and rioting followed in several nationalist areas. The army seemed only capable of making things worse.

Chapter 6

Both wings of the IRA, by the summer of 1970, had demonstrated their willingness to fight soldiers on the streets, with petrol bombs and with guns. And they were refining their weaponry, introducing grenades like nail bombs, which, lobbed from the middle of a rioting crowd, might be taken for just another lump of rock yet land at a soldier's foot and shred his leg.

To maintain the wars they had commenced, they needed the compliance of the people they lived among. The people in these communities had to be taught that they would be killed if they betrayed the IRA, exposed its arms dumps or gave information that would cause volunteers to be arrested. Both wings generated a paradox, insisting that they represented their communities while having to put those communities in fear of betraying them.

After the Falls curfew the Officials posted notices on walls of the area urging, 'Don't Fraternise'. They reinforced the message by humiliating women who dated soldiers, tying some of them to lamp posts and pouring pitch and feathers over them.

But in the summer and autumn of 1970 very few republicans in either faction had had direct experience of killing anyone, informer, liability, soldier or any other species of enemy or threat.

The first close-quarter shootings were, as we have seen, of Protestant men in Belfast on 27 June, after the riots against Orange parades on the Springfield and Whiterock Roads. The next first-bloodings of killers were in November and against Ballymurphy neighbours who had not joined the Provisionals and who were seen to be obstacles to their freedom to operate.

Alexander McVicker and Arthur McKenna had stopped in

a car to speak to a friend on Ballymurphy Road when an IRA man stepped out and shot both of them dead. Author Ciaran de Baroid says they were 'alleged criminals'.[1] Others say they ran a gambling outfit. De Baroid believes that the IRA was concerned to improve life for the community by removing criminals. The most significant result of the killing was a message to the wider Catholic community that the IRA was watching and would kill its own neighbours if it wanted to.

If the Provisionals had to monitor careless talk among teenagers in pubs and cull the criminal elements, they also had to worry about the Official IRA, the Stickies. Two armed militias living side by side would inevitably quarrel, whether over resources or girlfriends or conflicting strategies and ideologies. And when they did, the clash would be bloody and people would die.

Hanley and Millar's account[2] traces the first fighting between the militias to the shooting of John McGuinness, whom they describe as an Official IRA auxiliary. Provisionals thought McGuinness had access to weapons and wanted them. They had called at his house on the day before the shooting and been turned away.

This was in February 1971. McGuinness was walking home in the dark. A group of Provisionals accosted him at the corner of Westrock Drive. This time they were armed. Some of them wrestled McGuinness to the ground and held him while another shot him in the neck, paralysing him. The Officials understood that the shot had been fired by Tommy 'Todler' Tolan.

McGuinness would live another seven years confined to a wheelchair.

The Chief of Staff of the Official IRA claimed him as a member and accused the Provisionals of being 'more concerned with shooting republicans than fighting the British army'.

Now there was a feud on. The feud would be fought between neighbours and former friends. The Officials first retaliated against the Provos for the shooting of McGuinness by wounding a young Provo in the arms and legs. The Provos then beat up two Officials and that group returned in kind by beating up two Provos. This was all happening among people who lived in the same city, who could not return to barracks like the British soldiers to be relatively safe from attack. The targets now were men drinking in pubs, whose home addresses were known to each other, men who had been friends in school together, some of whom had been in the same companies in the IRA before the split.

Brendan Hughes wrote an account of the feuding on the website *The Blanket*.[3] Hughes was a prominent lower Falls Provo who would be a long-term friend of Gerry Adams.

The word came down from the leadership to all D Company volunteers to go into immediate stand-by mode and to open all arms dumps. A decision was taken by leadership to torch two drinking clubs run by the Official IRA . . . The Burning Embers was to be made to live up to its name. It was located directly facing Charlie's house. [Charlie Hughes, Brendan Hughes's cousin and Officer Commanding (OC) of D Company.] The assembled volunteers prepared to move out. They did so reluctantly. None wanted to be involved in fighting other republicans . . .

In The Burning Embers, Jim Sullivan, the Official IRA OC, was drinking with Paddy Devlin, one of the founders of the SDLP, who had himself been a member of the IRA when Gerry Adams's father was active. The Provos walked in with guns and petrol bombs in their hands and ordered them out and tried to burn down the club.

Or, as Brendan Hughes put it,

The volunteers asked all present to leave in order to avoid injury. They declined. They were then ordered to leave. They refused. At that point Charlie gave the order to 'burn it'. But he told all the volunteers to throw their petrol bombs behind the bar and not anywhere near the customers. The purpose was to frighten them out rather than harm them physically. It succeeded.

Paddy Devlin drove Sullivan and his wife home to Leeson Street. While inside the house his car was 'raked with machine-gun fire'.[4] He says that on the next day he got a gun licence and bought himself a Browning 9mm, which was his constant companion after that. Public figures and even journalists were arming themselves legally for their own protection.

Once the Burning Embers [Hughes continued] were well and truly on its way to becoming little other than embers the order was given for the Provisional IRA unit to move up to the Cracked Cup in Leeson Street, another of the Official IRA's drinking dens. But already alerted, the Official IRA were waiting to ambush the unit. A gun battle broke out and two volunteers were shot and injured.

One of the Officials who was there, JL, recalled the experience of having bullets pass close to his head. 'It's pretty hairy when you can't move and you don't know what else is out there.'

Brendan Hughes wrote:

Shortly after this incident a ceasefire was agreed and the volunteers of the Provisional IRA dispersed to their billets while a strategy meeting was arranged to take place in Squire Maguire's house in Cyprus Street.

Charlie Hughes was then ordered by the Brigade staff to put away weapons for the night and to prepare for negotiations to end the feud, but he retained his gun and 'feeling ultimately responsible for the safety of all volunteers in his area positioned himself behind a lamp post to give them cover. A shot rang out. The Official IRA had broken the agreement and IRA volunteer Charlie Hughes lay dead.'

The group of Officials who opened fire on Charlie Hughes was led by Gerry Adams's old friend Joe McCann. This was also, almost certainly, the first occasion on which McCann had killed anyone. Fighting that had been started by the Ballymurphy republicans had culminated in Adams's old friend killing a Provo.

A truce was established but there was one more shooting, in Ballymurphy. A group of Officials who had spent the night on Black Mountain, and had not been informed of the truce, encountered Provo Tom Cahill, brother of Joe Cahill, on his milk round the next day and shot and wounded him.

Gerry Adams says that many people were torn by 'conflicting emotions' during the feud.[5] He cites the old friendships that had been in place between senior republicans on different sides of the split, Proinsias MacAirt and Billy McMillen, and the fact that his own sister Margaret had joined the Officials.

He is coy in his writings about the fact that he was appointed by the IRA leadership to negotiate peace with the Officials. 'MacAirt suggested that I could help end the feuding and I found myself witness to a meeting between Billy McMillen and Billy McKee, at which an arrangement of sorts was hammered out.'[6]

He would, in fact, be a negotiator for the Provisional republicans in successive feuds with the Officials. These meetings would be held in Clonard Monastery in the Falls area and he would settle terms with other gunmen on how they might rub along together without shooting each other. By his own version of these events, he was, however 'acting as an individual' with 'no authority in the situation'.[7]

Adams was among old friends when he was negotiating in Clonard.

Clonard is the main monastic centre for the Redemptorists but their magnificent church serves the surrounding community. Less than a mile away from the imposing St Peter's Pro-Cathedral, it represents a separate Catholic authority in the area, adhering to a religious order rather than taking its lead from the bishop. The priests there were able to draw closer to the IRA and Gerry Adams because they did not implicate the bishop in their work and they were not vulnerable to being moved by the bishop if he objected to what they were doing. And the Redemptorists moved about among parishes and knew the wider scene in ways that a local parish priest would not. They ran the Lenten Missions that packed churches every night for a week of hell-fire sermonising in those days. To the outsider the contrast between the grandiose church and the little houses round it might have suggested a wealthy clergy draining resources from the poor, but the Catholics of Clonard liked the monastery and felt that the priests were more accessible and flexible than those appointed by the bishop. This is where the Adams family went to mass. It was a place in which Gerry Adams could comfortably be a practising Catholic while sparring with the bishop, William Philbin.

Indeed, Adams occasionally organised protests against Philbin.

Philbin had not been well prepared by life to be the spiritual leader of Belfast Catholics and a challenge to the Provisional IRA. He was a Mayo man who had found his vocation at the age of seventeen and for most of his ministry he was a professor of dogmatic theology at Maynooth near Dublin, training other seminarians for the priesthood. He was timid but he had seen it as his job to condemn the violence of the IRA and had dismissed 'immoral orders' directing the riots in Ballymurphy.

Adams knew exactly how to capitalise on that and embarrass him. He rallied the women he had used against the army in previous protests. He sent them to picket the bishop's home at Lisbreen on the Antrim Road, to make the point that a smug prelate who lived in isolated comfort in another part of town was in no position to comment on the community in Ballymurphy and its relationship with the IRA.[8]

The strategy was to assert proudly the case of the rioters, concede no apology or equivocation and dare anyone to refute the case. The picket of the bishop's house was led by Tess Cahill. Claiming to represent the women of Ballymurphy, she handed in a letter declaring their pride in the men and boys who fought the army.

The men you spoke of last Sunday are needed here to keep our estate free from crime, protect our homes and keep us from being trodden into the ground . . . peace protests carry no weight in this city. No one seems to care and so we rely on our own men and boys and back them in their efforts. God guide them all they are doing a great job.[9]

Adams's evolving political method was to assert that the community had a coherent voice and that he understood it better than his critics did. 'No one in positions of power can hide behind a smokescreen of selective condemnation or denunciation and expect to have any positive effect on any conflict situation.'[10] Yet 'selective condemnation' is what he specialised in himself.

The Provos killed their first soldier in February 1971. Between themselves and the Officials, they went on to kill nine soldiers that year before the state escalated its response with the introduction of internment without trial. The media had anticipated that the government at Stormont would eventually resort to its Special Powers as the trouble became more and more unmanageable. This left Adams vulnerable. On a bright August morning, British army raiding parties searched hundreds of houses across Northern Ireland and arrested men for interrogation. There were no charges against them. Soldiers pulled them from their beds, dragged them from their homes in their pyjamas and vests, and by the time most people woke up it was over and an apprehensive silence changed the normal feel of a summer day. Ironically, many of those the army had lifted had lived with no sense that they were in such danger, and those like Adams who were politically alert and knew they were likely to be wanted were able to protect themselves for a time by sleeping away from home.

Adams says that he was lying on the floor in the dark in a house in Ballymurphy's Glenalina Road, just behind his family home, with Colette McArdle, listening to paratrooper raids and occasional gunshots, and that he had whispered to her that he would marry her if they got out of there.

But he had work to do first, and that included generating a propaganda stunt to demonstrate that the IRA had survived the first internment raids.

Adams says he escorted Joe Cahill from a Ballymurphy press conference to put the Belfast OC of the IRA in front of television cameras even while the army was looking for him. This was an impressive stunt based on the principle that ultimately the IRA had only to survive while the British had to win. The IRA summoned journalists and camera crews to a school in Ballymurphy and there Cahill told the cameras that their losses had been 'very slight', thirty men arrested, two killed and eight wounded. (Adams, always an adept propagandist, afterwards took Cahill to meet a journalist.[11]) If those figures are correct then only a tenth of those lifted in the first raids were actual members of the IRA. Internment appalled the wider nationalist community. It had come about after the July 1971 withdrawal from the Stormont parliament of the SDLP, the political party representing most Catholics. The British army, they felt, had disgraced itself with several shootings of innocent people; they demanded an inquiry into the shooting of two young Catholics in Derry. When that was refused, the SDLP withdrew. Within weeks, internment was introduced. Soon rumours of torture surfaced. The SDLP encouraged public servants to strike in protest, and tenants to withold rent and rates.[12] Internment was exposed almost immediately as a failed strategy. It did not crush the IRA and it alienated the greater number of Catholics who opposed the IRA and whose co-operation would be needed for a political settlement.

Adams interpreted the nationalist anger at the suspension of the normal legal process as evidence that most nationalists now endorsed armed resistance as 'a legitimate tactic'.[13] He was wrong. Most continued to vote for the SDLP, which continued to plead with the IRA to stop. But the refusal of the SDLP to participate in the governing of Northern Ireland cost the Stormont parliament all credible legitimacy.

A second calamity, in January 1972, was Bloody Sunday. The army had deployed battle-ready paratroopers on the streets of Derry to suppress a banned civil rights march. These included the same men who had killed civilians in Ballymurphy during the first week of internment raids. In Derry, they killed fourteen unarmed people, causing deep outrage.

The IRA campaign was a burden on its own but the state was unable to secure the endorsement of those who opposed the IRA while it was suspending human rights and unleashing the savagery of the parachute regiments on the streets from which it operated. Yet the IRA was killing as many of its own members as the army was. Half of the IRA members who died in the early 1970s died in accidents, sometimes cynically described as 'own goals'.

Most IRA activity at this time was directed towards getting bombs into the city centre. These bombs were made in sheds and private homes in residential areas and then delivered to their targets. Those targets were mostly shops and bars, newspaper offices, government buildings.

Adams wrote in *Before the Dawn*, 'Belfast republicans were in the midst of the storm and, whether in armed actions or in accidents, or as victims of British or loyalist assassination, they were paying a heavy price.'[14] They were paying their heaviest price for their own inexperience and for the willingness of the IRA to get young teenagers to assemble and deliver these bombs.

As many IRA members were dying in accidents as by any other cause. Four boys aged between sixteen and twenty, Tony Lewis, Gerry Crossan, Sean Johnston and Tom McCann, blew themselves up in a house in Clonard Street in early March 1972. They were members of the Second Battalion. They had been making a bomb and had accidentally detonated it.

And others were in the 'storm' too, the people killed and injured by those bombs that got delivered to their targets, like Janet Breen and Ann Owens, killed by an IRA bomb in the Abercorn bar the previous week that injured 130 others, including two women who lost their legs. Two young women had delivered the bomb to the bar and phoned in a warning that came too late for the bar to be evacuated in time. Adams doesn't even mention these deaths or the ineptitude of those bombers in his memoir.

Chapter 7

Adams got married to Colette McArdle while living on the run and trying not to get arrested and interned. Margaret, his sister, also got married at this time to Micky McCorry, a member of the Official IRA. And in both cases, the traditional niceties were observed with the men formally seeking the permission of the women's fathers. These were people trying to overthrow the state but they were not rebels against a conservative social order.

And while they expected soon to be jailed or killed, they set up homes and imagined lives for themselves in which they had children; all this while never living at home but billeting in safe houses guarded by lookouts.

At times Gerry Adams is a bit glib and sentimental about the Troubles. For example, he tells a story about having to go out in the night to get ice cream for Colette while she was pregnant, and wondering how, if he was caught by the army on this mission, he would explain to others in the movement why he had put himself in danger.

But he may just have been propagandising for his own humanity. He does a lot of that in his writings.

One of his lighter yarns concerns the family dog, Shane, an Alsatian, which he says was kidnapped by the army from the house in Ballymurphy. Soldiers had been seen walking the dog around the estate, perhaps hoping it would lead them to him. One day, skulking round the city streets, Adams says he spotted an army foot patrol with Shane. He should have turned back and gone the other way. But he had a plan to recover the dog. 'They had him on a lead and I waited until they were a good distance from me before I whistled him, the way I whistled for him: one long, three short, then one long whistle, all in one breath; he went mad, broke away and came to me.'[1]

And he was able to run with the dog and take him home to live with him and Colette in their new home.

When he was eventually arrested in March 1972, in the week that the four boys died by their own bomb, he was sent to the *Maidstone* prison ship anchored in Belfast Lough. The prisons were full. The internment camp at Long Kesh outside Lisburn provided shoddy accommodation in crowded Nissen huts that had been built during the Second World War. The housing of internees on a ship had been tried before in Belfast in the 1920s on HMS *Argenta*.

Adams says the *Maidstone* 'sat in its own sewage'. It also sat in oil and waste from the city. This was on no scenic shore. The *Maidstone* was within sight of the shipyard and an oil terminal. The men heard the gulls but they were living with the noise and stench of industry.

Adams says he organised internees to make statements to the press about their conditions and bad food. The prisoners staged a solid food strike in protest against soldiers being mobilised in riot gear against them. Richard O'Rawe, who was also detained on the ship at the time, recalls 'a full-scale hunger strike, with food being thrown into the sea; it was awful'. Relatives made statements to the press, and media interest forced a change. Suddenly, says Adams, they had 'marvellous food', 'a whole side of ham glazed with honey', 'wonderful desserts'.[2] This is a curious note for Adams to strike. For once, he is ready to present the enemy as acting generously. He prefers to take the credit for winning a great feast for the men than to underscore again the suffering and injustice of life in resistance to British rule.

But Richard O'Rawe, who is no fan of Adams, remembers 'no big fucking change in the quality of the grub'. He says there would only have been two dinners anyway, at most, between the end of the hunger strike and the prisoners being moved to Long Kesh.

He contradicts other details in Adams's account. Adams says that he was the last prisoner to leave the ship when the prisoners were moved out. 'It's not true,' says O'Rawe. 'I was in the same helicopter as him and we were the first off.'

The theme of great craic continues through his account of the time in Long Kesh. Adams told Press TV that going to Long Kesh was like getting to Butlins' Holiday Camp. There he was reunited with his father and his brother Liam, where the men were so giddy at the sight of the sky over their heads that they fell into endless childish games of water-bombing each other. This extended to drenching men who had just changed into their best clothes to receive a visit. It was all just hilarious until an older man was brought in to impose order on them. Then the lads suggested they had another hunger strike to support Billy McKee who was starving himself in Crumlin Road Gaol for political status. That lasted fourteen days.[3]

The spring and early summer of 1972 had been turbulent for Gerry Adams. He had got married, lived on the run, visited his wife in family homes, which shifted too; Colette had conceived then miscarried; he had been arrested and beaten up; he had been through two prisons, one a junk ship moored in Belfast Lough, the other a wartime army camp; and he had participated in two hunger strikes. He was twenty-three years old and still he seemed to be coping, even impressing others with his clarity of thought and his mannered and disciplined demeanour. A possible exception to that is the giddy phase in Long Kesh when he was water-bombing his comrades and streaking naked through the cages. Perhaps he had reacted hypomanically, as anyone might, after a concentrated period of emotional turmoil, hunger and danger.

He writes also that he was taken by surprise when he was called to the gate for release, to be met by Marian and Dolours Price, two members of the IRA who would later be imprisoned for bombing targets in London in March 1973. They took him to be briefed on forthcoming negotiations with the British government and the newly appointed Secretary of State, William Whitelaw, now governing Northern Ireland directly.

The Official IRA had already called a ceasefire, though Joe McCann and others had opposed it. Joe was dead now, gunned down by paratroopers shortly after Adams was taken off the *Maidstone*. What chance was there he wouldn't be shot too in the same way? He can hardly have had high hopes of reaching his thirties.

The life that he had been living on the outside, before his arrest, was similar to that of McCann's. Anthony McIntyre, who was Joe McCann's lookout and scout as a fourteen-year-old member of the Fianna Éireann, says that McCann was heavily disguised on the day he died. McIntyre had spotted a uniformed policeman in Essex Street and visited McCann in his safe house to warn him. He escorted him from there to a pub. McCann parted from him and assured him that he would be OK. McIntyre was playing football by the Lagan when he heard the shots. 'I didn't take much notice.' Then later he met the woman who sheltered McCann. She was distressed. 'Joe McCann's been shot. Joe McCann's been shot.'

The Price sisters drove Adams into a city that was a war zone. They took him down the motorway past the spot where two years earlier, before the Provisionals had even been formed, he and Liam McParland had come off the road and McParland had sustained injuries he would not survive. They moved confidently through areas he could only have previously passed through in disguise, but he had safe passage now and could even go home to spend a short time with Colette. The army was still on the street, heavily armoured against attack. Paratroopers crouched in doorways and followed suspect cars in their sights, ready to blast them at the first suspicion of a gun barrel prodding through a side window.

The road outside Andersonstown police station had had large tarmac ramps laid to slow down passing vehicles, and they bore the scrapes of the exhausts they had already dented and battered.

Now there were even more ramps, lower but spread further. The city was sculpted for defence, with high fences now built above the police station walls to deter grenades and petrol bombs.

Adams could see that the whole city was like a prison now, that everyone was nervous and in danger, that for a few days anyway he would be the only free person in it, that so long as no soldier was twitchy enough to shoot him on sight, he could deal with any who tried to arrest him with the simple news that he was on his way to talk to state officials.

For a couple of nights he was billeted in the home of the SDLP MP Paddy Devlin.[4] Devlin was a basic socialist who was contemptuous of sectarian warriors and he saw Adams as trouble. But his party had urged the government to meet the IRA to try to agree a ceasefire and now he had one of the negotiators in his home with his wife and children, and his own gun safely locked away.

Why Adams? Some of the internees he had left behind in Long Kesh asked the same question. Mick Donnelly, a fellow internee, put the question years later to Ruairí Ó Brádaigh, who had been a member of the IRA army council, and Ó Brádaigh told him that he didn't know who had picked Adams; he had thought a selection had been made by the internees themselves.

The British wanted a ceasefire. They had suspended the Stormont parliament in March 1972 and were preparing the ground for inter-party talks on a new way to govern Northern Ireland that would give more power to the Catholic community. They needed peace for those talks to work, so they had to talk to the IRA. One wing, the Officials, had called a ceasefire in May, ostensibly in response to the demands of the Catholic community, sickened by the burden of death and danger. That ruled them out of the negotiations and made it easier for the Provos to suspend their campaign and sit down to parley. The clubbable, plummy and supercilious William Whitelaw was now in charge, as Secretary of State, governing Northern Ireland like a Viceroy. He wanted to find a political solution. He also wanted to end internment and to head off a possible escalation towards what was now widely feared: open sectarian civil war.

He was prepared to trade with the IRA for peace and the prospects of a political breakthrough. Billy McKee was now on hunger strike for political status. Whitelaw could concede to that demand or something like it. He could end internment and release internees. He could offer a face-to-face meeting between himself and the IRA leadership. So he had much to barter with.

The IRA had objectives and things to trade too.

It was getting better at killing British soldiers as each month passed – eight in April, nine in May and thirteen already by 20 June. It would get another six before the end of the month, even with a ceasefire approaching. Surely, the IRA reasoned, the British would concede something to save their soldiers.

There had never been a time when the IRA campaign looked so much like a clash of armies. Against this, there was also a growing exchange of sectarian killings with the loyalists more active than before. There was also the routine bombing campaign. The Provos had been blitzing the business community and killing civilians. A problem for them was that they were killing as many of their own activists as the army were. And they were killing many of the Catholics they were pledged to be defending. One was Martha Crawford. She was hit in crossfire in Andersonstown and there was pressure on the IRA from her neighbours. This fitted with political pressure to stop.

The IRA wanted a commitment from the British that they would leave Ireland to govern itself as a unit. It wanted political status for prisoners. It wanted recognition of the IRA's legitimate right to be armed. And it could offer to stop killing soldiers and destroying property. Republicans could agree to call that stoppage a ceasefire if the army stopped all actions against them.

And the IRA had difficulties of its own. It needed to present a renewed justification for the campaign to the Catholic community, which was growing weary of it. So republicans couldn't simply refuse to acknowledge a political opportunity; they had, at least, to test it.

The British government sent two envoys to meet the IRA's appointed delegates. These were a fifty-year-old former army captain, Philip Woodfield, and Frank Steele, an MI6 agent. Woodfield had left the army after the Second World War and had had a varied career in the Home Office. One of his jobs in the mid-1950s was helping to prepare Nigeria for independence. Steele had dealt with Kenya's founding father Jomo Kenyatta. So both of these men had had significant experience unravelling colonial attachments.

Gerry Adams and Dáithí Ó Conaill, a senior IRA man, met them at the home in Derry of Colonel Sir Michael McCorkell who, like Woodfield, had served in the Royal Artillery. At the time of the meeting McCorkell, a Donegal man, was a colonel in the Territorial Army and an aide de camp to the Queen.

The IRA delegates were accompanied by a solicitor, P. J. McGrory.

Before the meeting, Billy McKee had called off his hunger strike in Crumlin Road Gaol. The British had agreed that the IRA prisoners would be classed as Special Category, a compromise on the demand for political status that had satisfied McKee. The British were at an immediate disadvantage now because they had delivered their main concession just to get this meeting agreed and to persuade Billy McKee to come off hunger strike when his health was deteriorating. Had he died before the negotiations got under way, that would have soured the mood of the Provisionals and made negotiation difficult, perhaps impossible.

So Steele and Woodfield walked into the living room to meet Adams and Ó Conaill, knowing that their best card had already been taken off the table. They were diplomats, men of cultured civility who would be pleasant in their manner, for the sake of the job at hand.[5]

At the start of the meeting, Ó Conaill and Adams tried to test their adversaries with a challenge. They asked Woodfield and Steele to call the prison governor and get a senior member of the IRA to come to the phone to confirm that their conditions had improved. Woodfield was wary. He argued that the negotiations had to be secret and that this would jeopardise that secrecy. The republicans conceded the point, but the British envoys must have wondered if Adams and Ó Conaill were trying to create a leak and a breakdown of the talks, satisfied that they had already got most of what they were going to get.

Woodfield patronised the republicans, teasing out the definitions of what they asked for. When they asked for assurances that British army harassment would stop, Woodfield explained that 'harassment was a vague term'. They boiled it down to a question of whether the army would seek to arrest those IRA members they had not been able to arrest before. Woodfield agreed that the ceasefire should not be used as a chance to make arrests. Then Adams and Ó Conaill asked if IRA members would be able to carry 'side arms' for their defence.

Woodfield tried to sidestep the question.

If they were stopped and found to be carrying arms, would they be arrested? I said that this was a question I would report back but that the object was to produce a situation as soon as possible when people no longer thought they needed to carry firearms and that if persons were going about on normal peaceful business they would not be subject to arbitrary stopping and searching.

At a later stage in the discussion Woodfield qualified this in terms which suggested that the army would not be obliged to stay out of any defined areas like Ballymurphy or Andersonstown. Adams and Ó Conaill offered to provide a list of sensitive areas for the army to avoid. The discussion was around the danger of riots being triggered by schoolchildren and then escalating.

Woodfield reported, 'We replied that any specific proposal

genuinely designed to help would be carefully considered but that there could be no undertaking that the Army would simply avoid being in areas listed by the IRA.'

Woodfield asked for the ceasefire to endure for ten days including two weekends before the IRA would meet with Whitelaw. Adams and Ó Conaill agreed to the ten days and also agreed that Whitelaw would be the judge of whether the ceasefire was holding. The two republican delegates then asked Woodfield and Steele to help them open discussions with the loyalists of the Ulster Defence Association (UDA), which was rapidly growing in Protestant areas and erecting barricades at this time.

Woodfield's report says:

The IRA then asked if the Northern Ireland Office would be prepared to use their good offices to introduce them to representatives of the UDA. They clearly recognised the UDA as a potentially dangerous power centre in Northern Ireland and implied that if a meeting could be effected they might get along better than some people would expect.

This was an outlandish idea and had the British gone along with it they would have confirmed loyalists' suspicions that ministers were in talks with the IRA. Woodfield reminded the delegates again of the need for secrecy.

Adams and Ó Conaill also asked for the release of Billy McKee and two Protestants who are not named in Woodfield's report, and they were told that this could only happen if judicial procedures decided that they had been wrongly arrested.

But the British delegates also tried to coax the IRA delegates into conceding beyond their remit. There must have been times in that meeting when the two sides were nudging each other, gaining a little familiarity, working for more latitude than formal engagement allowed.

Woodfield asked if it was possible that Seán MacStíofáin, the IRA Chief of Staff, might be left off the delegation to meet Whitelaw. He was probing to see if they would acknowledge that MacStíofáin was a difficult man; trying to compromise Adams and Ó Conaill by cajoling them into undermining the authority of their own Chief of Staff. Ó Conaill said that that idea could be considered and he hinted that MacStíofáin probably wouldn't want to come anyway, but MacStíofáin would join the delegation and, by Adams's account, brought a pistol with him.[6]

So there were enough strong hints in the proposals of Adams and Ó Conaill that they were using the negotiation to stretch the British, to put them in difficulty, to exact from them a clear recognition of the IRA's legitimacy, its right to be armed in nationalist areas, and to make the terms of the deal public.

Yet Woodfield seems to have been overconfident that he was dealing with good-natured amateurs. He wrote in his report, before the commencement of the ceasefire:

There is no doubt whatever that these two at least genuinely want a cease fire and a permanent end to violence. Whatever pressures in Northern Ireland have brought them to this frame of mind there is little doubt that now that the prospect of peace is there they have a strong personal incentive to try and get it. They let drop several remarks showing that the life of the Provisional IRA man on the run is not a pleasant one.

Their appearance and manner were respectable and respectful – they easily referred to Mr Whitelaw as 'the Secretary of State' and they addressed me from time to time as 'Sir'. They made no bombastic defence of their past and made no attacks on the British Government, the British Army or any other communities or bodies in Northern Ireland. Their response to every argument put to them was reasonable and moderate. Their behaviour and attitude appeared to bear no relation to the indiscriminate campaigns of bombing and shooting in which they had both been prominent leaders.

So Woodfield, reporting to the Secretary of State, William Whitelaw, described Gerry Adams as a 'prominent leader' of 'indiscriminate campaigns of bombing and shooting'. Adams denies that he was ever in the IRA but, given that Woodfield was writing confidentially to his minister, one may assume that he was speaking out of genuine belief and with no intention to exaggerate or propagandise.

The envoys left that meeting impressed by the young 'Gerard Adams'. They perhaps hadn't understood yet how little they had exacted from him. Every time that Adams and Ó Conaill were asked to recognise British difficulty they opted for the least sensitive response, yet Woodfield construed their manner as obliging, amenable and naive. He and Steele went away trusting that they had been dealing with people who were much less experienced and adept than themselves. Yet Adams and Ó Conaill had located points of anxiety for the British and, instead of working with them to assuage those anxieties, had in all cases aggravated them.

The IRA announced its ceasefire four days in advance and kept busy right up to the midnight of the Sunday before it, killing five more soldiers and an RUC man between the meeting with Woodfield and Steele and the cessation. They timed the ceasefire to start on a Monday, perhaps specifically to deny the British their requirement that two weekends should pass in the ten days before the meeting with Whitelaw.

The ceasefire freed Gerry Adams to sleep at home with his wife but it was not a peaceful time. The two weeks it lasted were even more violent than those that preceded it, but this violence was purely sectarian; the IRA did not attack the army or bomb commercial property and the British conceded that this satisfied their conditions for a meeting with Whitelaw.

Woodfield had understood that the ceasefire would include avoidance of conflict with the loyalists, but the loyalists were not a party to the agreement and the IRA continued to exchange attacks with them. The British had put themselves in the position of having to stay out of any clash that might arise between loyalists and republicans, or at least to being free only to take on the loyalists.

The bottom line for Adams and Ó Conaill was that the IRA could conduct itself as a legitimate army and the lawful authority in republican areas and would act on that understanding, blatantly. That the government and the army did not then contest them on this amounted, in effect, to a huge advance in the IRA's claim to legitimacy.

As a demonstration of that legitimacy, the Provisionals set up roadblocks in Catholic areas. They shot dead two people who tried to drive through checkpoints, just the way the British had done. Bernard Norney was killed in Ballymurphy and Samuel Robinson in Cavendish Street. Adams had been incensed that British soldiers had previously shot two sisters he was friendly with in the same type of incident. Maura Meehan and Dorothy Maguire had been driving round the Raglan Street area sounding their car horn to alert IRA members to the presence of British soldiers. A foot patrol fired on them and shot them both in the head.

Adams had problems with one of the Ballymurphy IRA men, Jim Bryson, an eager gunman whose father had been a British soldier. Adams is rumoured to have been wary of Bryson. Bryson had been sceptical of the ceasefire and Brendan Hughes had had to visit Ballymurphy to meet him and persuade him to keep it.[7]

Bryson was at the heart of a dangerous confrontation with the army in Ballymurphy that came close to escalating into an exchange of fire. 'Some of the local units got a Land Rover, painted IRA on the side and began to patrol West Belfast.'[8] The army entered the estate to intercept it. Adams dealt with this, he says, by calling on the solicitor P. J. McGrory to intercede.

But there was no one to intercede with the loyalists. When some of them killed two Catholics and dumped their bodies in Westway Drive, republicans shot two random Protestants and dumped their bodies on waste ground off the Cliftonville Road. In the two weeks of the ceasefire, loyalists and republicans (including Officials) killed sixteen people between them, but Whitelaw accepted that the IRA was still on ceasefire despite this and his meeting with the leaders went ahead. He must have felt, however, that things were not exactly as Woodfield and Steele thought they had agreed.

The delegates for the London talks with Whitelaw gathered in Derry again. They were taken by car to a field on the edge of the Shantallow estate, a short distance from the house in which Adams and Ó Conaill had met Woodfield and Steele, and an army helicopter descended to airlift them to Aldergrove airport. Those flown to London to meet Whitelaw were Seán MacStíofáin, Dáithí Ó Conaill, Seamus Twomey, Ivor Bell, Martin McGuinness, who later acknowledged to the Saville Inquiry that he was a member of the IRA at this time, and Gerry Adams. When their limousine stopped in Henley-on-Thames to allow Seamus Twomey to find a toilet, Adams and others 'went for a brief dander'.[9] He was dressed down for the occasion, he says, wearing a jumper with a hole in it and they all enjoyed the consternation they created among their escorts.

The meeting was held in Chelsea at the home of Paul Channon, Minister of State at the Northern Ireland Office. On a T-junction, facing Chelsea Embankment, this was a location that was easy to secure. If anyone had been rash enough to shoot Whitelaw and rush from the building, he could only have gone in one direction, up Cheyne Row, against the flow of the traffic and therefore with no prospect of hijacking a lift. The republican team had brought Myles Shevlin, a solicitor, as a note taker. Whitelaw and Channon were accompanied by the emissaries Philip Woodfield and Frank Steele.

To start off, Seán MacStíofáin read the republican position paper, requiring the British to make a public declaration of the right of the Irish people, acting as a unit, to decide the future of Ireland and to withdraw all forces from Irish soil by 1 January 1975. They demanded a general amnesty for all political prisoners in both countries, for internees and detainees and all who were on the run. They also wanted proportional representation for all elections in the North and an end to oaths of allegiance to the Crown.

The IRA delegates had authority to negotiate a political compromise short of Irish unity and MacStíofáin is said by

Bishop and Mallie[10] to have been offended that they were not provided with conference facilities. Yet no one had elected the IRA to represent anybody. The leaders understood themselves to be the legitimate government of the whole of Ireland, drawing their authority from the 1918 general election, which Sinn Féin, at the time, had interpreted as giving it the right to establish a breakaway parliament. But neither the British nor the Irish government nor any of the Northern Irish political parties would acknowledge that the IRA leaders had that status and defer to them in it. They had nothing to barter with other than their power to end the IRA campaign and thereby enable others to negotiate a political settlement that would inevitably fall short of their aims. Republicans would have had no seats by right at those negotiations.

Adams understood the problem. The last time before this that the IRA had negotiated with the British, when led by Michael Collins in 1920, 'they had represented a revolutionary government with massive support'.[11] The men who met Whitelaw represented only an IRA that had no government behind it nor any electoral mandate.

Whitelaw wanted to have further meetings. Adams says that MacStíofáin was excited and thought they were going to have their demands met. Bishop and Mallie say that MacStíofáin believed that he could convene a conference of Irish organisations including the Protestant churches to discuss the future of the North and that this would create a momentum for change that would force the British to discuss withdrawal. This was fanciful nonsense.

The Provos could not have summoned any but their own members to a conference. But they had enhanced their credibility as a coherent force. They had proven that all the IRA guns could be silenced in a moment. They had shown that they could make the British treat them like a real army at war with them and that they could exact compromises in principle from them.

And Gerry Adams learnt an important lesson, that his best bargaining chip was the violence and the leadership's ability to contain it and that no assertion from a Prime Minister that he or she would never talk to terrorists need ever again concern him.

The IRA had no intention of entering a prolonged ceasefire. It understood, at the same time, that backing for a war against British rule was so slight now that it could not just resume the campaign on the grounds that the British had refused to withdraw. Many of those who supported the IRA sympathised with a need to defend communities or to punish the army for excesses or to prepare for war against the loyalists, but would never, in normal times, have supported an IRA armed struggle simply for British withdrawal. If the IRA was to resume attacks on the army and on civilian commercial property, it would have to have a local issue on which it could break the ceasefire and with which people who were not fully committed republicans would sympathise.

The Ulster Defence Association provided the occasion. It was threatening to block Catholics from being moved into houses in Horn Drive at the bottom of the Lenadoon estate in west Belfast, at the fault line between the Catholic and Protestant communities. The British army based at Woodburn held several rounds of negotiation with the IRA leadership at the end of the first week in July to try to persuade them that it would be better if the Catholic families did not take the houses. The IRA declined compromise. It could now break the ceasefire on an issue in which the problem was clearly the threat from loyalists and the failure of the British army to defend Catholics. That's what it chose to do.

On the afternoon of Sunday 9 July a lorry with furniture belonging to the families presented itself at an army barricade at the bottom of Lenadoon Avenue. It was a sunny afternoon. This was in a new estate of white houses with gardens in narrow streets, at the foot of Black Mountain, just south-west of Ballymurphy. Seamus Twomey, who had been part of the delegation to meet Whitelaw, demanded that the army give way. Both sides knew that IRA gunmen occupied a row of houses facing down the avenue, waiting for a signal from volunteer Tommy Gorman.[12]

Gorman got the nod from Twomey and waved to the gunmen. Jim Bryson was in a bedroom in a house with a view straight down Lenadoon Avenue. He had his Lewis gun. Suddenly the air was crackling with gunfire and the ceasefire was over. And this all happened in front of an audience of hundreds who had come to watch or support the families, who scattered now over garden hedges and between houses to escape. The men at the top of Lenadoon Avenue, Bryson, Tolan and others, were Ballymurphy republicans, old comrades of Gerry Adams, though he says that he was taken by surprise by the breakdown of the ceasefire. 'It more or less crept up and took me unawares, and then I was off out of the house and on the run again.'[13]

Chapter 8

Bloody Friday started after lunch on a warm and sunny day when office workers had just returned to their desks and counters after browsing shop windows or stretching themselves for an hour on the lawns around the City Hall. It was 21 July 1972. Belfast was always tense in those days but it was still in many ways a normal British or Irish city. People had either had their summer holiday and were settling back into their routines or they were still looking forward to getting away, to Spain if they could afford it. The sound of the first bomb would merely have been a little disheartening for most if they were not close enough to have been stunned to silence by the loudness of it, thrown off their feet if they were closer still, or worse, scalded or felled or ripped by shrapnel.

In their offices they were safe so long as they were not directly hit. But there were people in Belfast then who had been close to bombs before and some of them had started screaming and would fret the whole afternoon as blast followed blast. By the routine but inexplicable logic of violence, most of the bombs killed nobody, then one, at Oxford Street bus station, killed two soldiers and four employees of the bus company. Three of the dead were teenagers. Another bomb, an hour later on the Cavehill Road, killed two women and a man.

You could read the memoirs of Gerry Adams and hardly know that the IRA put more effort into its daily bombings at that time than to any other project, but he acknowledges that these bombings did actually occur. He says that the IRA gave adequate warnings to the police and the army but accepts that the intensity of the bombings was a 'mistake', whether the British were 'overstretched' or 'failed to act in relation to two of the bombs'.[1]

The Provos detonated twenty-six bombs in less than ninety minutes on Bloody Friday and blamed the police and the army for the deaths, arguing that they should have been able to evacuate people in time at every location. In fact, the IRA had come close to managing the day's attacks without deaths and on the following day it planted several bombs in Armagh without causing any deaths at all.

Some have viewed Bloody Friday as a calamitous blunder by the IRA. However, it demonstrated logistical co-ordination between IRA units right across the city. It provided the world media with images of Belfast as a city under attack, with pillars of smoke rising from several locations at once. That is, it presented an inflated image of the power of the IRA and the scale of its war.

Brendan Hughes, who later told the Boston College Archives that he had helped organise the bombing, gave a rationale for the city centre bombing campaign when speaking on a documentary film, *Behind the Mask*, in 1991. He said that the purpose was two-fold: to draw British forces out of communities to protect the city, thereby exposing them as more interested in protecting capital than protecting people; and to damage the economy.

He gave no credence at that time to the argument that the IRA might have created a bigger problem than the police and army could handle. 'They say they could not handle it because of so many bombs in the town? I don't believe that. They can walk into a place like Ballymurphy, completely seal it off and search every house in it yet they try to tell us that they couldn't empty the city centre.'

Just an hour after the last bomb the IRA Belfast Brigade staff press officer was calling newspaper offices to put the blame for the casualties on the army, which, he said, had been given enough time to clear the streets.

But Hughes told the Boston College Archives that the IRA had been 'over-zealous'[2] and that he regretted the deaths. Though he had taken the lead role and could have stopped the bombings had he wanted to, he said that those who agreed the plan at leadership level, 'Twomey, Adams or Bell', bore as much responsibility as himself.

Again, this counters the oft-repeated denials of Gerry Adams that he was ever a member of the IRA.

Adams was free and on the run again between June 1972 and July 1973. He might genuinely have thought for a time that he could bring the violence to an end and find a more stable life for himself, but his only available futures now were going to jail or getting killed. He was moving and working in secret and has left little or no evidence of his actions or his thinking during this time.

This was a significant period in the evolution of the IRA. The ceasefire had ended. The British government and the IRA leadership had each sounded the other out and had each returned to trying to defeat the other by force. What we find in the IRA strategy of the time is an approach that was sensitive to public opinion and geared towards showcase or spectacular acts of carnage, a leadership that was willing to deceive the people it presumed to be acting on behalf of, and which was careless with the lives of its volunteers.

The British army had anticipated a major bombing attack as a 'curtain raiser' on a renewed IRA campaign. A report to the Secretary of State from the General Officer Commanding, Sir Harry Tuzo, warned that the IRA would have gained in strength during the ceasefire and was likely to resume its campaign with renewed vigour. He estimated that the Provisionals and the Officials between them had two thousand men. The army should now, he thought, be ready for a major 'firefight' to demoralise and neutralise them. He did not think that British public opinion would accept a long campaign against the IRA and therefore recommended that the job of wiping it out should be completed in a matter of weeks.

He wrote, 'It is unrealistic to think in terms of total elimination; complete demoralisation and surrender is the best we can hope for.'[3]

This operation would be based on intelligence gained from selective arrests and interrogation. Interestingly, he says that interrogation was the best source of information about the IRA.

The massive offensive planned against the IRA would have to be accompanied by an information policy that would persuade Catholics that this escalation was in their best interest. 'Indeed our Information Policy would aim to attract support from Catholics in the North as well as in the Republic, for ridding society of a force which would otherwise bring about a civil war, with dire consequences for Catholics in Ulster, and every likelihood of spreading south of the border. The fact that low key military operations and sincere political proposals have been tried and failed must be emphasised.'

But the British escalation when it came did not proceed as Tuzo had foreseen. He had planned for a warning being delivered to the communities that an invasion was on its way. Schools and other buildings would be requisitioned for a major occupation of republican areas. And the army would engage the IRA in a firefight that might last days, inevitably sustaining higher losses than before.

The first part of the plan went as intended. William Whitelaw went on television to announce that the army would move against the IRA no-go areas and remove the barricades. It practically encircled west Belfast with army camps and occupied the Gaelic Athletic Association's sports ground at Casement Park. This gave it a reach inside these communities that enabled it not only to patrol the streets more thoroughly but to recruit spies.

The army was now sitting on top of the IRA. Having penetrated the areas in which it was based, it was better able to gather information, question people on the streets or during house raids, and recruit informants.

But the gun battle didn't happen. Whitelaw may have tempered Tuzo's strategy. There are key parts of it that were not conceded. For example, Tuzo wanted the army to be free to use heavy weapons like the Carl Gustav, a type of anti-tank bazooka, in offensive operations against the IRA. These were never used and it is alarming that the most senior army officer thought they could have been used in the housing estates of Belfast. But the IRA had no intention of standing its ground and fighting the British and getting wiped out anyway. By the simple expedient of not turning up for the battle it undermined the plan.

The flaw in Tuzo's reasoning was imagining that the IRA would conduct itself like an army holding territory. But the IRA lived in the territory, was part of the civilian population. Tuzo had argued that the Catholic population should be given a chance to reject the IRA or to vacate the republican areas before battle commenced. This thinking flowed from a misunderstanding, a sense that the IRA was distinct from the community.

Practically, all the IRA had to do to avoid the battle Tuzo had planned was to stay home and watch television, or go out to work as normal, perhaps take the kids to the seaside. These were full-time civilians and part-time guerrillas.

Tuzo had grasped that the IRA was not necessarily representative of the community but had failed to understand the implications of it being an integral part of it. Adams, on the other hand, more ambitiously sought to argue that the IRA was the community and was representative of it.

He knew better than anybody, however, that the IRA had always to be wary of the community for it could pool knowledge about its movements and leak that knowledge, even unintentionally, to the security forces. One part of the problem was careless talk; another was the diligent paid informer who could spy on neighbours in the IRA and report their movements. And then there were people who believed that their duty as good citizens was to pass information on anything suspicious to the police.

In the mythology of the IRA with which Gerry Adams had grown up, the informer was a loathsome traitor to his people who deserved to be executed. By virtue of being almost demonic he was also easily presumed to be rare. That drama had been played out in fiction, as in Liam O'Flaherty's 1925 novel *The Informer*. The IRA was finding out now that some people might be easily turned against it. It would therefore have to kill a lot of suspected informers to be safe from infiltration and it might find that difficult to explain to the Catholic community. For want of a way of confidently announcing that it had to kill local people, the Belfast leadership was approaching a decision to conceal the execution of informers by secretly burying them.

The sharpened focus on the threat of espionage and infiltration followed the discovery that the British army was running a group called MRF. There are different accounts of what these letters stood for, whether Military Reconnaissance Force, Military Reaction Force or even 'mmediate Reaction Force. This unit was, inexplicably, stirring up trouble by shooting at civilians on the street and, to more purpose, gathering information about the neighbourhoods through operating a laundry service. Adams says in his memoir that the phoney laundry would test clothing for explosive traces and even check the collar sizes of shirts against those living in a house to see if men on the run were taking refuge there.[4] It's hard to imagine how he could have known this detail.

The IRA attacked the laundry van, killing three soldiers who manned it, after two members confessed to being informers and explained the operation. Seamus Wright and Kevin McKee are the first known victims of the IRA to have been 'disappeared'. Much has been made of the disappearing of executed informers as a disgraceful breach with the tradition of the IRA, but at this time there was little or no tradition governing how informers might be dealt with. There may have been a reasonable calculation made by the IRA leadership that the public disclosure of executions would cost it popularity and respect in the Catholic communities. Not everyone would believe an IRA statement that a person had been working for the British or the police. The IRA had killed other Catholic civilians but most of them by accident in snipings or explosions. Where it had deliberately targeted them, it had sometimes represented them as criminals, as with Alexander McVicker and Arthur McKenna in Ballymurphy. Three times the IRA had just dumped the body and said nothing. That's what it did with John Kavanagh, Martin Owens and Sam Boyd, all of whom had had some links with the IRA either as vigilantes or members. Those killings have never been explained.

Some Catholics were killed in feuding with the Officials, like Des Mackin and Charlie Hughes. Only Edward Bonner, killed on the same October day that Wright and McKee disappeared, was named by the IRA as an informer at this time. One might cite that as evidence that the IRA was willing to kill informers publicly and without reserve or shame. Bonner's killers went into the club where he was drinking and lined the customers and staff up against a wall then picked him out and shot him in the head in front of the others. This was clearly intended to be a public statement. The IRA could hardly have been more open about it. Nor could it have done more to dramatise its warning to the community and to spread the message. But perhaps to have killed three in one day might have been thought too shocking, might have presented the IRA as more of a threat to its own base than it could risk, if it was to retain support. It might even have seen the shooting of Bonner as a means of deflecting curiosity about Wright and McKee. But the IRA was not candid about the degree to which it had been infiltrated and about the number of people in its own communities, turning against it, whom it was feeling obliged to wipe out.

The best-known of the disappeared is the widowed mother of ten Jean McConville. She was not a member of the IRA and, though the researches of Ed Moloney[5] persuade him that she was spying on the IRA for the army, other investigations insist that she wasn't and give credence to the suggestion that she was killed because she had gone to the aid of a wounded soldier. (Incidentally, the author's own mother tended to a wounded soldier in that same month in Riverdale, across the street from the safe house in which several IRA men were billeted. Grateful and tactless army officers later brought flowers to her at home but she was never threatened or abused by republicans for this.)

Jean McConville was kidnapped from her home and shot in the head and buried on a County Louth beach. Two of those involved, Brendan Hughes and Dolours Price, have since accused Gerry Adams of making the decision to have Jean McConville buried in secret, though he has repeatedly and emphatically denied that he had anything to do with it or indeed that he was ever a member of the IRA. Hughes told the Boston College interviewers, 'There was only one man who gave the order for that woman to be executed. That man is now the head of Sinn Féin.'[6] Adams was arrested and questioned for days about this and the Public Prosecutor found that the police had insufficient evidence to charge him. He has, of course, emphatically denied any involvement in the killing. He has described the killing since as 'wrong and a grievous injustice'.

Brendan Hughes did not disapprove of the decision to kill Jean McConville. He believed that she was an informer. He says others argued that she should have been shot and left where people would find her and the message would be plain, a warning to all informers.

Dolours Price told a journalist that she had driven Jean McConville to her execution and she also offered to help the Independent Commission for the Location of Victims' Remains to trace the bodies of Seamus Wright and Kevin McKee.[7] She has since died. The bodies were found in the summer of 2015 in a bog in County Meath.

The disappearing of informers was essentially a deception perpetrated on the people for whom the IRA claimed to be fighting. Adams often described the IRA as a people's army, representing the grievances of an oppressed community. The community is described as coherent and principled, often even noble in its resistance to the brutality of the British and the predations of loyalist paramilitaries and other criminal gangs. Such a vision of the relationship between the people and the IRA depends on an assumption that the people knew the IRA and trusted it. But the IRA lied several times about its activities and motives.

It disowned some embarrassing operations. In Claudy in south County Derry on the day of Operation Motorman, in which the army dismantled barricades and set up new bases around the troubled areas, three car bombs exploded without warning, killing eight people, half of them children. The IRA simply denied that it was behind the attack. This promoted speculation that loyalists or a British army dirty tricks unit was responsible. And many Catholics believed this for there had been unclaimed murders by the army and loyalist bombs. Even still the IRA has not acknowledged responsibility for those bombs and deaths.

The government and the Church were also implicated in concealing the truth about Claudy. That is because the chief suspect was a Catholic priest, James Chesney. The Secretary of State, William Whitelaw, met with Cardinal Conway to discuss suspicions about Chesney[8] and he was then shifted to a parish in north Donegal, out of reach of the RUC and away from his close IRA associates.

Whitelaw's fear may have been that arresting a priest at that time would have further outraged the Catholic community, and, without clear evidence, interning him might have been the only judicial option. Conway's fear was probably that if a priest was exposed as a bomber that would have seemed to loyalists to confirm their prejudice that the Catholic Church was implicated in the IRA campaign. Armed with that confirmation it might have treated all priests as legitimate targets.

The IRA had previously disowned other killings of civilians, notably the Abercorn bomb in March 1972 and the premature detonation of one of its bombs in Anderson Street in the Short Strand area in May, when Gerry Adams was interned in Long Kesh. Eight people were killed and two houses destroyed by that bomb. The deaths of known IRA men were explained in a cover story that said they had been guarding the street against loyalist attack, that they had seen the suspicious lorry and had moved to intercept it then been caught in the blast. It was a lie. They had been transporting the bomb to a target and it had exploded prematurely.[9]

Denying attacks and accidents like these had the double effect of lifting the blame from the IRA and passing it onto the loyalists or the army. An IRA blunder could turn immediately into a propaganda advantage, particularly in a culture in which the IRA had an undeserved reputation for integrity, for being led by decent and principled people who were honest about their failings. The deception that the Anderson Street bomb had been a loyalist sectarian attack provided the rationale for further attacks by republicans in loyalist areas.

In some cases the truth was never acknowledged; in others it emerged years later. Terry Herdman was a teenager who hung out with young members of the IRA on the Riverdale estate in Andersonstown. The key IRA figures in the area when he mixed with them included Bobby Storey, Tommy Gorman and Tucker Kane, men who worked closely with Jim Bryson and the Ballymurphy IRA. Terry Herdman had witnessed IRA actions in the area and knew the people involved. He knew the safe houses and the likely location of arms dumps. This was at a time when IRA activity behind barricades was hardly discreet. Herdman moved away to live near the border with County Monaghan but IRA members visited him there in June 1973 and took him away for questioning, then shot him dead and left a note on his body describing him as a 'tout', an informer.

Libby Abrams, his girlfriend of the time (their daughter was born twenty-seven days before he died) asked Sinn Féin in 2010 for a fuller explanation of the killing. After several meetings she was told that the IRA conceded now that Herdman had not been an informer but a 'liability'. The IRA still stood over the decision to execute him, however.

Dolours Price, who confessed that she had driven Jean McConville to her executioner, was also on the bomb team that struck in London in March 1973 with her sister Marian and Gerry Kelly, now a senior Sinn Féin politician. Dolours Price claimed that Gerry Adams ordered that mission, that he had addressed a group of IRA members and called for volunteers and that few had come forward, given the risk of serving a jail term in England. Adams denies that.

The IRA leadership ordered the bombing of London for propaganda value. Just another bomb in Belfast would not get onto the front pages; even the smallest bomb in London would. And the IRA now wanted publicity.

There were, essentially, four planks to the Provisional IRA strategy at this time. One was to maintain sufficient support, or, for the want of that, fear, in the communities in which it operated. Another was to make Northern Ireland too expensive for Britain to govern by bombing commercial targets. The most important was killing soldiers. A fourth would be propaganda of the deed, the spectacular that might have no inherent military value but which would bring global media attention.

The IRA in the early 1970s believed that the killing of soldiers was the tactic that would be most likely to produce a British withdrawal from Ireland. It believed that Britain would only stomach so many losses and would then start looking seriously for an exit. This strategy is set out in Tommy McKearney's *The Provisional IRA: From Insurrection to Parliament*. McKearney says that early belief in the prospects of a decisive victory gave way to a hope that the British electorate would want a withdrawal when casualties were high.[10] Previous to that rethink, he says, many volunteers in the early 1970s 'were carried along on a wave of optimism', sincerely believing they could defeat the British by military means.

Maria McGuire, who was close to the Dublin leadership of the IRA, says in her book *To Take Arms* that the army council's 'first target' was to kill as many soldiers as had died in the Aden campaign.[11] Over ninety died there.

McKearney, who was on the IRA Executive in the mid-1970s before his arrest, says the IRA was never going to be able to kill enough soldiers but in the early days it did think that it might. Gerry Adams tells us in *Before the Dawn* that this question of how many soldier deaths would be enough to destroy the British will to stay in Northern Ireland was actually discussed with a British official on the plane back from the ceasefire talks with Whitelaw. He says the official told them, 'We can accept the casualties; we probably lose as many soldiers in accidents in Germany.' It appears that a British official, showing some understanding of IRA thinking, was seeking to dissuade the leaders of their core motivating theory.

And Tuzo's report to the Secretary of State, setting out military options, lists one of the advantages of the strategy preceding the ceasefire as 'low force penalty'. The army did not feel that it was suffering a significant loss of soldiers.

In that year, Gerry Adams was free and on the run. Volunteers were busy with commercial bombing, killing soldiers, producing spectaculars and culling spies.

Anthony McIntyre's account of his life in the IRA provides some insight into the daily operations of an armed activist at that time. At the end of 1973, McIntyre joined the Provisional IRA for a chance to shoot soldiers. He was sixteen years old and was soon busy as an active sniper in south Belfast. He says now that he was 'let out' far more often than he should have been but confirms that 'every death, even a civilian death, was thought to be another straw that would break the back of the British occupation'. A problem for the IRA was that many of their members were not actually keen on trying to kill soldiers, certainly not as keen as Anthony McIntyre was. He says that, apart from his OC, others who would assist in taking over a house for an ambush would melt away before the actual shooting started. Later, when he was OC himself, he had problems with quartermasters relying on him to hide weapons for them. He told them that if they couldn't find dumps for the guns themselves and insisted on passing the responsibility for weapons back to him, then they had no role within the IRA.

There was another enemy to worry about, the reorganised loyalist paramilitaries who were killing Catholics. At first the scale of this activity was hard to assess because it could easily be confused with IRA killings of civilians and with attacks by the nebulous MRF, the military unit operating undercover and occasionally opening fire at people on the streets. Some unionists argued that the unexplained killings were the work of the IRA, disciplining its own members and dumping the bodies in Protestant areas to make loyalists look bad.

In the period that Gerry Adams was free, between 20 June 1972 and 19 July 1973, fifty-three members of the Provisional IRA were killed. Nineteen of them blew themselves up with their own bombs. One was killed in a shooting accident and four died in car crashes while on active service, according to the IRA's own figures.[12] Twenty-four were killed by the British army and five by loyalists.[13] So the IRA killed precisely as many of its own members as the British army did.

The IRA killed 107 soldiers in that period, a much higher number than it lost, this in a time at which the General Officer Commanding had envisaged that the army could humiliate and neutralise the IRA by killing huge numbers. Adams will have faced arrest with a sense that the IRA was inflicting more damage than it was sustaining. Given that all these figures are minorities within the overall death toll of 461 in the period, one might suppose that the IRA would have made a stronger impression if it had not conducted the bombing campaign alongside the effort to kill soldiers. It could then have made a cleaner argument that it was fighting a war, and winning it.

One of the last IRA operations of Adams's period of freedom was the bombing of the pub he had worked in, The Duke of York, in Belfast's Commercial Court. The bar was demolished by a massive bomb in a tea chest, delivered in a van with a twenty-minute warning to the staff and customers to get out. The Belfast *News Letter* led with the bombing the following day, 15 June 1973, and inserted in heavy type a little item of information that had perhaps come in too late to be included in the main text of the story. It said that Gerry Adams, recently a barman in the pub, was 'the leader of the IRA in Northern Ireland', which he denies, though he was on the run at the time and in no position to refute or correct this.

Chapter 9

On 19 July 1973, Adams tells us in his memoir, he had arranged to meet Tom Cahill and Brendan Hughes in a house in the Iveagh area of the Falls Road. Hughes told the Boston College Archives that they had been holding a meeting of the Belfast Brigade staff to plan attacks and robberies, and that most of the staff had already left the house when it was raided. It would have been a cramped meeting in one of those small redbrick terrace houses, built in the nineteenth century for mill workers. Adams says that his 'sixth sense' told him something was wrong. From inside the house he watched two republicans check a parked car. Hughes says he had been suspicious of the vehicle and had gone across to nearby Beechmount to order a volunteer 'to get a squad together and pull this car in'.[1] What they didn't see, according to Adams, was that when the republicans approached the car, men sitting inside produced a submachine gun and threatened the republicans before driving off.

The whole area was staked out by the army, and a soldier knocked at the front door. Adams says the strategy was to send the least well known of those inside to deal with the caller. In this case they judged that that was Tom Cahill. Gerry Adams and Brendan Hughes then tried to get out the back, but they were ensnared.

Adams says he then lit his pipe.[2] Hughes, he says, was philosophical about being arrested.

The *Irish Times* journalist and author Colm Keena, drawing on interviews with Adams, says that initially he fought back against a beating from the arresting soldiers and even broke a soldier's wristwatch.[3] He also says that when the soldiers prepared

Adams for the trophy photograph, they dried his clothes on a boiler and brushed his hair. So, if these pictures emerge we need not expect Adams to look as badly beaten in them as he says he was. When the prisoners were driven in a convoy to Castlereagh Detention Centre, a soldier held a pistol to Adams's head, he says, throughout the whole journey, assuring him that he would be shot if the convoy was attacked.

The arrest of Gerry Adams came after a period of gradual decline in the monthly death toll from violence in Northern Ireland, from ninety-six in July 1972 to twenty-nine in June 1973. On the same day Adams, Cahill and Hughes were arrested, according to Ed Moloney,[4] the entire staff of the Third Battalion was scooped in Ardoyne, making that a hugely successful day for the British army. The British were getting a result without Tuzo's battle plan.

In his writings about his second spell in prison, Adams represents himself as good-humoured and resourceful, getting on well with his comrades, even enjoying himself a lot of the time. Recalling prison life he celebrates not just the camaraderie and the banter, the streaking antics and the scheming, but the food, the occasional expressions of love for him from other prisoners, meeting up again with Shane, the Adams family dog, which he believes had been shanghaied by the army again.

Shane had moved in with him and Colette after they got married, 'but in 1973 he vanished, captured by the Brits, though I was to meet up with him briefly later'.[5] One day, Adams thought he saw Shane near the gate of the Long Kesh cage with an army dog handler. 'I shouted out to him but he didn't move.' Shane had been too long with the enemy and had forgotten him.

'Then I whistled.' One long, three short, then one long whistle, all in one breath. Now the dog tensed, ears cocked. 'He jerked towards me and I thought he was going to break free, as he lunged forward . . .' But a soldier intervened and shoved Adams round a corner and into the hut. 'I could still hear Shane crying. It was the last I saw of him.'

Mick Donnelly, also interned then, mocks Adams's account of streaking in Long Kesh, saying that anyone who ran naked about the place for fun would have been looked at askance, but Tommy Gorman recalls that he ran streaking with Adams himself, but 'he wasn't completely naked because he had his boots on'.

Prison allowed Adams to regress and make up for years of playfulness lost to him when he was younger. Life among young men like himself provided him with the chance to live out a boyhood he had missed while living with his granny and uncles in a small house.

Yet, both his allies and his critics agree that, in prison, Gerry Adams was estranged from many other prisoners. The countrymen and other IRA prisoners who had not known him before his arrest regarded him as odd and gauche. There was a circle around him who saw him as a leader and there were other prisoners who were bewildered by this adulation.

Mick Donnelly remembers Belfast republican Danny Morrison as one of those who seemed to need the approval of Gerry Adams. 'Danny Morrison had a nice wee personality and we used to talk tactics and he was all for propaganda and I saw the value of that and we would walk round the yard and talk and he was forever talking about Gerry. Everything he done was about Gerry; "I must talk to Gerry about that." And I said to Danny, "Danny why don't you do it yourself? What do you have to talk to him about it for?"'

Tommy Gorman, who had previously escaped from the *Maidstone* prison ship, says Adams was not regarded as a hands-on operator. His main contribution was strategic thinking but this didn't impress the men who had killed and laid bombs. Adams, of course, has always denied being a member of the IRA.

Gorman says, 'A man was giving a lecture on the workings of an AK-47, and people were surprised to see Gerry there and asked him why he had come and he said, "Oh, I only want to keep my hand in," and they laughed even louder at that.'

There are many stories like this in circulation. Some contradict each other in ways, but the common thread is an image of Adams as an awkward and self-important man whose ungainliness drew mockery from prisoners famous for their cruel humour.

Gorman says, 'One half of the hut was for handicrafts but we occupied it all and we were cutting a door out of the plaster wall. Adams says, "Stand back," and he took a run at the wall and he put his two feet through the wall and he was hanging upside down. And we slapped the face off him.'

They would, however, have slapped anyone who had made himself look foolish in the same way. Slagging or mockery was part of the culture, but Adams attracted particular disdain because he was seen, especially by those from outside Belfast, as not being a true militarist. While his critics in later years would attack him for not admitting to having been a member of the IRA, many in the IRA mocked him for not really being one of them at all.

The representation of life in Long Kesh as high jinks and banter isn't unique to Gerry Adams's writing or the stories about him. Several others who were imprisoned there describe the same practical jokes and playfulness, punctuated by horror, the deaths of comrades and the beatings from the 'screws' and British soldiers. While there, Adams helped plan escapes and draw up a training manual for republican activists on how to resist interrogation. He is credited by Sharrock and Devenport with being the 'prime architect' of a cell structure for the organisation,[6] though how tightly organised it really was in later years is questionable, given that people on housing estates always seemed to know who the local IRA members were.

Former IRA man Gerard Hodgins says the cell structure is a myth. 'There was never a time when I was in the IRA and only knew the three others in my cell. It might be how Adams envisaged the IRA would work, but it never did work like that.'

Some of Adams's stories from that time are retold in differing, contradictory versions. His attempt to escape from Long Kesh in 1973 is a good example of this.

Tommy Gorman says, 'Gerry Adams in his wisdom found a blind spot in the cage from which you could not be seen from any of the watchtowers, so he was going to attempt an escape with Marshall Mooney and Marty O'Rawe. Tommy Tolan might have been there. From our cage you want to go right. We were the last cage before the sentenced men. In his wisdom he decided to go left, the long way, and they were caught.'

Gorman doesn't believe that this was a serious effort to escape at all. He says that the incident provoked a punishment of the other prisoners in the cage, what Gorman calls 'a bad tanking'. 'I doubt very much if this was a serious attempt to escape because the chances of success were infinitesimal. Maybe Adams wanted to get shifted up to the sentenced end.' He says, 'His other attempt at escape was as ridiculous. He shaved himself and then taped the beard all back on again, swapped places with another man who was a foot smaller than him.'

Mick Donnelly says he also witnessed Adams's escape attempt in which he got arrested with Mooney, Tolan and O'Rawe. 'We had a tunnel out of Cage 5 and were all set to go and somebody looked out the window and said, "Look at those boys". And there was Adams and co cutting the wire. And what was the point of that? At that stage you were in the walkway that the Brits used to patrol. They got to the point that anyone could have got to but what was the point because the lookout post would have seen you?'

He says, 'I believed they were just trying to get themselves arrested. My first thought, seeing them out the window was, Bastards. People were shouting at them, "Fuck you, what are you doing standing there?" They didn't go to the next stage, the tin wall. They weren't going to cut through that. What were they going to do, climb over the top? Pretty well impossible to do.'

Donnelly thinks that Adams wanted to go to the sentenced end for an easier life. Another possible reason, however, might have been more practical; in the sentenced area Adams would be among senior IRA members. There he would be with men who would be central to his future strategies, Bik McFarlane, Bobby Sands, Brendan Hughes. And he would be appointed OC of Cage 11.[7]

Adams himself gives two separate accounts of the escape attempt, though he never describes it as anything other than a serious effort to get away from Long Kesh. The first account is in *Before the Dawn*. He was with Tommy 'Todler' Tolan, Marshall Mooney and Marty O'Rawe from Cage 6, where they were interned. They had been calculating from the lines of sight from watchtowers where there might be blind spots close to the wire, had hoped in vain for fog, but went ahead anyway, in camouflage clothing, with wire cutters. It was Christmas Eve. They crept through a gap between the cages for the internees and the sentenced men and crawled towards the fence. But they were quickly spotted.

Adams writes that Marshall Mooney stood up and tried to deflect the attention of the guards from the others, even started cutting the wire in plain view of the soldiers. Then Adams, by his account, got up and tried to provide further distraction to help the other two to get away.

Marshall and he 'took bad beatings'.[8] Adams writes, 'I was wearing a pair of glasses, which I had tied on, and a very senior official pulled my glasses down and when he realised they were not coming off he gouged my face.'

Marty and Tommy escaped being beaten by confusing the Brits with their antics, we're told. 'Tommy had hit on the trick of shouting at Marty O'Rawe in a British accent, and marching him up to the punishment cells.' He was apparently pretending to be one of the arresting soldiers and hoping that the real ones wouldn't notice.

In the version of this story in *Before the Dawn*, British soldiers are depicted as crass and inept, easily belittled by the humour of the republicans. The arrested men were stripped naked and put in separate cells while dogs were loosed in the corridors. 'We feared that at any moment soldiers and warders would descend on us.'

From the windows of their cells, Marshall and Todler taunted the soldiers. Marshall would shout, 'My name's Tommy Todler and I'm going to knock your bollocks in.' Next day a doctor came to check them and Adams asked for cream for his face injury. '"What's wrong with your face?" he replied, looking straight at the ugly wound.' Adams says he said 'Happy Christmas' and left it at that.

Another account of the same escapade in a collection of his journalism, *An Irish Eye*,[9] serves a different message, not that the British are brutes but that humanity prevails, even among heartless soldiers, at Christmas time.

In this account Adams goes to the window of his cell in the punishment block, naked and wrapped in a blanket, to see soldiers lined up with dogs, shouting abuse at him. 'Get down, ya Fenian bastard.' The soldiers outside now speak like bigoted Ulster Protestants.

Tommy Tolan now shouts out from his cell, 'Fuck up, ya bollocks. My name is Gerry Adams and if you come in here, I'll knock your melt in.'

Gerry curls up on his bed and prays that Tolan will stop. 'Jesus, Mary and Joseph, tell him to shut up.'

Now the dogs are in the corridor and the soldiers are banging the doors with their batons, more details that were missing from the account in the memoir written ten years earlier. Missing too is the amazing behaviour of one of the soldiers. The dogs have gone. A soldier stands in his cell door. Gerry braces himself to fight. The soldier then flings a packet of cigarettes onto the bed.

'You want a light, Paddy?' [. . .]
  I sucked on the cigarette. 'My name's not Paddy.'
  'I know, Paddy. Happy Christmas.'
  I grinned back at him. 'Happy Christmas,' I said.

Adams was not the kind of activist who enjoyed violence for its own sake and that is evident from his limited participation in the one great act of rebellion by the prisoners, apart from the escape attempts – the burning of the cages, or compounds. Adams opposed the burning of the cages and played little or no part in the operation.

In a refusal to be bullied or abused, the IRA had held in reserve the option of burning down the camp and let the prison authorities know this. The threat may have had some value in restraining the army and the screws but, in its execution, it inflicted more pain on the prisoners themselves than anyone else, so Adams was wise to counsel against it.

A dispute had arisen in one of the sentenced men's cages over food. Bik McFarlane told a journalist years later that the trigger for the decision to burn the camp was a refusal of the screws to provide two packets of pancakes that were missing from a food order, though he acknowledged that there are other versions. Adams says in his memoir that tension had been growing around protests about the quality of the food and the laundry and soldiers being deployed in the visiting area.

Exchanges with the screws escalated to the point of the IRA men ejecting them. The governor then demanded that offenders be sent to the punishment blocks and threatened to send in the army. The IRA said it would burn down the republican cages if that threat was not lifted.

The fire plan expressed the great flaw in IRA thinking, the notion that hitting back was always preferable to enduring injustice, even when rebellion made things worse. In that sense, the burning of the camp was a symbol of the whole IRA campaign and its determination to make Northern Ireland ungovernable rather than allow it to be governed unfairly. The person most strongly associated with taking the easier course in Long Kesh at the time was Gerry Adams. Few of his critics would say now that he was right to oppose the burning of the camp, since the episode has entered the mythology of republican struggle, but none of them can point to much that was gained by it.

Mick Donnelly from Derry was the quartermaster of the interned prisoners, responsible for acquiring wire cutters and implements for digging tunnels. He says that the OC of the internees, George Gillen, was contemptuous of Gerry Adams, saw him as having gathered a clique around him who regarded themselves as standing apart from the command structure. Donnelly, whose version is disputed by other former prisoners, says Gillen understood that Adams was the chief opponent of the plan to burn the camp and would have to be pushed into playing his part.

'The night before, George Gillen said to me, come on and witness this. He went over to the wire and shouted across to Cage 2, "Tell Gerry Adams I want to speak to him." Adams wouldn't come out. Gillen called then for the cage OC and said, "Tell Adams I want to speak to him now."'

Adams refused.

In Adams's account the fire was started by the sentenced prisoners in another part of the camp but Donnelly claims that he and George Gillen took the initiative, ignoring advice from the sentenced prisoners that the plan had actually been cancelled.

'The next night they had the relay and we thought it was going ahead, but the message came from the sentenced men that the Brits had pulled back, it was all off. Gillen said, "It can't be." George turned to me and he said, "Did you hear him saying that the Brits have gone in and we're to burn it?" And I said, "Aye, that's what he said." George said, "That's the order then, Mickey, burn it." So I ran into the first hut and shouted, "Burn it, burn it." I ran round all the huts.'

Accounts by loyalist prisoners also say that the fire was started by the internees and not by the sentenced men with whom the decision should have rested.[10]

Adams had been at an IRA command meeting discussing

plans for the fire and arguing that it would only be worth doing if it could provide cover for a mass escape. He says he saw the first column of smoke rise up and heard the order passed along to burn everything and was taken by surprise.

Given that this was such a colourful and dramatic event, Adams says relatively little about it in the memoir and puts the fuller account of it in his book *Cage Eleven*, in the words of a different republican prisoner with the unlikely name 'Cedric', who kept a diary. This may have been part of a routine strategy of not providing evidence against himself.

Tommy Gorman says that Adams tried to stop the fire because he didn't know that an order had come down from the sentenced men to go ahead with the plan (though by Donnelly's account, it hadn't).

Donnelly says, 'I ran over to Cage 2 and shouted, "Burn it, burn it; it's going up." Then I went into our hut with Gerard Cooney and Sean Mullan and we burnt our hut. We were last out. They all went up very quickly.'

They were surprised by how quickly the huts filled with smoke, which rose up the walls and accumulated in the curve of the ceiling. Some of the men nearly didn't get out in time. One hung back trying to smash a television set because he wanted to see how the tube would implode.

Donnelly says the internees then went up to the part of the camp occupied by the sentenced men to break them out. 'Two men even ran into a UVF cage, not knowing where they were.' One captured a guard dog and tried to kill it. Donnelly says the dog was so docile and obedient that the men took pity on it and found food for it.

Donnelly believes that there had indeed been a plan to break out of the prison camp, as Adams had wanted, but that it was abandoned because the perimeter was secured by armed British soldiers. For him, further evidence that Adams was not properly committed to the fire was that he did not follow him up to the sentenced prisoners to help break them out. 'Why didn't he come across to us and up with me to the sentenced men?'

Adams appears to have anticipated this criticism when he was writing his account of the fire for *Cage Eleven*: 'Things were hectic for a wee while. Apparently, though none of us knew this, the idea was to try and join up with the sentenced men.'[11]

Cedric's diary, in Adams's story, says he was playing a Kris Kristofferson LP as the heat from the fire reached him and the singing of 'Me and Bobby McGee' got eerily slower and slower. Army helicopters hovered over the burning camp and soldiers fired gas canisters among the prisoners.

Cedric says he knew that the gas fired at them was CR and not CS for he knew the taste of CS. He says that swallowing the CR was 'like choking on balloons which inflate to fill out and smother your windpipe and your lungs'.

In the mayhem it was a character called Your Man who formed up the internees and drilled them to restore order, and then sent them out on 'foraging squads' to burn more.

Cedric writes, 'When everything burnable was burning, we just sat back and admired our handiwork.'

Adams's memoir repeats one of Cedric's stories, further suggesting that the diary is his own. Cedric says he met Dickie Glen, told him he'd love a smoke and Dickie went off and got him a Hamlet cigar. 'God alone knows where he got it.' The same story in the memoir uses proper names. 'Meeting Dickie Glenholmes, another comrade, I said I'd love a smoke and a few minutes later he returned with a Hamlet cigar.'

As so often before, the key point of many of Adams's stories is to indicate how others loved and respected him and how touched he was by their small favours for him. Cedric and those around him retired to Cage 4 with the wounded and older men. 'Every so often a watchtower would topple over and collapse in a great fanfare of sparks and flames.' Loud explosions bewildered him at first but turned out to be Kosangas bottles being detonated by the heat.

It was a long sleepless night for the prisoners in the wreckage of the camp, waiting for the army to attack them. In the morning the soldiers charged in. Cedric's account says they were squealing and whooping for psychological effect, and that the internees met them with silence, which 'had its psychological effect also'.

Accounts by loyalists also include the screaming of the soldiers but describe the republicans as broken and defeated. Some claim that wounded republicans were rescued from the battle by UDA men and brought to safety in loyalist compounds, this despite the republicans having broken promises to spare the loyalist parts of the camp.

Curiously, the loyalist accounts describe the brutality of soldiers retaking the camp much more vividly than the republicans do, the republicans perhaps preferring not to tell the story in terms that present it as a defeat. As recounted by Adams, the Long Kesh fire was a victorious and ennobling protest; as witnessed by the loyalists it was such a humiliating defeat for republicans that they took pity on them.

Cedric's story ends with a touch of whimsy. 'As we snuggled down together, Big Ted turned to me and said, "I'm glad we went out tonight." . . . Ted's getting a bit bohemian.'

According to loyalists, the soldiers came in and battered the men with clubs, forcing them to run the gauntlet between lines to receive food that they had already befouled and was inedible.[12]

William 'Plum' Smith writes, 'The troops who took over immediately began to brutalise the prisoners, making them run a gauntlet of batons and then throwing them against the wire fences. I had never seen such brutality in all my life.'[13] This is from a riot-hardened UVF leader who saw himself as being on the same side as the British soldiers. His account is not easily reconciled with Adams's recollection of sitting calmly in the midst of the turmoil, enjoying a cigar.

Chapter 10

What was the IRA for?

That was the question that Gerry Adams had to address in prison.

It saw itself as an army that would use military force to eject Britain from Ireland. It was structured in battalions and companies. Its aim was to batter the commercial infrastructure of Northern Ireland and to kill soldiers and police officers in the expectation that, eventually, the British government would be sickened by this and, unable to prevent it continuing, would negotiate a withdrawal.

And there was evidence, the leadership thought, that this was working. The British were negotiating and asking for another ceasefire.

At some point, whether before, during or shortly after that ceasefire, Gerry Adams concluded that the British had been toying with the IRA leadership, raising their expectations only to string them along to weaken them and ultimately demoralise them. He was among the first to see that the logic of winning by pitting military force against the British army, in order to secure a victory, was exhausted and had failed. If armed struggle was for anything, it was for something other than a classic guerrilla war that the IRA would ultimately win, because they were not going to win by those means.

Yet these were ideas he could not share candidly.

Among the sentenced prisoners he did not escape tensions and divisions of the kind he had experienced among the internees. This was largely because the IRA command had a different vision of the progress of the campaign; it was still thinking in terms of an armed insurrection that could achieve its aims by imposing an unsustainable physical cost on the enemy, the British state.

Adams, appointed OC of Cage 11, had to defer to the senior IRA command.

A charter for republican prisoners drawn up in 1989 defined the relationship between the prisoners and the IRA in bold terms. And its preamble described those terms as 'historic'; that is, descriptive of how things had always been in Long Kesh. So, though the charter was not in existence when Gerry Adams was in prison, it claims to encapsulate principles that were already well established then.

Our communities exist under the guidance and protection of the Army [IRA] itself. Its interest and pursuit of its objectives override all other considerations. While every attempt will be made to complement Army and civilian needs/requirements contradictions will occasionally arise. Where such does occur the Army needs will be explained (if feasible). Ultimately Army considerations will outweigh all others. In all such instances the Army is a final arbiter.

Adams has said that he took the post of OC in order to reconcile divisions between the men and that he concentrated mostly on a bookish life.[1] While there, he wrote an occasional column for *Republican News*, the Sinn Féin weekly, under the pseudonym Brownie and promoted education among the men. He has said that he persuaded the men to give up food parcels to enable them to receive books by and about republican thinkers, including James Connolly and Liam Mellows. He was now leader of a community of men who lived under the 'guidance and protection' of the IRA, and he directed their political education.

The most immediate embodiment of that command structure was the camp commandant, David Morley. He was a vain and naive man. Adams had little hope of converting him to a new way of thinking about how to direct the IRA campaign but he had to avoid clashing with him. When Brendan Hughes sought a meeting with Morley, he was disgusted that Morley received him while posing for a portrait. Hughes was contemptuous of Morley because he ran the camp on British army style discipline and even gave himself a white beret to distinguish himself as the most senior IRA officer.[2] Yet Hughes was, in some ways, closer to Morley than to Adams in his thinking, for he too wanted a war that the IRA would win by inflicting huge damage on the enemy. Hughes says he spoke to Gerry Adams about Morley and even raised the idea of dumping him over the wire and shooting the Belfast leaders, afraid that they were running down the IRA and letting the British manoeuvre it into sectarian warfare and an unproductive ceasefire in 1975. The IRA leadership at this time not only imagined that it was contending in a clash of forces with the British that it had a prospect of winning but that the British had already decided on a retreat to avoid losing more soldiers to IRA snipers.

In Long Kesh, Adams, Bell and Hughes had to act within the rules of the IRA while critical of the leadership. Adams's Brownie articles were vetted by Morley. Direct communication with possible sympathisers on the outside, like Brian Keenan and Martin McGuinness, was forbidden and would have attracted courts martial.

While Morley in the camp was trying to prepare the IRA for an early British withdrawal and the civil war that he expected would be triggered by it, Adams had reasoned that this was all folly, that the British had no intention of withdrawing and that a new strategy had to focus on a 'long war' fought by cell groups of volunteers who were sufficiently well educated never to be led astray again by a docile or incompetent leadership.

There were two major crises for the IRA while Gerry Adams was in prison. One was the Ulster Workers' Council Strike in May 1974 by which loyalists and unionists together brought down the power-sharing executive established after inter-party negotiations as a constitutional compromise. The other was the IRA ceasefire of February 1975, by which the movement was weakened.

The strike showed the potential for a loyalist mass movement that would combine political action with paramilitary threat. The British and Irish governments and the main parties had negotiated a power-sharing settlement without Sinn Féin participation. Unionists and nationalists, then represented mainly by the SDLP, would govern in coalition and a cross-border Irish Dimension would acknowledge that the Irish government had an interest in the welfare of the North. Loyalists opposed this and, backed up by intimidation, cut electricity supplies and threatened to make the region ungovernable. They were able to control the power stations and the food supplies. They barricaded the streets to stop people going to work.

Northern Ireland was on the brink of total collapse, with Harold Wilson's Labour government shrinking from the prospect of moving the army against striking workers. And the devolved assembly fell.

The meaning of all this for republicans was that loyalism was organised, had had political backing and had blooded itself not just by killing random Catholics but by vetoing a possible settlement.

After the UWC strike it appeared inevitable that a British withdrawal, if it could be accomplished, would result in civil war, though Gerry Adams argued then and later that most Protestants would reconcile themselves quickly to their being Irish. There was a strategic logic to this. No loyalist army would have been able to force Britain to come back, once it had gone, and in the interim, no loyalist army fighting Britain to oppose withdrawal would be likely to succeed militarily or to sway British minds on the question.

So, inside Long Kesh, when the IRA started to believe British hints that they were planning to go, the logic was plain that civil war would follow but that it would be winnable. Loyalist morale would be deflated by British indifference and the Irish army would fight alongside the IRA. Morley started training his men for that war, not a guerrilla war but a battlefield clash of forces. Yet, at the same time, the IRA outside the prison was losing its edge, allowing itself, as Hughes argued, to be channelled towards sectarian counter-attacks and factional warfare with the Officials. An IRA that foresaw the need to fight a major civil war was conducting itself like a street gang.

It was being bled by the 1975 ceasefire and losing its potential. There is a question over how well Adams read that situation. Hughes says that Adams was critical of the leadership. Anthony McIntyre argues that the leadership that got drawn into the ceasefire on the phoney promise of withdrawal were people Adams supported. Seamus Twomey was the Chief of Staff, Brian Keenan the Quartermaster. The easy myth afterwards would be that the northerners had to take over the IRA and regenerate a campaign that the southern leadership had been tricked into winding down. It's not so simple. They wanted a different kind of war.

Hughes feared that the IRA was being weakened by the ceasefire. He would later suspect that Adams liked it that way. Interestingly, Richard O'Rawe doubts that the IRA actually was in decline. O'Rawe was a member of the IRA in Ballymurphy and had been interned on the prison ship, the *Maidstone*, alongside Adams in 1972. He describes the state of the IRA as he knew it at that time as fit and eager. When he had conversations about this period in jail later with Hughes he found he could not agree with him on the analysis that the IRA had been weakened. 'I could only speak from a local perspective but in Ballymurphy with a glut of good men and women at our disposal, we never felt that we were staring into the face of defeat.'[3] O'Rawe wonders if the depletion of the IRA by the ceasefire was exaggerated by those making a case for shifting energies in the movement towards political activity.

O'Rawe said that at daily meetings in battalion 'call houses' he met the OCs from the other companies in west Belfast during the ceasefire. 'Never once did I leave with the impression that they thought we were on the verge of being defeated.'

Anthony McIntyre cites contradictory readings of the state of the IRA. He says that when he came out of prison in 1975 'the IRA was thriving; Martin Meehan thought it was thriving'. But he also recalls IRA member Pat McGeown telling him that by the end of 1974 the IRA in Belfast was on its knees, 'down to eight men holding the whole thing together'. Provos had had to borrow weapons from the Officials.

The reality is that the movement had been weakened by internment but that the ending of internment, as part of the deal for the 1975 ceasefire, had released a lot of enthusiastic volunteers.

O'Rawe says, 'In 1975 I had no doubt; it absolutely never entered my head that we wouldn't win this war. The Brits were talking to us. They'd been talking to us since 1972. They were weak. They were talking to the IRA leadership for whatever reason. That in itself was hugely encouraging. Because it showed you these guys are potentially pliable, if the tactics were got right.'

He says, 'I can only talk of what I saw about me. I saw four companies in Ballymurphy, maybe with thirty or forty guys each in them, very strong. They had guns. No reason to think for one second that we couldn't have gone back on the tools. You were reading stuff that said this is a disaster but I couldn't understand why it was such a disaster at the time.

'I didn't see disaster. If we had wanted to go back on the tools it could have happened within twelve hours. You could have put snipes out; you could have put blowies together for the town; I mean that was second nature, it wasn't a big deal. I had this out with The Dark [Brendan Hughes] and I said to him, do you ever consider that Big Gerry deliberately put this out to undermine that leadership?' (O'Rawe would emerge years later as one of the most ardent critics of Gerry Adams.)

'And he said, you know it crossed my mind. I said, it crossed my mind a few times because I'm not sure it was the big disaster you say it was.'

There was, of course, an obvious case for reform; it was that the IRA actually had no hope of a military victory. But it didn't want to hear that.

The discussion on the whole point of the IRA campaign was about to slip from the hands of the republicans themselves and be taken over by civilians who would pour onto the streets in a demand that the killing be stopped.

Danny Lennon, one of the Cage 11 men, was back on the street and trawling for soldiers to shoot one day in August 1976. Lennon was driving. John Chillingworth had the weapon. Whether he fired it or not is disputed, but soldiers he targeted on Finaghy Road North saw him take aim at them. Lennon had honed his political thinking under Adams's guidance but he was out of practice in the part of soldiering that mattered on the street. This was at the top of the Andersonstown Road, at right angles to it, cradling the Riverdale estate. They were probably hoping to get one good hit and then to speed down Finaghy Road North and to take cover in the narrow streets of Riverdale on the left or Ladybrook Park on the right.

This was a busy area. It would be hard for the army to give chase with so many people around. There was St Michael's Church on the corner, the St John the Baptist School beside that. People were shopping at the garage on the corner. Across the road from that was the Ballyowen day centre.

This was no place for an exchange of fire.

The soldier who spotted the Armalite at the side window of the car shot Lennon from a pursuing Land Rover, killing him and wounding Chillingworth just as the car was building speed to escape.

The car ran out of control, veered onto the footpath, outside the school.

Anne Maguire was walking along the footpath with four

children. She was pushing a pram with six-week-old Andrew in it. Her eight-year-old daughter Joanne was cycling alongside her. The car hit them. Joanne and baby Andrew died on the street. Two-year-old John was pronounced dead the following day. Her seven-year-old son Mark survived. So did Anne, though with serious injuries to her leg, pelvis and head. But the grief would overwhelm her and she would take her own life three years later.

This was insufferable. This at a stroke was the irrefutable illustration of the need for the killing to stop and a huge popular movement rose up against the violence. Betty Williams, Mairead Corrigan and Ciaran McKeown, founders of the Peace People, brought tens of thousands onto the street to protest. The common-sense logic of their case was plain; it was madness to have armed men fighting a war in towns and housing estates, endangering the very people they claimed to be representing.

The two women, Corrigan a devout Catholic and Williams from the Protestant community, came to symbolise an anti-sectarian response to the violence, a heroic uprising of protest from ordinary people against chaos and madness. To survive, the Provisionals had to refute them comprehensively.

Confronted with moral outrage at the untenability of a guerrilla war among civilians, the Provisionals chose not to concede that their struggle was too dangerous nor to lie low until the passion subsided. They saw a major protest had been rallied against them and they chose to fight it, and the voice raised against the new Peace People movement was that of Gerry Adams, even though he was still in prison.

Adams did what no one else would dare do at the time; he defended Danny Lennon. But Lennon was a difficult martyr to sympathise with, having taken three small children with him when he died for the cause.

Others spoke in defence of the Provos as vulnerable young men who had got caught up in violence, who barely understood the forces that had overwhelmed them. Adams wasn't going to bother with excuses like that. He wrote that Danny Lennon had made up his mind that he was a republican revolutionary and that he understood the cost. To some republicans, he might have been an embarrassment, his death a calamity best forgotten. Gerry Adams was determined not to be coy about his respect for a revolutionary who had studied under him in Cage 11.

Adams's first book was a pamphlet written in Lennon's defence: *Peace in Ireland: A Broad Analysis of the Present Situation*. The book was dedicated to 'Danny Lennon, who died for peace, and for the Maguire children who were killed with him.' Others might have thought the better strategy was to wind down the campaign until the emotional moment had passed. Adams preferred direct confrontation with those who demanded peace. He asserted that he knew better than stricken and anxious mothers what was good for the people. This took moral courage or blinkered vision. Adams was going to defend an IRA campaign that had had ghastly consequences for the very people it was supposed to be defending and at a time when thousands of women were on the streets calling for the killing to stop. He boldly told them they didn't know what they were talking about.

Adams accused those who called for peace of siding with the British army and effectively disqualifying themselves from the right to have an opinion. He reasoned in his pamphlet that he could give no quarter to the arguments against the IRA campaign. He accused those who demanded peace of being unfocused and politically naive. His case was that the IRA wanted peace too but that the problem was British imperialism. If the Peace People didn't identify the problem, it could not point the way to peace. He conceded no right to anyone to criticise Danny Lennon or to hold him to blame for the deaths of three children.

It was not to be the responsibility of the IRA to bring peace. The British were the cause of the war and only a British withdrawal could end it.

This was the emergence of a new way of defining the IRA's

purpose. It is not to be an army that can by force and attrition overwhelm the British will to stay in Ireland; it is not an initiative but a perpetual symptom of the problems created by unjust British rule. But Adams is not good at identifying the actual problems created by British rule other than to say that it is imperialism and conquest and produces a type of government that is 'corrupt' and 'mercenary'.

'The system which the Irish live under is not built for peace, and it is this which will defeat the desire which is being demonstrated at present.'

He argues that the peace campaigner should argue for the disestablishment of 'one of the most corrupt Imperial manifestations that humanity has ever known'.

But in this same pamphlet he started to shift the emphasis of his concerns towards social issues. He says the suffering caused by imperialist oppression and conquest includes unemployment and bad housing. He offers Ballymurphy as an example of this. 'Ballymurphy cannot cure itself of violence by a simple removal of the IRA from that area.' He writes that the demands of the people there are for 'freedom from heavy rents for homes they will never own'. They want 'employment, better housing, play centres, facilities for the aged, the handicapped and the young'.

That people in public housing estates in Britain and the republic also complained of unemployment and disadvantage seems not to have occurred to him as relevant. Nor did he provide an account of how the IRA campaign could improve things, and surely he at least knew from his reading that 'humanity' had known worse conditions than those in Ballymurphy under imperialist oppression, say in Bengal or the Warsaw Ghetto, in the Americas or Australia where indigenous populations had been almost eradicated. Adams insists on a point that he has returned to many times in his writing, that the demands for peace and justice, employment, fair rents and play centres 'have been refused because they cannot and could not, be conceded by

Stormont's political regime'.

The logic of republicans pursuing social change was that such a campaign would expose the real nature of imperialist oppression. He believed that the British government in Northern Ireland exercised discrimination and denial of rights to non-unionists because it had to do so in order to survive, that it would collapse if forced to be fair.

Anticipating the counter-argument, that Britain was held in Northern Ireland by its commitments to the unionist majority, who wanted British rule, Adams dismisses unionism as an instrument of imperialist oppression, a pact between Orangeism and the British government that has no purpose other than to preserve Protestant supremacy and which would have no substance after Britain did the right thing and unilaterally ended it.

He concludes that two states artificially imposed on Ireland by partition cannot by their very natures be just and peaceful, 'and, while this is so, revolutionary violence will continue to strive to overthrow them in pursuit of true justice, peace and happiness'.

This was the best case that the IRA could make at the time, and Gerry Adams was the best person to make it, but it is a weak one. If Northern Ireland was a colony, it was a strange one in that it sent MPs to the British parliament, elected under the British electoral system, and participated in the welfare system of the British state, receiving unemployment benefits and the National Health Service. India, which knew what it was like to be colonised, would hardly have thought the dole queue was evidence of 'one of the most corrupt Imperial manifestations that humanity has ever known'.

Nor was he clear on how an IRA campaign that inflicted such grief on the very people from whom it sought support was going to make things better.

Yet we have the beginnings here of a heresy within traditional republicanism, a hint that the grievances of the people under imperialism are social and material, high rents, lack of jobs and lack of play centres. We are hearing the voice of a political activist who is perhaps torn two ways, who is committed to the ideal of a free Ireland but who developed his political skills first as a campaigner on social issues and housing. He wasn't saying that social reform, employment and play centres would ever be enough to pacify Ireland. He was part of a movement that insisted that Northern Ireland could not be reformed, yet he was calling the IRA back to social action, trying to persuade it that this was also a route to undermining the Union and exposing its contradictions.

Adams made the argument that the Peace People had a naive idea of what peace was. He challenged them to be as vociferous in attacking the British army as the IRA; that is, to take a neutral position between the two. This was clever, for it effectively demanded that the supporters of the Peace People withdraw their assent to the British state, as a minimal precondition of having the right to criticise the IRA. And if they couldn't do that, they could be reviled for having a political agenda of their own, the endorsement of the status quo, the Union. He argued that the lack of peace was a symptom of the British imperialism in Ireland and could not be remedied by the cessation of attacks on the British by the IRA. In taking this line he eroded the argument of the Peace People, but he also raised, whether or not he realised it at the time, a challenge to the IRA's definition of peace as a united Ireland free of Britain.

The question could now be put to republicans: what do you mean by peace? British withdrawal? But most people, including themselves, expected that withdrawal would actually trigger a civil war.

Adams had effectively reframed the objective of the republican movement from Irish unity to peace, whatever that might mean. He had also begun to frame a political objective for Sinn Féin that would give it a bigger job than merely supporting the IRA.

Chapter 11

A little boy arrived in the visiting area with his mother. But how well did he remember his father, the prisoner? A friendly man approached them. His mother knew him. But he wasn't his father, was he?

'Aren't you going to give your daddy a kiss?' With this or some such expression of familiarity and intimacy, Cleaky Clarke teased the child of his comrade, Gerry Adams.

While in prison Adams and the others maintained relationships with their families, as far as this was possible, through receiving visits. Adams now had a son, Gearoid, who has spoken a little about those days for Bill Rolston's book *Children of the Revolution*. Gearoid says that Cleaky Clarke was 'winding me up that he was my real da',[1] extending the rough banter of prisoners to an infant. Perhaps Cleaky wasn't one of the more sensitive souls in the IRA.

Gearoid describes a life in the 1970s that was similar to his father's in the 1950s, going to the same school and often living with his granny. Other children of prisoners have been more scathing of their fathers for putting revolution before family life. Jeanette Keenan's father Brian Keenan was a long-term prisoner in England and later Chief of Staff of the IRA. She says, 'My daddy believed very much in family life, and part of his political struggle was that he was trying to create the best possible life for families where people could be nurtured.'[2] The problem was that he was neglecting the family he already had for the sake of other families in the future republic. Keenan came out of prison and returned immediately to the IRA, where his first loyalty lay. 'He owed us something and he wasn't going to pay up.'

Jeanette rationalises, in the end, that somebody had to fight the war and that she would have had a greater struggle to go to university if the IRA had not waged its campaign. 'In 1964 when I was born, people were still fighting for things like voting rights. That's only in my lifetime! That's how I manage to say it was worth it.'

But it clearly wasn't. She could have got her university place without the IRA's help. Gerry Adams, like Keenan, also went straight back to the struggle when he was released from prison in March 1977. He went first to his mother's house and met 'another old friend'[3] who wanted him to go to Dublin to meet Seamus Twomey, the Chief of Staff, who was on the run, 'to discuss the political situation'. He and Colette and their son set off that evening so that he could meet with Twomey before going for a couple of weeks' holiday in County Meath.

Adams says that the child 'had no problem at all adjusting' to his being out of prison. He could recognise him now. 'There wasn't even a transition period.' Gearoid puts it differently. He says that 'that's when the relationship started'.[4] And 'all of a sudden there's changes'.

Gearoid Adams told Rolston that even now he feels guilty that he didn't join the IRA himself given that so many others in his family did and that there was always one or other of his uncles in jail. He grew up in a home that was routinely raided and searched. His job as a little boy was to try to stay awake, sitting at the top of the stairs, watching the soldiers to be sure they didn't plant anything.

Many other children had older relatives on the run and maintained contact furtively. Máiría Cahill says she would visit her uncle, Joe Cahill, in Dundalk where he lived safely on a housing estate, though he couldn't cross the border into the North. He was managing the finances of the IRA and living parsimoniously. 'Annie his wife always seemed to have a pot of soup on when we went in.'

But members of the Provisional movement like Cahill and Adams were in danger not just from British soldiers and the law but from other republicans, the Officials or Stickies, and from loyalist paramilitaries.

That feuding had caused tension in the Adams family while Gerry Adams was in Long Kesh. One night in August 1973, Jim Bryson and others drove round Ballymurphy looking for members of the Official IRA, at a time when a feud was stirring between them. They had information that the Officials intended to kill Bryson. Micky McCorry, the husband of Gerry Adams's sister Margaret, was in the area and hiding from them. One of the gunmen with Bryson was Patrick Mulvenna, husband of another sister, Frances.

The feud between the two wings of the IRA was dividing the Adams family.

A British soldier in a secret lookout post overlooking a part of Ballymurphy called the Bull Ring saw Bryson and Mulvenna and another man armed in a car but was spotted by them too.[5] Both sides opened fire. The soldier killed Mulvenna and wounded Bryson so badly that he died days later.

Local people assumed that the men had been ambushed by the Official IRA. The Officials put out a statement on the night claiming the hits as their own. Someone had assumed that their plan to kill Bryson had gone ahead. Provos were mobilised to take on the Officials that night. The army was able to arrest a member of the Officials and recover a 'grease gun', claiming afterwards to be acting on information from a Provisional source. This was reported in an account of the incident written for the Royal Green Jackets' annual *Chronicle* by Captain R. G. K. Williamson.[6]

The gossip went round that Micky McCorry had killed Mulvenna. The assumption was that one Adams brother-in-law had killed another Adams brother-in-law. Margaret had to go to her family home and sit with them where Patrick Mulvenna was lying dead at a time when people were saying her husband had shot him.

Margaret herself was in danger during these feuds. A caller at her home in Braemar Street handed her an envelope. He had been asked to deliver it by an IRA member. Inside was a single round for a .357 Magnum pistol. One of her brother Gerry's closest friends had sent it to her.

The Officials were seen by the Provisionals to be encroaching in their areas. They would test the ground by selling their weekly newspaper the *United Irishman* in estates where the Provisionals were strong. That meant taking it into Ballymurphy. Once they were selling at the top of the Whiterock Road when Gerry Adams senior came out of Kelly's bar. He bought a copy of the paper, says one of the Officials who were selling it, and then tore it up in front of them. The Official says that he thought Adams senior expected to be thumped and to get credit back in the bar for standing up to their republican rivals but they just laughed at him.

But these tensions got bloodier still. On Easter Sunday 1977 the different republican factions lined up for their separate parades to Milltown Cemetery to honour their dead. There had been clashes between them before but Easter Sunday was felt by both to be a time for reverence and respect, not for violence. They trusted that they could safely bring their children to the parade. The Officials assembled under the banner of the Republican Clubs, emphasising the political rather than military facet of their movement.

A loyalist gang had left a bomb on the windowsill of Kennedy's bakery. There was no precision in the targeting beyond the hope of killing anyone at all who might be there. It exploded among those gathered for the parade, a horrific blast just yards away from most of them, the building itself directing the force of it out towards the crowd. At first people crouched in panic. Some of them were old bombers themselves, but few if any had the resources to contain the shock through the people, even after a planned and expected blast, let alone this brutal eruption on a city street on a Sunday afternoon.

Only those close to the bomb could see the immediate result and they were the ones most staggered by it. A boy was dead, ten-year-old Kevin McMenamin. And as the news of that went through the panicked crowd, some drew their guns.

Micky McCorry, the husband of Margaret Adams, was at the front of the parade in Logan Street, leading the colour party and, incidentally, chatting to the father of the boy who was killed when the bomb went off. He thought it best to start the parade and get his men away from the scene, but further up the Falls Road they were accosted at the gates of Milltown Cemetery by jeering supporters of the Provisionals and IRA auxiliaries throwing stones at them. Several of the men in the parade drew pistols and fired in the air to scatter their attackers and get through the cemetery gates to hold their ceremony at the graves.

After the ceremony, John Short, the dead boy's uncle, was on his way with others from the cemetery to visit the McMenamin family. Suddenly a car screeched to a halt beside them. Armed men stepped out and opened up on them, killing Short and wounding another. Having wrongly taken the blame for the murder of the child, the Provos appear to have been keen to strike first in an inevitable round of tit-for-tat killings that they knew would follow, to demonstrate that those who had drawn guns at the scene of the explosion and threatened to kill Provos would not get away with it. This was a dangerous moment but that brief feud was settled quickly by negotiators. Then there was another round of killing in July with four deaths in five hours, starting with a Provo attack on Trevor McNulty, a twenty-nine-year-old father of one from north Belfast, and ending with the death of Tommy 'Todler' Tolan.

Adams in his memoir elides the two outbreaks of killing into one. He had mediated in feuds before but tensions between the two movements had worsened with a round of killing in 1975 while he was in Long Kesh. Still, he had authority to settle this feuding finally on behalf of the Provisionals. A meeting was arranged at Clonard Monastery. Micky McCorry was the delegate from the Officials.

He said, 'First of all, you clarify if you are here to make decisions. If we agree that it ends here can we stop it? Once you see Gerry there you know that they are serious. We talked it through and ended it.'

The last of those killed by the Officials, Todler Tolan, had been with Adams on the farcical escape attempt from Long Kesh. A man who was a member of the Officials said, 'Tolan was a great hit. We regarded him as a Stickie-hater.'

Adams had lost a friend but he was pragmatic. He brought the feud to an end without avenging Tolan. In effect, he allowed the Officials to have the last shot, the Provos having rashly taken the first by shooting John Short.

As they were leaving Clonard, Adams told McCorry that he had narrowly missed being shot himself. The team that had gone to shoot yet another Provo had passed Adams on the road and failed to recognise him, 'but they could have got out of that car and shot me.'

Within weeks of being released from Long Kesh, Adams had the power to commit the IRA to deals with the Officials and to stop feuds. This would be impressive in one who had been off the streets for four years let alone in one 'acting as an individual' and not as a member of the IRA, as he puts it himself. He still wasn't thirty years old.

And it was time to tell the foot soldiers how the IRA leadership had misled them into a ceasefire on the delusion that the British were leaving.

Every year, republicans gathered on a Kildare hillside, at Bodenstown, to honour the man they claimed as their spiritual founder, Theobald Wolfe Tone. Tone had led the revolution of the United Irishmen and tried to establish a republic in Ireland following the inspiration of Thomas Paine and the example of the

United States and France. He had tried to land a French army in Ireland to face the English. The weather had been against them. But Tone's idea of how a war was fought was wholly different to that developed by later generations of republicans. He had sought a clash of armies on a battlefield. Republicans had since developed guerrilla tactics. Now that prospect was exhausted too.

Adams was going to have to find another means by which IRA weapons could advance republican objectives.

He wrote the annual Bodenstown speech to be delivered by Jimmy Drumm whose wife Máire had recently been shot dead by loyalists in her hospital bed. The speech explained to the assembled faithful that they had been wrong to assume that the British were leaving. Republicans had viewed the departure of major industries from Northern Ireland as confirmation that the British were packing their bags. The speech told them that this was all explained, in fact, by the economic recession and that Britain's objective in Northern Ireland was to stabilise the region and stay. The import of this was that the leadership had got it wrong. They had fallen for British hints that they were ready to go. The IRA had called a long ceasefire and let the organisation decline because it had been tricked into thinking it was winning. This speech was, in effect, a manifesto for a long war in which republicans had to reconcile themselves to not forcing the British out just by killing soldiers and crippling the economy. It was now time for the more politically astute to have their day. They would have to build a radical and energised Sinn Féin party.

They had failed through political naivety. Now they needed to develop a political movement that could capitalise on IRA gains.

At this time, Adams appeared to believe that an invigorated IRA campaign and a political movement could work together in the interests of each other.

J. Bowyer Bell, in *The Irish Troubles*,[7] says that Adams was Chief of Staff of the IRA in 1977 after his release. This clearly contradicts Adams's own insistence that he was never a member. Bowyer

Bell's researches in terrorism led him to believe that the man who had been sneered at by hard-edged militarists in Long Kesh was now in charge and ideas that he developed for the redirection of republican efforts while he was in prison were now accepted by the IRA at the highest level.

That these included the principle that Sinn Féin would be under the 'control' of the IRA (the words used in an IRA Staff Report captured by the Gardai in 1977) appears to undermine any insistence he has made since that the two were separate. Perhaps he was phrasing his plans tactfully for IRA members who would have been wary of a shift of energies from armed actions to political campaigning. The insertion of a reminder of the IRA's primacy in brackets in a line in a document found on Seamus Twomey when he was arrested in Dublin, urging the radicalisation of Sinn Féin, reads like an afterthought: 'Sinn Féin should be radicalised (under army direction) and should agitate about social and economic issues which attack the welfare of the people.' Subsequent events suggest that Adams was more ambitious for the growth of Sinn Féin than for a military victory.

In the mid-1970s, when the IRA was demoralised by the ceasefire and then humiliated by the campaign of the Peace People, Gerry Adams gave the movement a project and a purpose. He showed the IRA a logic by which it could continue in the face of the failure of the armed campaign to eject Britain from Ireland and a huge popular movement pleading with it to stop.

It would be wrong to attribute the shift in the emphasis towards political action entirely to Gerry Adams. He clearly had allies in the movement, like Danny Morrison, who had published Adams's Brownie column in *Republican News*. Morrison was rewarded when the paper merged with the Dublin-based *An Phoblacht* in 1979, and he became the editor of both. Adams would also establish a Republican Press Centre with Morrison at the head of it.

Morrison and those around him had already acquired political experience during the ceasefire, managing incident centres with hotlines to the civil service, and they had discovered that they could enhance their influence within their neighbourhoods by directing complaints to government offices.

But the IRA was still busy in the old work of bombing and killing. And Adams would enjoy family life only intermittently with Gearoid and Colette and would soon be back in jail.

Chapter 12

The bombers used a meat hook to hang a blast incendiary on the window grille of the La Mon House hotel. In February 1978 north County Down was the more salubrious part of Northern Ireland, where middle-class Protestants lived. Many of them farmed the rich fertile plain by Strangford Lough, sheltered from the din of Belfast by the Castlereagh Hills to the north. You could live here and do your shopping in Comber or Newtownards and have little sense of the Troubles at all.

The IRA had sent a team to stake out in advance the best way to destroy the building. Their explosive was designed to work like napalm, to blow in the window and throw flaming petrol from four attached cans around the dining hall. It worked.

Inside, members of the Collie Club were enjoying dinner and talking about their dogs when they were engulfed in a fireball sixty feet in diameter. Viewed one way, this was an advance on the IRA's campaign to attack commercial property but with regrettable deaths. Viewed another, it was a savage sectarian massacre made flimsily deniable as such by a useless warning. The IRA accepted afterwards that a nine-minute warning given to the police was inadequate. In fact, it had given less than seven minutes' notice. Police who took the message and phoned the hotel found that the bomb had already gone off.

A waitress quoted in *Lost Lives* said, 'People were on fire, actually burning alive . . . I could smell the burning flesh.'[1] She described men pulling down the curtains and trying to wrap burning people in the fabric to smother the flames.

The IRA smugly allowed that it would accept criticism from

'the relatives and friends of those accidentally killed and from our own supporters who have rightly and sincerely criticised us'. No one else, in its opinion, had any right to a say in the matter. But this was a hopeless effort to stem a wave of outrage at the worst atrocity of the Troubles up to that time. Twelve people were killed, seven of them women, some so badly charred they could only be identified by their teeth or blood samples.

Gerry Adams, by his own account in *Before the Dawn*, was at home with Colette and Gearoid when the news came through. He had been out of Long Kesh less than a year. He had anticipated that he would be arrested, he says, and failed to act to save himself. He had been engaged at the time in 'regrouping', urging the IRA to 'fight in a more cohesive way and in a manner which encouraged the development and building of a popular struggle on a thirty-two county basis'.[2] He felt that that work was going well. The IRA had been firebombing commercial targets 'in an intensive series in twenty different towns two months earlier' and adequate warnings had been given, but not this time.

'Shocked by the death toll I despondently sat up to get the late news reports. I was depressed by the carnage and deeply affected by the deaths and injuries. I could also feel two years of work going down the drain.'

The police came for him in the morning.

He was charged with membership of the IRA.

While he was in custody, Danny Morrison, the publicity director, organised a leafleting campaign, putting out the line that Adams had been 'interned by remand', that his arrest was politically motivated.

After days of interrogation, he was sent first to the old Victorian stone-built Crumlin Road Gaol. In his memoir he moves quickly on from the horror and grief at the deaths of dog lovers to entertaining his readers with accounts of how the absurdity of prison life amused him, from the manner in which screws tried to formally march him into the governor's office to his appreciation of the food, particularly the custard and porridge.

Richard O'Rawe, who was in 'the Crum' around this time, paints a more vivid picture of republican prison culture in his book *Blanketmen*. He says that first-time prisoners often fell for a practical joke in which they were told that they would have to receive the sacrament of confession before they could be fully assimilated. The 'priest' would be another prisoner who would probe their sex lives. O'Rawe had fallen for this himself in an earlier spell in jail.

Adams describes how 'scores' of republican and loyalist prisoners exchanged 'the most obscene verbal abuse' from the cell windows.[3] By contrast, O'Rawe says that the loyalists in the cell above his 'seemed a decent bunch'. When he and his cellmates received a food parcel they would pass some meat on a line up to the loyalists and the loyalists would reciprocate when they had food gifts. 'Later on, we found out that two of them were members of the Shankill Butchers gang and realised how careless we had been.'[4]

Life was bleak and routine in the prison and a new crackdown by Roy Mason, a hardline Labour Secretary of State, had rounded up most of the Sinn Féin leadership and put them in danger of the death penalty through charges of high treason, which remained on the statute books until 1998. So, as before for Adams, being sent to prison felt like a reunion.

The republican prisoners gathered together in the dining hall and in the exercise yard when they weren't confined, mostly, two or three to a cell. They observed a general rule that they would not defecate in the cells, though the prison was then run on a slopping-out routine, where prisoners would use buckets and bring them out each morning. When a republican prisoner needed to relieve himself, he would squat over newspaper and throw the waste out the window into the yard. These were jokingly called 'surprise packages' but the unpleasant content was no surprise to the screws gathering them up in the mornings.

The Provisional IRA OC at the time was Hugh Brady from Derry. Each of the prisoners arriving in the jail had to send him their depositions, the legal papers relating to their case. Tommy Gorman, for a lark, embellished his. He wrote at the bottom that the prisoner had been asked to explain why there were so few IRA operations in Derry and answered that there was no one there capable of organising them, a jibe at Brady himself.

At a dining-hall table the men discussed whether or not they should recognise the courts. It had previously been a strict rule in the IRA that members refused to acknowledge that Northern Ireland was part of a British jurisdiction and took no part in their own trials. Tom Hartley, Gerry Adams, Gerry Brannigan and others were there. Brannigan was arguing that it made no sense to refuse to recognise the court and to create the near certainty of being convicted. Hartley objected, but Adams cut across him and one who was there claims to have heard him say, 'Shut the fuck up, let the man speak.'

If Adams refused to recognise the court, the others would have had to follow and the entire leadership of Sinn Féin would have been convicted without offering a defence.

IRA members still agonised about recognising the court nearly ten years later. Dominic Adams, the youngest of the five, sought the advice of his older brother Paddy. Some prisoners advised pleading guilty in the hope of getting a shorter sentence. But Dominic decided that this amounted to recognising the right of a British court to judge him and pleaded not guilty while declining to offer a defence, taking the risk that he would annoy the judge by prolonging the trial for no legal advantage.[5]

After the failure of his bail application Gerry Adams was transferred to the Long Kesh H-Blocks, now called the Maze Prison, while the police worked in vain to gather evidence against him. This was a new modern prison built on the site of the old Long Kesh camp that the IRA internees had burnt down; it was a symbol of the resolve of the state to treat paramilitary prisoners like ordinary convicted criminals, even though most were now being tried in single-judge Diplock courts, convened on the understanding that juries would be intimidated and were therefore best dispensed with.

By this time the IRA prisoners in the Maze were protesting against the withdrawal of Special Category Status by refusing to wear the prison uniform. This protest had evolved into a refusal to wash. Adams was spared having to join this protest while on remand, being allowed to wear his own clothes, and he was given a cell to himself, 'which I quite enjoyed after the overcrowding at the Crum'.[6]

In his nostalgic recollections of prison life and the spirited resistance of the men, Adams, as we have seen, occasionally contradicts himself. In *Before the Dawn* he describes the prisoners recreating the sound of bin-lid protests against army raids by banging on the pipes in their cells. This was on 9 August 1978, the anniversary of the first internment raids. The screws ordered them to be silent and conducted a headcount. Adams says an 'eerie silence' settled over the wing when the headcount was finished. 'Suddenly a voice rose in song from one of the cells near me.'

A prisoner was singing 'We're on the One Road'.

Another voice joined in, then another and soon the whole wing was singing, 'We're on the long road, maybe the wrong road, but we're together now, who cares?' Which is perhaps not the best representation of republican conviction they could have come up with.

So when he retold that story on video to promote a later book he changed the song to 'Always Look on the Bright Side of Life', from Monty Python's *Life of Brian*. Actually that song, and the film, were only released a year after his spell on remand.

He also described the headcount as 'a brutal incursion' in which 'the prison officers beat everybody', though he makes no mention in the memoir of anyone having been beaten. In that first account the screws were merely loud and abusive.

Adams was housed alone and escorted closely yet he had a weekly 'soirée' with the other prisoners and was able to provide them with cigarettes and polo mints, he says. He was transferred back to Crumlin Road Gaol before his trial, to have secure access to the court through the tunnel under the road, and there he met Tom Hartley again.

On the morning before the hearing he says he and Hartley sang 'The Creggan White Hare' together in the custody cell. He can be forgiven for recalling in a tweet thirty-seven years later that the song was 'Slieve Gallion Braes', but surely not for the claim that he and Tom Hartley got 'thrown out' of prison for singing it. Had it been possible to get thrown out of prison for singing, they'd all have been at it.

Adams always likes to recreate a folksy and comedic account of the Troubles.

At his trial, he was charged with having been a member of the IRA between 1 April 1976 and 25 February 1978 and also with having professed to be a member of the IRA. His solicitor was P. J. McGrory, the one who had accompanied him to negotiations in Derry on the terms of the 1972 ceasefire. McGrory asked Lord Chief Justice Sir Robert Lowry to consider a little-used legal device called an entry of No Bill in the Crown book, on the grounds that the depositions to be submitted did not amount to a viable case. By using this device, Lowry spared Adams even being arraigned, and the embarrassment of pleading and thereby recognising the court.

Lowry acknowledged that formerly 'the Grand Jury required to be satisfied that there was a prima facie case before finding a True Bill. Here the onus is reversed because the trial ought to proceed unless the judge is satisfied that the evidence does not disclose a case sufficient to justify putting the case on trial.'

From his reading of the depositions, the judge ruled that there was indeed no basis for a prosecution. But he did disclose what the evidence was and some of it is interesting. The greater part of it came from a British army sergeant major who had been posted at Long Kesh during the time Adams was held as a sentenced prisoner.

On Easter Sunday most of the prisoners were formed into three ranks. There was a colour party with republican flags. Each compound had its own flag and compound 9 had a C Company flag. Half a dozen men came out of a hut and faced the parade. The accused stood in front and faced the parade, and the colour party led the parade past him. In most respects this parade had the appearance of a military parade.

Lord Chief Justice Lowry said that the behaviour of Gerry Adams in receiving a tribute from IRA members formed in parade with flags was not evidence that he was himself a member of the IRA, but only that he had republican leanings. It was conceivable, he reasoned, that he was receiving this tribute as a supporter who was not a member.

Nor is there any warrant for holding that a man who occupies a top position in Sinn Féin and may be (as the Crown suggest) dedicated to supporting violence is necessarily or even probably a member of the IRA, because he, so to speak, takes the salute at a march past of a parade (whether all those on parade are IRA members or some may be just sympathisers or people who conform with the conventions of the compound).

A prison officer was also on hand to provide evidence that Adams, 'when awaiting trial on the present charges, was on a parade in the rear of two ranks, which commemorated two Provisional IRA volunteers who had recently been shot by the army'. This similarly was viewed as insufficient to demonstrate that he was an actual member of the IRA at the time.

On the second charge of having professed to belong to the IRA, the depositions included transcriptions of a speech Adams had delivered at the Sinn Féin Ard Fheis in October 1977. Adams had told the party members, 'We could not survive almost eight years of war unless the people wanted to billet us, to look after us, to drive us about, unless they wanted to support us.' This, the judge decided, could not necessarily be read as Gerry Adams describing himself as a member of the IRA; he may just have been using the military language that is common in revolutionary politics.

There was also evidence that Adams had attended a meeting between the Official and Provisional IRA to help end a feud.

In his argument, Lord Chief Justice Lowry said that, Adams being a paid official of Sinn Féin,

It would be passing strange if the accused, who is one of the two Ulster members of the Ard Comhairle and actually on the pay roll of Sinn Féin, does not endorse its general policy and also the particular policy of supporting violence as manifested by the poseters [*sic*] at the Belfast headquarters.

All this is not to say that there is prima facie evidence that the accused is or professes to be a member of the IRA.

Support for violence, he reasoned, was not proof of membership.

Gerry Adams came out of custody in 1978 to comment on the food, which had not been as enjoyable as that in Crumlin Road Gaol. The prisoners he had left behind had food on their minds too. Those he had met in Long Kesh, protesting against the loss of Special Category Status, were planning a hunger strike.

Chapter 13

If Gerry Adams had been convicted on the charge of being a member of the IRA, he would have been sent back to Long Kesh. There he would not have been granted the Special Category Status that paramilitary prisoners had been given since his negotiations in 1972 with Philip Woodfield and Frank Steele. That status had been withdrawn by a Labour government in London that wanted IRA attacks clearly classified as criminal. A new, clean, modern prison replaced the old huts. Prisoners did not wear their own clothes. They were issued with a prison uniform. More than half of them were refusing to wear it, insisting on their right to be political prisoners.

Adams would have been faced immediately with the choice of joining the protesting republicans or seeing out his sentence as a conforming prisoner.

Had he joined the protest he would have taken his place in an escalating standoff between the IRA members and the state. The first stage was refusing to wear the uniform. The second was refusing to use the toilets. The third was hunger strike. But for the ruling made by Justice Lowry that taking a salute from assembled IRA members did not prove that one was a member of the IRA, Gerry Adams might have died on hunger strike in the Maze Prison at Long Kesh in 1980. He would not have come out of that experience eulogising the food and the antics and the naked streaking.

He has written about the prison protest he had seen in Long Kesh in the tone of an interested observer inclined to be helpful. He says that before he had been jailed himself, on remand, he had believed that the prisoners had started their 'dirty protest' as an escalation of their campaign of refusal to wear a prison uniform. '. . . in fact the prisoners had been forced into a no wash protest because their toilet facilities had been withdrawn from them.'[1]

Richard O'Rawe, who participated in the protest, wrote in *Blanketmen*, 'The idea was the result of discussions between The Dark [Brendan Hughes], Bobby Sands and Tom "Nail-bomb" McFeely from North Derry.'[2] He says it was modelled on a protest by the Scottish lifer Jimmy Boyle, protesting his innocence of a murder charge, who had 'smeared shit on the walls and on himself'.

Gerard Hodgins, another protesting prisoner, says the dirty protest was a clearly agreed strategy, though it is true that the screws were abusive and made slopping out difficult. 'The screws that you have with you were mostly pretty hostile to you. Many were loyalists. Some ex-Brits were bitter but mostly with the ex-Brits it was about getting a living wage, it was never as personal as with unionists or loyalists. So you would have the incidents of screws being heavy handed, brutal, but it was also a strategic decision, we're going to do this.'

After his own release from remand on the failed IRA membership charge, Adams appointed Gerry Brannigan from the Clonard area as the link man to a newly formed committee representing the protesters in the prisons, Long Kesh, Crumlin Road and Armagh women's prison.

Brannigan visited Long Kesh on the first available visit and saw Tomboy Loudon, a cellmate of Bobby Sands who had operated alongside him in the IRA. Loudon later, while performing on stage at a hunger strikes tribute, told the audience that Bobby Sands was his best mate, 'but he got caught first because he was a stupid cunt'. Brannigan's visit was held in a quiet area of the old internment block. He told Loudon that he would need to speak to Brendan Hughes, the OC, and to the OCs of all the wings. He was going to tell them that there was no significant propaganda effort around their protest and that it would take time to build one up. To facilitate that, some things would have to change. And there was no point in starting a hunger strike until a co-ordinated campaign was well established.

He explained that the prisoners would have to accept visits so that messages, 'comms', could be smuggled out and in. Family members of prisoners were asked to conceal messages or small packages in body orifices, to remove them in the visiting area and pass them across to brothers, sons and husbands who would conceal them again in a similar way.

Messages were mostly carried in the anus and vagina but some prisoners and visitors learnt to hide them up the nose or in the sinuses from which they could be dislodged into the back of the throat with a snort, coughed up and passed with a kiss.

For the visits the prisoners would have to wear the prison uniform. Brannigan would work through the Republican Press Centre on the Falls Road, sifting those messages for possible news stories that could be worked up for the media or form the basis of political statements. Brannigan says many of the men did not want visits for they did not want their families to see the state they were in.

Brendan Hughes, according to Gerard Hodgins, had argued against the whole protest at first. He had been one of the prisoners with Special Category Status but lost it when he was convicted of an attack on a screw along with Cleaky Clarke and transferred to the H-Blocks. There he immediately became the OC.

'And the first thing he said was, "See if we all put that uniform on tomorrow, they will not be able to control us". But we were in no mood for any of that auld talk. We were diehard and we'd never wear a criminal uniform and that. To up the ante, the dirty protest was inaugurated.'

Hughes argued against the blanket protest but joined in and led it because that was the only way he could keep the respect of the men. 'A lot of men took the uniform and conformed. Brendan didn't do that because then he would have been acting as an individual and he would have been rejected. Once you step out of the herd, the herd goes, phut!'

Gerard Hodgins, Richard O'Rawe, Tommy McKearney, Tommy Gorman and three hundred other prisoners were now living naked in shared cells. The toilet was the corner of the room and they would mop up their faeces with a piece of sponge torn from the mattress and smear it onto the cell wall, progressively destroying their beds. One day O'Rawe noticed movement in a pile of foetid discarded food. Maggots had hatched out overnight in all the cells on the block. Cleaky Clarke ordered that they were not to be killed, he says. Gerard Hodgins says this was probably meant in fun, 'Cleaky acting the wag'. O'Rawe disregarded the order anyway. The maggots were difficult to kill until he made a mash of the leftover food and their crushed bodies and smeared it on the wall over the shit. Some prisoners, he learnt later, adapted more easily to life with the maggots. Hodgins says he would wake in his bed with them crawling over him. Sometimes he organised little races for them that went on for hours because they were so slow. 'Boredom is a marvellous thing.' This is what men were reduced to. The H-Blocks were hell, a hell created by the prisoners who refused to wear prison clothes, wash or slop out their waste but which demanded tenacity, camaraderie and courage.

Gerry Brannigan's propaganda endeavour in time got the protest into the local and international media, but many on the outside were sceptical of a protest in which the worst conditions were self-inflicted. A joke went round Belfast. A man is walking up the Falls Road with two buckets of shite. His friend says, where are you going with that? Oh, says the man, our Jimmy is getting out of H-Blocks this week so we're doing up his bedroom for him.

Not that republicans indulged such humour.

The men were at war in the prison. The prison authorities had also become obsessive in their determination to break the protest. Liam Clarke's analysis in *Broadening the Battlefield*[3] is that the standoff was exacerbated at every stage by harsh and ill-considered discipline by the prison authorities.

Gerard Hodgins describes the beatings. 'I got beaten a lot in prison, a lot. A doctor would go round and say to you, I recommend that you have a bath, knowing that we weren't going to do it. And then you'd get brought down to the boards and dropped into a bath of freezing cold water and then you'd have two screws, medical officers, with a big long handled deck scrubber each and they would scrub you with that, and that's fucking sore.' He says the doctor would stand and watch.

He can joke about it now. 'If you find yourself in a situation where you know you are going to get beaten, the best thing is just to resign yourself to it. Hopefully you'll get a dig in the head that will knock you out and you'll not feel it.'

He says that, at first, it was immensely embarrassing to shit in the cell in front of another man but that the prisoners got used to it. 'Wanking? Some men would try to be discreet and some would just pull a blanket over themselves and get on with it.'

This grim protest was proving almost impossible to maintain. Nearly half of the IRA prisoners had agreed to conform to prison rules and wear the uniform. The IRA faced the possible humiliation of the protest being progressively eroded. When more prisoners were conforming than protesting, it would be difficult to argue that this was a united struggle fully endorsed by the movement.

The prisoners made five demands. Their slogans and the street graffiti insisted that they were prisoners of war entitled to political status but they compromised on this from the start. The five demands, if implemented, would allow them to claim a victory but would equally allow the government to claim it had not restored Special Category Status, which had, itself, been a compromise on the idea of political status.

The demands were for: (1) the right to wear their own clothing at all times; (2) exemption from all forms of penal labour; (3) free association with each other at all hours; (4) the right to organise their own recreational and educational programmes; and (5) full restoration of remission lost through the protest. A sixth demand, not listed, became part of the discussion later and that was that republican prisoners would be segregated from loyalists. Some argue that that is implied in the idea of free association. The government was caught on a principle, that conceding under the pressure of protest would look like weakness and grant a victory to the IRA.

Richard O'Rawe says it was not the prisoners themselves who framed the five demands. 'The outside leadership drafted them, and there was little or no input from the average Blanketman.'[4] Which was probably for the best. The obsessive determination of blanketmen would have inclined them to pitching their demands too high. A list of demands that started with compromise invited compromise from the other side. The demands were devised by the politically astute in the movement, not by the confrontational. The strategy appears to have been to suggest to the British that a deal was attainable. This may have been tactical, a hint that republicans would be more amenable than they actually intended to be, but many involved in the campaign at that stage will have hoped that agreement would be reached and that no one would die.

Hughes, Tommy McKearney and five others started refusing food in the autumn of 1980. Bobby Sands took over as OC from Hughes, who expected to die before Christmas. The first hunger strike failed because Hughes called it off rather than let a man die on the brink of a possible deal. Sean McKenna had gone into a coma. Tommy McKearney was close to coma. A priest mediator known as The Angel, Father Brendan Meagher, had come to the hunger strikers to tell them that a document was on its way from Aldergrove airport with government proposals.

Tommy McKearney believes that a deal was indeed imminent, even that the principle of prisoners being allowed their own clothes had been conceded before the hunger strike started.

The prisoners had agreed that no deal would be made unless Gerry Adams and Danny Morrison were present to approve it. But now it was clear that there was a weakness in the strategy. Hunger striking would always fail as a tactic if people were not ready to die, not just for their core demands, but for tiny incremental elements of them and to preserve the procedures around approving a settlement. Would a man be allowed to die to give Adams and Morrison time to reach the prison and to read and discuss a document? If not, the strike could easily be compromised.

The H-Blocks committee was now run by Jim Gibney, replacing Gerry Brannigan, who says he was thought to be too close to the prisoners. The prisoners were told that Brannigan had had a mental breakdown. The committee promoted a line that the strike had ended with a deal and that the British had broken their commitment to it. This wasn't true, according to O'Rawe, who says that Sands reported back to the prisoners that they had got nothing.

Tommy McKearney says it is not so clear that the first hunger strike was a failure. 'You're talking about language here, the language of pressure and despair.'

Bobby Sands went on to devise a new type of hunger strike, one in which men would die in series rather than all together. Four would start in fortnightly intervals, then each would be replaced by another prisoner when he died.

The first strike had been predicated on the prospect of the government saving lives by conceding and it had failed because Brendan Hughes had previously promised to save Sean McKenna and couldn't wait for clarification.

Bobby Sands wasn't going to risk a strike falling apart because an OC would rather save him than wait for a message. He appointed Bik McFarlane to replace him as OC of the prisoners when he planned the second strike.

McFarlane said later:

I actually went through this session with him on a Sunday morning at mass and I said to him, look, I am not even number two or number three or number four in the chain of command in here and I mentioned Seanna Walsh who was the vice OC. And there was an adjutant and an intelligence officer, there was all this. And he said to me, 'What you don't realise is Seanna Walsh is my best mate. And when a crisis arrives and if they do decide to negotiate and you have to say no, he'll not let me die.' And I said, 'Well, by extension then, you're saying that I will.' 'Oh yeah,' he said, 'you have to. And that's just the size of it.' And I said, 'Well, thanks for the compliment and your confidence in me.'[5]

Sands had recognised qualities in Bik McFarlane that had been lacking in Brendan Hughes, a serious killer who, nonetheless, had proven unable to let a comrade die to preserve the strike.

The second hunger strike was predicated on the near certainty of men dying and of the need for the strike to continue beyond that. Men would now be tested on their resolve before they entered the hunger strike and would formally affirm their determination to let their lives go.

Richard O'Rawe says, 'The logic of the stepped system was to instil loyalty to the guy who died before you, so that you would go too. All the responsibility for everything was on your shoulders, the responsibility for three hundred blanket men, the responsibility for your comrades who had already died. You were looking behind you and they were standing there, waiting on you passing over. Right? There was a psychological imperative or a trap, straitjacket might be a better word. You were almost compelled to go the whole way. To pull out would have been seen as abject cowardice, particularly after some of the men had already given their lives.'

In future, if a striker ended a fast, there would always be another striker behind him and more time to play with. And the pressure would keep piling on the government. But strikers wouldn't break this time. They would hold their resolve and die.

The pressure on the government to settle would be the appalling routine of prisoners dying and each funeral would be a rallying point of public support for their demands. There was another difference. Gerry Brannigan had urged Bobby Sands not to join the first hunger strike on the grounds that a strong man would be needed as OC to make the call on whether to end it or proceed to let men die. Hughes made the call in the end, and called wrong. Sands would lead the second strike, being the strong man who would be sure not to weaken at the end and thereby provide an example to those behind him. Having let Hughes scupper the first strike short of a deal, he would have to show that he could hold his resolve at the end in a way that Hughes had not. But that left Bik McFarlane as the OC who could call the strike off. And he would never be able to do so because, as is clear in his letters from the prison, he deferred in everything to Gerry Adams.

Chapter 14

Bobby Sands died in May 1981 after sixty-six days without food. He was twenty-seven years old. A huge support campaign had built up around the prison protest. His slow starvation and death became a global story and a rallying point for street protest and riots. Loyalists responded by attacking key members of the campaign on the outside. In January a gang had shot Bernadette Devlin several times in an ambush on her family home, a country cottage, and she tossed the child in her arms to her husband as the bullets ripped into her. She survived. Others, including the academic Miriam Daly, were killed. A loyalist gang went out to kill Gerry Brannigan but attacked the wrong house and killed a young neighbour.

The high profile of the hunger strike was turning its leaders into easy targets and the sectarian warfare escalated. The IRA campaign against the state continued its routine momentum but the real changes presaged by the hunger strike were political.

The support strategy developed with an electoral opportunity. Frank Maguire, the sitting MP for Fermanagh South Tyrone, had died suddenly. Adams conceived the idea of a dying Sands fighting for the seat from prison, with Sinn Féin running his campaign. Those who depict Adams as supremely Machiavellian must concede that he could not have anticipated this opportunity at the start of the hunger strike, but he seized it and used it well.

After Sands's success, anomalous republican graffiti in Belfast read: 'Rt Hon Bobby Sands MP'.

Gerry Adams advised on the direction of the hunger strike through smuggled letters to the prisoners' OC, Bik McFarlane.

McFarlane had been in Cage 11 with him and with Bobby Sands and clearly loved him. He often signed his own letters out to Adams with 'xoxox'. Adams himself often signs cards and greetings in the same way. The letters that Adams sent into the prison were destroyed by the prisoners and there is now a dispute between McFarlane and his press officer in the prison, Richard O'Rawe, about one of them.

Three men had followed Sands onto the strike at fortnightly intervals. A fourth, Joe McDonnell, replaced him when he died.

By July 1981, the first four were all gone and the second wave of deaths led by McDonnell was about to begin. Joe McDonnell as a lad probably never imagined himself becoming a martyr for Irish republicanism. He was a short, wiry, handsome and cheeky man who had kept prisoners' spirits up with his wit. He had been five years in jail throughout the whole blanket and dirty protests, refusing visits from his family because he would have had to wear a prison uniform for them. He had not volunteered for the first hunger strike but had found the resolve to join the second. He had pledged that he was willing to die and he had surrendered to his OC, Bik McFarlane, the right to save him or let him go.

McDonnell probably reassured himself on his long hungry days that the IRA leadership would save him at the end. A strike that had not achieved its aims after four deaths was unlikely to win after more. As he weakened and wasted in the ninth week of his fast, both sides were looking for a compromise that would stop the routine of passive suicide.

In two books, *Blanketmen* and *Afterlives*,[1] and in much journalism, O'Rawe has insisted that a deal was offered to the prisoners on 5 July 1981, after the first four deaths, and that he and McFarlane had agreed that it was sufficient to end the strike and save McDonnell and the others coming after him. O'Rawe had, the previous day, issued a statement clarifying the position of the prisoners, saying that they were not, as was being assumed, seeking special treatment. They were happy that their gains through the strike be shared with all prisoners. 'I just wanted to save lives,' he says.

O'Rawe wrote that statement, passed it to McFarlane who contributed little to changing it, then released it to the media as a smuggled 'comm'. From that moment a protest which had started as a reaction to the withdrawal of Special Category Status was just about a general improvement in conditions for all prisoners in Northern Ireland. There was now an opportunity for the British to make an offer that did not compromise their insistence that the men were criminals, like other prisoners.

In response, a compromise offer was mediated to the prisoners from the Northern Ireland Office through a body called the Irish Commission for Justice and Peace, made up of some Catholic clergy and nationalist politicians. It was reinforced by a message from the Foreign Office through a secret channel, the Derry businessman Brendan Duddy, nicknamed The Mountain Climber. The British offer said that the prisoners would have their own clothes, subject to the approval of the prison governor, that parcels and visits would be on the same basis as conforming prisoners, that there would be flexibility on prison work and 'further developments'. But the British insisted that none of this was negotiable and would only come into effect when the hunger strike ended.[2]

The Taoiseach or Irish Prime Minister, Garret FitzGerald, argued in his autobiography that the British had made a crucial mistake in adding an extra minor clause to the version of the offer that went through Duddy, offering prisoners access to Open University courses. This, he believed, led Adams and Morrison to think that they could do better in direct dealings with the British than through the Commission.

FitzGerald wrote, 'we [. . .] had known nothing at all of the disastrous British approach to Adams and Morrison.' And he claimed that the IRA had attempted to 'raise the ante by seeking concessions beyond what the prisoners had said they could accept'.[3]

So the Taoiseach's understanding was that the IRA had taken the initiative away from the prisoners.

Duddy – codenamed SOON – advised the British that very few top republicans were competent to make an agreement. Thomas Hennessey has recounted his exchanges with the British in his book *Hunger Strike*. SOON advised, writes Hennessey,

that if the key to accepting any agreement was persuasion, education and knowledge, then that was not available outside the very upper echelons of the Provisional movement. It was not even available as of right to the entire Sinn Féin leadership. This, SOON claimed, posed a problem. In response to HMG's request for suggestions of Provisionals who would fit this description, SOON produced Danny Morrison, Gerry Adams and Martin McGuinness as the only three candidates. After consultation, HMG said that it would accept Morrison but would on no account accept either Adams or McGuinness.[4]

Duddy had passed the offer to Martin McGuinness. Danny Morrison brought it into the prison and explained it to McFarlane. O'Rawe says he and McFarlane agreed between themselves that this was sufficient to warrant ending the hunger strike. McFarlane denies this.

Danny Morrison came in and said, 'The Brits have opened a channel. There's a possibility for a negotiated settlement here,' and he knew the elation in my face was nearly – you could almost physically grab it. And he cautioned me and he says, 'Look, keep your feet on the ground because this might be just part and parcel of what they do because, see if they build you up to that height and then they slap you down, you'll hit the ground harder than you came off it in the first place.'[5]

McFarlane's account acknowledges that a message was indeed relayed to the hunger strikers by Danny Morrison and that Morrison dampened his enthusiasm for it and urged caution.

Danny had a session with the hunger strikers and then I went in with them and they said to me that there wasn't enough in what the British were prepared to talk about here. There were five demands; there weren't even near two or three of these; that they needed to flesh things out; they needed also to send somebody in and spell out in detail, you're getting a, b, c or you're not getting a, b, c.

They promised to send someone in.

They didn't send anyone in.

O'Rawe says that Bik wrote to Gerry Adams saying there was, in fact, enough in the offer to enable them to end the hunger strike and that Adams wrote back expressing his disappointment with them and saying the hunger strike had to continue.

O'Rawe says, 'When McFarlane and I accepted the offer they just blew us out of the water. "Get out of the way; it's got nothing to do with you." From then on they didn't even tell us what the content of the conversations were with the British.'

Nor was there much insistence from the dying prisoners that they should.

'You have to understand the discipline of the IRA. You gave them your life to do whatever they wanted with it. The discipline was the discipline and the authority was overbearing and omnipotent.'

But it wasn't just about discipline; O'Rawe says it was about the regard in which Adams was held by the prisoners. 'One, we had absolute faith in Adams. Adams to us was a God, an intellectual giant walking among midgets. Right? And two, the Brits had circumvented the problem of talking to the prisoners by talking to the leadership on the outside, so there was a sort of a logic that this is probably an expedient way of doing business.'

O'Rawe says the men revered Adams. 'Absolutely. That was founded on the sort of way he took the movement on a leftward direction in around 1977–78. It was founded on a belief that he had almost single-handedly saved the IRA from the disastrous '75 ceasefire. And that he had been the visionary who had seen the pitfall that was in the '75 ceasefire, that the British were not withdrawing. Then he had shown a degree of leadership and started saying that . . . what we need is a socialist republic. But all of that there endeared him to the ordinary volunteer and he seemed to be a man of wisdom and he was a very charismatic man into the bargain.'

The Prime Minister's offer, made via Brendan Duddy, was rejected by Adams and the close coterie of senior republicans around him who had a full grasp of the protest and the conditions. It was a statement of concessions that would be announced immediately if the hunger strike was called off. Margaret Thatcher insisted that there could be no discussion about this, simply a yes or no answer.

But Gerry Adams doesn't do yes or no answers.

He moved quickly to monopolise the negotiations. He met members of the Irish Commission for Justice and Peace who had been mediating basically the same offer to the prisoners from the Northern Ireland Office. There was the small difference between the offers that Garret FitzGerald mentioned. Adams told them that they were cluttering the field, that they were being used for intelligence gathering and that he had a direct channel to the British with a better offer on the table.[6]

He also told the British he wanted to bypass Brendan Duddy, The Mountain Climber, describing the links through Duddy and the Commission as 'the worst possible channels'.

The republican reply to Margaret Thatcher reveals that Adams viewed her offer as a possible first step in a negotiation process, not as the only and final move she would make. Adams had secured a connection to Thatcher and his political instincts told him to try to keep her on the line and work to influence her further. He had seen the failure of the 1972 ceasefire. He had sat and faced a British minister, but the team of IRA leaders he was with then had found no way to extract an advantage from that or to keep communications open. He was having another try. He wrote back, 'We are always prepared to facilitate a more practical and confidential means of conducting this dialogue.'[7]

McFarlane had written to Adams on 7 July, the day before McDonnell died, when Adams was exploring the potential for dialogue, assuring him that the Irish Commission for Justice and Peace would not now be taken seriously by the prisoners. 'If we can render them ineffective now, then we leave the way clear for a direct approach without all the ballsing about.'[8]

In his memoir, Adams says he was on the phone to a British official at the moment McDonnell died.[9] This suggests that the British had responded in some measure to his call for another route for talks. The 'direct approach' that McFarlane mentioned was made. Having already told the prisoners to reject the offer, Adams was teasing out with the British some prospect of it being made more acceptable.

Papers released to a *Belfast Telegraph* journalist, the late Liam Clarke, on a Freedom of Information request, disclose that some exchanges with the IRA leadership did follow the first letter. Perhaps that phone call was one of them. And perhaps the man at the other end of the line was a diplomat close to the exchanges, Philip Woodfield, one of those who had met Adams in Derry in 1972 to negotiate the first ceasefire.

The Adams line ever since, reiterated at the time of the death of Margaret Thatcher, is that the British were stubborn to the end and are to blame for the deaths of ten hunger strikers.

Richard O'Rawe says, 'I don't give a shit what Adams or Morrison or any of these guys say, the Brits were genuinely looking for a way out of this. And that actually contradicts the general assumption that these things always go to the brink.'

Critics of Adams's management of the hunger strike see him as a Machiavellian manipulator working to a plan for political power. Tommy McKearney takes a more circumspect view. 'You have to be careful of thinking of Sinn Féin as this incredibly prescient, all-knowing machine. But I suspect there was a lot of ad lib, off-the-cuff, panic in decision-making taken at that time. Not necessarily to exonerate but you were finding that they were making it up as they were going along. The one criticism that I don't draw back from is that the ending of the hunger strike should have been a decision by the army council of the IRA. The army council abdicated its responsibility.'

The IRA was letting Adams and a coterie around him manage the whole strategy.

Adams was doing what any negotiator might have done had the stakes been lower. What is appalling is that they were bartering with men's lives, and those men had assented to their lives being used like this.

There is another trace of those extended negotiations in documents released to Liam Clarke and reproduced in O'Rawe's second book, *Afterlives*. A letter from Downing Street to the Northern Ireland Office, updating the Secretary of State for Northern Ireland on the exchanges, describes the republican response. The message had come back from the IRA asking for 'a good deal more' and fishing for further dialogue. The British understanding was that the hunger strikers were under IRA orders and that it made more practical sense to deal with their contact, that is, with Adams, than with the hunger strikers themselves. Downing Street made clear to the IRA that declining the offer effectively marked 'the end of this development' for they were refusing to be drawn. A briefing note for the Northern Ireland Office said, 'This had produced a very rapid reaction which suggested that it was not the content of the message which they had objected to but only its tone.'[10]

In a public meeting in Derry discussing O'Rawe's claims, in May 2009, Brendan Duddy joined the panel to explain the offer and its aftermath to an audience including many former blanketmen. Duddy told O'Rawe that he had never before heard this message about 'tone'. It had not been passed through him. This objection to the 'tone' of the British offer was communicated directly to Downing Street, presumably by Adams; either that or there was even another channel open. After hearing the quibble about 'tone', Downing Street agreed to get back to the IRA with a draft statement, in the hope that the leadership would then order the men off the hunger strike.

But there were some in the leadership of the protest who would not have been assuaged by a change of tone, for they saw the hunger strike by this stage as integral to the whole IRA campaign, the cutting edge of it.

Bik McFarlane saw the hunger strikers as 'front-line troops' in a war that the IRA was winning. This was no longer just about prison reform. Two weeks after Joe McDonnell's death Adams briefed McFarlane on the moves the British were offering to make, following the end of the hunger strike. McFarlane agreed with Adams then that to accept them would be to capitulate and that, though the cost was high, they should continue.

He wrote, 'Yet I feel the part we have played in forwarding the liberation struggle has been great. Terrific gains have been made and the Brits are losing by the day.'[11]

This was an absurdly optimistic reading of the state of play between the IRA and the British government, but then presumably even the men on the outside would not have been pursuing a war without hopes of winning, however tenuous and ill-informed those hopes were. In his letter to McFarlane Adams had asked him to consider the price they would pay. McFarlane wrote, 'we are fighting a war and we must accept that front-line troops are more susceptible to casualties than anyone.'[12]

Gerry Brannigan says that this thinking informed the hunger strike plan from the beginning. 'The hunger strike was never just about five demands. In my opinion, it was a chance for the IRA to rebuild.' But, as he sees it now, the men died for 'constitutional nationalism'; that is, 'they were sacrificed for principles they opposed'.

In war men must, of course, be willing to die.

There are other stories from IRA members about their willingness to sacrifice themselves for the cause or for comrades. Peter Rogers, one of the seven who escaped from the *Maidstone* prison ship in Belfast Lough in 1972, says that each of the men had pledged not to shout for help if he started to drown. 'We made a pact with each other. If anyone got into difficulties in the water they were not to call out and ruin the escape for the others. It was a pact, which really meant that you had to go under, to drown for the sake of your comrades and the success of the escape. Thankfully, no one was put to that rigorous test.'[13]

So the danger that he might have to die for comrades on an operation was already ingrained in the IRA man's understanding of his responsibility.

Gerard Hodgins, the last of the hunger strikers, says that he was willing to die because the life he was giving up 'wasn't that great'. He had been a blanketman for five years. He had nothing but the comradeship of other men, and they were willing to die for him.

But what was it he was to die for – the prisoners or a united Ireland or the political growth of Sinn Féin? Tommy McKearney says he joined the first hunger strike on the clear understanding that the welfare of the prisoners was the sole concern. 'My clear understanding is that it was a prison issue. We weren't naively thinking a hunger strike in the blocks wouldn't have political implications but I remember putting it very clearly to Brendan: Is this more or less than a prison protest? And he was very clear that this was a prison protest.'

Dixie Elliott, a Derry IRA man who was close to Bobby Sands, says, however, that the strike was integral to the wider struggle. 'These were courageous men willing to die for a cause they believed in. We in fact believed at the time that winning the prison issue was the final phase of the struggle. Once we defeated criminalisation we had more or less won.'

There is clear division of opinion among former blanketmen on whether they were fighting for their own conditions or actually pursuing the wider struggle by other means. The second hunger strike became a proxy for the whole IRA campaign. The men had limited freedom to come off the strike but were so mesmerised by obsession that they did not know that. They believed that their leaders had more right than they had themselves to choose whether they lived or died.

Adams and McFarlane knew that these men who were volunteering to die would, if they weren't in jail, be out risking their lives for the IRA anyway and many of that generation of republicans had low expectations of living into their thirties and beyond. For McFarlane, the hunger strike was an integral part of the IRA campaign and about more than the five demands. Adams understood that the OC in the prison, leading the men, viewed it that way. And McFarlane, when sharing that vision with Adams, trusted that he was dealing with a friend who agreed with it.

Political tactics alone seem a weak explanation for the resolve of these men to die. Brendan Hughes later spoke, with some difficulty, of the love between the men, unique in his experience.

There was an almost loving comradeship developed over a period of years among them, something that to me is unique, that deep solid comradeship. They are all ordinary people but that comradeship, that suffering, that unity, brought about something in those people, in us, that we felt so tied, so committed to each other. Some people would refer to them as saints. I think that's sloppy; they weren't saints. They were just ordinary. They missed ordinary things. We talked about sex. We used to talk about how you missed freedom. Then at night we'd have talked about the stars; we'd have talked about God – is there one? We'd have talked about the beauty of the stars and the moon. And that whole period, coming through all that enabled ten people just to walk to their deaths.[14]

But they didn't just walk to their deaths. They were encouraged.

There are several hints in the 'comms', the letters smuggled out of the prison, that the men were being manipulated. The second to die, Francis Hughes, had written to his family explaining that Jim Gibney, Adams's mediator who had replaced Gerry Brannigan, would be coming with them on every visit to him in the prison. He clearly did not like this. 'Don't say to anyone other than John that I don't want this Jim boy up on every visit. OK, it's probably all for a good reason.'[15]

Towards the end of July, one of the hunger strikers, Pat McGeown, started suffering from an internal wound and this raised the question of whether he should have medical treatment. McFarlane reported this to the outside. 'I explained to him that so long as it was non-vitamin or glucose based, then that was sound enough.'[16]

Then McFarlane wrote to Gerry Adams explaining further difficulties with keeping McGeown 'on the line'. 'I explained that independent thought was fine.'

But he let McGeown know the limits of what free thinking was permitted: '. . . once it began to stray from our well considered and accepted line, then it became extremely dangerous.'

Rogelio Alonso, an academic specialising in the study of terrorism, applies Groupthink theory to the management of the hunger strike and the wider IRA campaign.[17] Everyone was caught up in a shared determination to stand over the initial resolve, having once agreed that it was right, even when it was leading to calamity. By this reading, no one had autonomy, neither the prisoners nor the army council who, Alonso believed, were directing them and who could have ordered the hunger strike to end. But was it the IRA army council that was directing them?

Richard O'Rawe says, 'He [Bik McFarlane] was under Adams's control. He was a Cage 11 man, as was Bobby, as was The Dark; they were all Cage 11 men, so they were guys that he was comfortable with and whom he would have a certain degree of control over.'

Gerard Hodgins says, 'Bik effectively handed control of the jail to Gerry Adams. And he became our OC then and he ran it for whatever his objectives were. And we're seeing the outworking of that in the political growth and development of Sinn Féin.'

Without being able to read Adams's letters to McFarlane it is impossible to say which of the two men was more focused, more determined to prolong the hunger strike and who would have let more men die, but there are many clues that Adams was the lead mind. O'Rawe and others plainly believe he was in charge. When McFarlane, for instance, contemplated joining the hunger strike and sacrificing his own life, he turned to Adams not for guidance but for permission.

The original argument against McFarlane joining the hunger strike had been that he would attract little public sympathy because he was serving time for an attack on the Bayardo Bar on the Shankill Road, and had killed civilians. But in a message to Adams[18] he said he would like to be one of those 'front-line troops'. He wrote that he was willing to give his life, but that he would leave the decision entirely to Gerry Adams. 'I know I'd die sin é [that's it]. I'll abide by your decision as I can do little else. If it's negative just say no.'

Adams has said little in response to any of the claims that he managed and directed the hunger strikes, but O'Rawe quotes a letter he wrote on a Sinn Féin Twitter feed on 8 October 2009. The article had been removed soon after posting and was then posted briefly again on the *An Phoblacht* website and once more removed.

The Adams letter emphasises that the hunger strikers 'were not dupes',[19] that the British were not trusted because they had reneged on a deal to end the first hunger strike, a point disputed by O'Rawe but accepted by McKearney, and that O'Rawe had never left his cell during the whole period and, by implication, couldn't be trusted to know much.

Pat McGeown was told bluntly by McFarlane that he had no freedom to question the decisions of 'the Big Lad'. He was ordered not to share his doubts with other hunger strikers and later expressed regret that he had 'not been more honest' with Tom McElwee, who had wavered and then gone on to die.[20]

If the kind of Groupthink that Alonso sees in all this included Adams, then maybe he had limited freedom himself to break from the momentum of routine suicide. Yet, knowing more than the prisoners did, and having established direct contact with British officials, he may have been the only player with the freedom to act as an individual and make a decision that would have saved lives.

But Tommy McKearney is sceptical of the view that the British had made a clear offer that was sufficient and rejected. 'If the British government was anxious to bring an end to the hunger strike then and made a genuine and half acceptable offer, and given that the British cabinet is a sophisticated machine that can analyse situations, they would have very quickly realised that the IRA was playing a game, attempting for the IRA's own ends to prevent an acceptable settlement. Why would the British not then take the deal that was on offer, bring it quietly to Cardinal Ó Fiaich [Archbishop of Armagh], John Hume, Ted Kennedy, the Taoiseach and through them to the families of the hunger strikers?'

Maybe the British were not as sophisticated as McKearney thinks they were. But they were emphatic that the deal had to be secret, that they would only move to implement some of the five demands after the strike had ended. Thatcher was willing to provide the prisoners with an escape route from the trap they had placed themselves in; she was not going to prise it open and lift them out. But there are indications that the British did try to reach the prisoners by influencing families and other visitors. McFarlane was struggling to deal with the prisoners and their families when word reached them through members of the SDLP that an offer had been made and that conditions would improve radically if the strike ended.

He reported this in an almost frenzied tone to Adams.

I said that we should keep firmly on our line, not deviate in the slightest, because to do so spelt danger . . . I then explained how you were on the ball every day . . .

I said that you were in the best position to advise and read the situation and that you had agreed that my presence was a must at any talks. Also that you'd ensure 100% effort and more to steering the propaganda effort in the right direction . . .

I told them that I could have accepted half measures before Joe died, but I didn't then and I wouldn't now. I told them that the price of victory could be high and that they might all die before we get a settlement.[21]

Even as the hunger strike dragged on without progress, more men volunteered for it as those in front of them died. One of those later strikers was Gerard Hodgins. Hodgins now shares Richard O'Rawe's view that the hunger strikers were manipulated by Adams and his committee. He says, 'We did firmly believe that we could change the British government. We still believed right up to the end in fighting on and keeping the hunger strike going. Thank God that we didn't. We were overruled on it. The great mythology is that we were the supreme authority on the strike, the prisoners, that's a load of nonsense.'

But he also says, 'There were people prepared to go on with it.'

In his own writings, Gerry Adams contradicts himself on the purpose of the hunger strike. In his memoir he says it was simply about the five demands. In *The Politics of Irish Freedom* he says that the prisoners knew that they were involved in a fight with the British government that went beyond prison conditions. 'They were pitching themselves with the only weapon at their command against the Imperial power.'[22] And they felt that their deaths were going to be 'politically productive for the republican cause'.

Others on the outside were using different weapons and the prisoners approved. Bik McFarlane joked about killings in a letter to 'Liam Og', Tom Hartley. 'Have just heard about that cunning little operation in S. Armagh. O, you wonderful people.'[23] The 'cunning little operation' was a landmine attack on a British army vehicle near Bessbrook, which killed five soldiers on 19 May 1981. McFarlane bragged that he would personally 'whack Concorde'.

The strike was brought to an end by a Tyrone priest and school headmaster, Father Denis Faul. His nickname, The Menace, had followed him from the school, St Patrick's, Dungannon. Faul had known many of the prisoners as pupils and he cared about them.

He had come to be regarded as a problem, not just by the IRA but also by British officials for his campaigning on justice issues. He was a lump of a man, oblivious to his appearance, and he spoke with a lisp. He was a theologically conservative Catholic priest yet was seen by much of the media as a strident radical. He opposed integrated education. He once told a journalist that he would, of course, refuse communion to a divorced person who was in a new relationship but that he would not refuse it to an IRA bomber. 'Who am I to say that I know the state of that man's soul?'

He did not comport himself aggressively like a fighter and was slightly bumbling in public speaking yet Faul was the one to take on Gerry Adams. He met Adams and persuaded him to go into the prison and talk to the men. Adams has provided an account of this meeting in his memoir. He denies that he had the power to call off the strike, though he says that Faul had 'almost persuaded' some of the families that he could order the men to end it.[24]

He went into the Maze with Owen Carron, the new candidate for Sands's seat in Fermanagh South Tyrone, and he met Bik McFarlane with six of the hunger strikers in the hospital canteen. Two of the strikers were too weak to join them. Adams says, 'As they smiled across the table at us, all my fears and apprehensions vanished.'

He says all the lads were 'crystal clear' that there was 'no basis for a settlement'. He told them that the British were 'still persisting in their refusal to move meaningfully on work, association and segregation'.

In fact, segregation had not been one of the five demands. The British had conceded that work might include educational programmes and that free association would be permissible within the wings.[25]

Adams says he was brutally harsh with them in telling them that they all might die and that nationalist Ireland might be demoralised, but he was testing their resolve, not challenging it. He says that the meeting descended into banter. 'Tom McElwee was trying on my glasses. Somebody was seriously and genuinely concerned that Bik might miss his tea.'

Adams says that the men were committed to the protest until they had all their demands met. He is emphatic in his book that the men had made a rational political decision; they were not merely dying to pay a debt to those who had died before them: '. . . each was personally committed to the five demands and the hunger strike.'

It would be hard to be absolutely sure of that.

At least one of the hunger strikers meeting Adams had had doubts about the strategy and about his willingness to die but had not aired them. Pat McGeown was under orders from McFarlane not to share his doubts with the other prisoners, and the one person who could have prompted him to speak frankly, and who knew about those doubts from Bik's letters, was Gerry Adams. But perhaps by the time of the meeting he thought that McGeown's doubts had been assuaged. McFarlane challenged McGeown on why he had not raised his doubts with Adams when he had come into the prison to meet them and he said he hadn't because he was afraid the room was bugged.

As for Adams's insistence that the men were not bound to the routine of dying out of loyalty to each other but by political conviction, it was precisely this loyalty that McFarlane played on to get McGeown back in line. He sent McGeown a written message arguing that his doubts would damage the morale of the other men if they knew about them. McGeown then replied with an assurance that he had overcome his doubts and was back on track.

But the meeting with Adams was not the great candid meeting of brave souls that he describes because the men who were preparing to die did not feel free to speak frankly.

In August Owen Carron was elected to parliament in the seat vacated by the death of Bobby Sands.

Denis Faul found the weak link in the hunger strike plan. At the very end, usually two days before death, the prisoner would slide into a coma. He would then not have the power to summon food or medical assistance; that responsibility would pass to his next of kin. Faul told the wives and mothers of the dying men that they could save them by consenting that they be fed and given medical assistance at that stage. Pat McGeown was taken off the fast by his wife when he started to lose consciousness and the strike began to break down with other families committing themselves to the same action.

There was opposition to the strike growing within the IRA leadership too. Mick Donnelly, a former Derry OC, believes that there may have been an intervention from John Davey, a member of the IRA army council. He says, 'John Davey and I met at Mickey Devine's funeral and walked along together and talked about the hunger strike. At this stage, it was fairly obvious nearly to everybody that they were managing it outside and you'd various bits and pieces from Father Faul and you started to have an idea what was going on. Then John Davey spelt it out: "That crowd are managing the whole thing but this will be the end of it; there'll be no more after this." And I remember me saying, "But how are you going to stop it, John?" And he got very excited. He said, "I'll stop it".'

Yet, cynical as some in the IRA now were about the management of the hunger strike, some prisoners wanted to continue. Gerard Hodgins had a plan to circumvent the danger of families asking for their men to be fed when they lost consciousness. He suggested that the striking prisoners should marry IRA women who would then be the next of kin and could allow them to die; they could indeed be under IRA orders to allow them to die. Bik McFarlane rejected the plan. Hodgins thinks that he was 'in the loop' and knew that the strike was coming to an end.

The hunger strike ended formally on 3 October 1981. Three days later, on what Adams reminds us was his thirty-third birthday, the British announced the concessions that they had offered three months earlier.[26]

The O'Rawe version of the deal offered to the hunger strikers has been supported by Charles Moore's biography of Margaret Thatcher[27] and others, yet refuted strongly by Danny Morrison, who claims that if a deal had been rejected, the British would have sought propaganda advantage from that, 'stopping the struggle in its tracks'.[28] It's a strong point, but the British had other interests to defend, primarily perhaps the integrity of future negotiations. Their offer had been a secret one and they kept that secret for decades ahead.

Gerard Hodgins had been expecting to die and had been ordered to start eating again. He says, 'On the day that we did end it, it did feel like a defeat. We hadn't achieved any of our objectives, we had lost ten people, three of them off the wing that I was on, which is a high proportion. It would be a lie to say I wasn't relieved. You get a surge of relief over you and you say, I'm not going to die. Then you have a whole new appreciation of life. But at the same time you had the feeling that we gave up.'

Part Two

Politics Takes Over

Chapter 15

One day in the early 1980s, Gerry Adams, Tom Hartley and a member of the IRA's Belfast Brigade staff were meeting when Hartley raised questions about a protest in the Iveagh area of the Falls Road by the political units. The political units were set up to absorb the energies of those who wanted to help but not to join.

The man from Brigade staff says, 'We had had a policy in the IRA that if some guy wanted to join, the RO, the recruitment officer, would test that resolve by trying to talk him out of it, let him see how hard and how dangerous it was. And then if the applicant realised he couldn't hack it, that was fine. There was no criticism of that decision, no attempt to sway him; we just let him go and no hard feelings. But we were losing talent that we could have made some use of so we changed it.'

He proposed the creation of 'political units', groups of people who would not be sworn into the IRA or 'Green booked' but would be organised to provide help. 'Now applicants who changed their minds about becoming full members would be invited to help in other ways, storing weapons, joining protests, providing billets. These political units were under the direct management of the IRA; however, they were not Sinn Féin members.'

He claims the members of the political units were later absorbed into Sinn Féin on the orders of Gerry Adams when he was working to build up the party.

At the meeting, Tom Hartley and the IRA man argued about who was doing more on the ground. The IRA man said the protest was needed because 'Sinn Féin is doing fuck all'.

He says, 'Gerry tried to calm the situation, said we'd reconvene later. A couple of days later an order came through from GHQ that the members of the political units were to be absorbed into Sinn Féin. That was the end of them. But you have this myth that Gerry fashioned Sinn Féin out of his own native genius for inspiring people; in fact, he just took over something that we in the army had already set up. Adams took the credit, naturally.'

Sinn Féin had been developed to serve the purposes of the IRA but was now evolving a separate identity with separate objectives, under the guidance of Gerry Adams. And the IRA let this happen because it had already accepted that it did not need to expand but to maintain a low-level campaign. It was no longer dreaming of being an army that would erode British power but sought to be a constant irritant that would sap British will and make political compromise impossible.

Richard O'Rawe, who had been the press officer for the republican prisoners during the hunger strikes, came out of prison and went home resolved that his IRA career was over. Then one day a car pulled up outside. It was Gerry Adams and Tom Hartley. Adams sat in the car. Hartley came into the house. They had a job for him. They wanted him to come and work at the Republican Press Centre and help organise Sinn Féin election campaigns.

The Press Centre was then run by Danny Morrison. O'Rawe took the job and was paid £40 a week and drew the dole as well. IRA activists at the time were getting £20 a week from Joe Cahill, the man with a tight hand on the funds. Much of the money was gathered through robberies and protection rackets, though the party had wealthy friends and supporters in the United States and other countries, but IRA volunteers were expected to sign on for unemployment benefit.

Gerry Brannigan says he once had to talk to Cahill because he was cutting money to a group of men on the run in the South. The men had to wait six weeks before they qualified for the dole in Dublin and received an extra subsidy until then, but Cahill had cut it a week early, leaving them short. Brannigan says he took Cahill to a pub and said to him, 'If these guys have to go back up north because they are broke, and they get arrested there and interrogated, do you think they are still going to feel they owe a debt of loyalty to you after you dropped them in it?'

They got their money, says Brannigan. His story illustrates how the IRA needed welfare payments from the enemy. Those same welfare payments subsidised the Press Centre too.

O'Rawe's job was to write press statements for candidates, many of whom, he says, 'didn't know what they had said until they read it in the paper themselves'.

He wrote statements for Gerry Adams too at first, but Adams took him aside and said he would do his own. 'He was good at that. Gerry Adams is nobody's fool and he can write. He was a savvy sort of a guy. Some of the guys we had up hadn't the intellectual wherewithal to know when to put a statement out, how to put it out, so a wee bit of help did no harm.'

The staff in the Press Centre needed to think like professional journalists, to anticipate what an editor might regard as a good story, to know what questions to expect from reporters. O'Rawe had to generate copy for the local papers working at the level of a senior press officer who would have been earning more than three times as much in another party or with a government department. To do his job properly he had to be acquainted with the policy objectives of Sinn Féin and to be attuned to the ways in which story angles could be directed to serve its interests.

'I was at a few of the meetings of a small politburo, IRA and Sinn Féin together. It was all leadership. We would discuss, how are we going to handle this, what is our line here? I had already come to the conclusion around then that the war wasn't going to work so I didn't have a problem with Sinn Féin developing as a political party.'

But he was relieved when Danny Morrison told him that his own 'operating days' were over. Nobody was going to ask him to do a robbery or deliver a bomb. He was answerable to IRA GHQ but no one ever insisted he attend meetings. 'No adjutant general was coming up to you and saying there's a meeting down in Dublin for the GHQ staff and you have to be at it.'

But he believed that the work of the party was integral to a broader strategy that included the IRA. 'I thought it was a dual strategy and I had thought it would work. The one thing that united us was that constitutional politics would not be enough to drive the British out. There had to be more; there had to be armed conflict. And to get the support of the people for armed conflict, you had to offer them something more than the ideology. You needed to offer them bread and butter advice and remedies. That was the thinking of that whole stratum as far as I could tell. I had no idea Gerry was already on the peace quest. Gerry must have realised that there was only one destination and that was an end to armed struggle.'

Someone who claimed to see the way things were going was Eamon Collins. Collins was a senior IRA man in south Down and part of the IRA's internal security department alongside Freddie Scappaticci, later outed as the British army agent codenamed Stakeknife. In his book *Killing Rage*,[1] Collins says that he saw the inevitable contradiction between armed struggle and party politics.

He met with the Quartermaster who agreed with him that Sinn Féin was the movement's 'Achilles heel'.[2] These senior IRA men believed that allowing Sinn Féin to grow as a party and to enter elections showed that the current leadership around Adams was 'at best, inept and, at worst, on the verge of ending the military campaign, albeit by stealth'.

Avoidance of electoral politics was pure orthodoxy for the IRA, he says. Republicans knew that constitutional nationalism was 'the most potent political force in Irish history'.

'They also knew that the IRA did not, could not, engage in constitutional politics.' Collins says he was agonising about his role in the IRA and that by the time he wrote his book he was convinced that Adams had been running down the IRA and had been right to do so. But he crossed Adams and lost any prospect of being accepted by his coterie in Belfast.

This happened in August 1984, when Collins was part of the IRA colour party for the funeral of Brendan Watters, a young volunteer killed by his own grenade. Adams was at the funeral. When the main cortege met a line of police vehicles, the local republicans started stamping their feet and creating a confrontation. Francis Molloy, a Tyrone republican, stepped forward and asked them to stop. Collins wanted the confrontation and thought that it would make a good image in the media. So what if there was a scuffle or worse? The images would go round the world in minutes. So he urged the men to continue with the foot stomping.

Collins reasoned that the desire for a peaceful funeral, when violent confrontation could only have provided good propaganda for the IRA, 'only made sense if the war was over'.

Collins's view then was that there were potentially two great traps for the armed struggle and the revolution. One was that republicans would be wooed into electoral politics and would divert their energies away from violent action. The other was that a concentration of leadership in a small group, like that around Adams, would give that group the power to call off the armed campaign.

Adams rebuked Collins after the funeral, commenting that it had gone well, without serious trouble, 'apart from this man here'. Collins says he turned and defended the stomping. Adams, he says, thought it smacked of militarism and fascism.

Collins said, 'That's like something the Sticks [the Official IRA] would come out with.'

Later he was asked to a meeting in Belfast at Sinn Féin headquarters and was rounded on by Danny Morrison for insulting Adams in such a way, though Adams never brought it up with him again.

While the IRA was avoiding escalation and had decided not to expand or take territory, it did seek to run a 'Civil Administration' in the areas in which it operated. Sinn Féin centres like Connolly House on the Andersonstown Road, where Gerry Adams had his office, provided more services than the average political party. They took in complaints about criminal and anti-social activity. Often those complained about were shot in the legs by local IRA teams acting as vigilantes in the area.

In the 1980s, the IRA shot more bullets into the limbs of young men in the nationalist housing estates of west Belfast, Adams's constituency, than it did into soldiers or police officers, its supposed primary targets.

Within the Civil Administration Sinn Féin and the IRA were most like a single organisation, Sinn Féin councillors receiving the complaints about car thieves and drug dealers, the IRA shooting them.[3] The Civil Administration fitted with Adams's idea of usurping the state by replacing its functions in a parallel system. It also provided work for IRA men at a time when the idea of escalating the campaign had been abandoned.

A senior member of Belfast Brigade staff at the time says that they 'pulled in' several criminals and got them to sign statements pledging themselves to stopping their criminal activities and acknowledging the right of the IRA to execute them if they went back to their old ways. He says that some IRA operations had been disrupted by criminals or joyriders drawing the police into the area. This man argued within the IRA that they should be using the talents of these criminals. 'If they were good at stealing cars, they could steal them for us.'

The statements signed by the criminals were stored in a safe dump, in an area where there was no visible IRA activity, and three criminals, judged to have broken the terms of their amnesties, were murdered by the IRA in 1980, at the start of this project.

Nor did the policing of joyriders bring order to the streets; it may indeed have exacerbated the joyriding problem as many of the joyriders accepted the threat from the IRA as a challenge to be met and fought back, targeting the homes of members, defacing them or revving engines outside and daring them to give chase.

The IRA aimed to undermine the authority of the police by replacing them.

Anomalously, however, those whose cars were stolen by the joyriders had to report the thefts to the police in order to get insurance payouts on their losses; that was one part of the service the IRA could not provide.

Richard O'Rawe doesn't believe that Gerry Adams was active in IRA operations at this time but he does believe, despite Adams's frequent denials, that he was at the top of the organisation. 'Gerry didn't do operations, ever. Gerry was a sender-outer. He was up to his balls in it. And he needed to be because the IRA controlled Sinn Féin. Everything was subject to army authority.'

O'Rawe describes a frenetic media operation at the Republican Press Centre. 'I was meeting journalists. Some journalists would come and literally plant themselves in the office and fucking get themselves a coffee and have a smoke and chew the fat. They felt very comfortable there.' He says some journalists, like the *Sunday Tribune*'s Ed Moloney, were regarded as more astute and well informed than others. When one of these was due to come in, staff would get instructions to be more wary and would be given fuller briefings on the party line.

'The Sinn Féin political machine was like a monster, soldier ants all over the place, putting up posters, knocking on doors, impersonating punters and all of this business.' Party members and sympathisers were given multiple identities and driven round different polling stations to vote at all of them.

'I wouldn't have a problem with it,' says O'Rawe, 'don't get me wrong, a vote's a vote whether you steal it or get it legit. Know what I mean? That was the attitude, but I didn't know it was huge. It was on an industrial scale, thousands of votes going astray. There were van loads driving people from one place to another, circling all the time. This has always gone on in republican politics. We did it in 1917 too.'

O'Rawe liked Adams. He had been interned alongside him in the *Maidstone* and regarded him as an easy prisoner to share time with. 'No, he was just one of those guys that you liked being around.'

Gerard Hodgins worked at a later stage in the Press Centre and tells a story about the humour among staff and the culture of the place. 'In the run-up to the election in 1987, there was a girl who worked in the Press Centre with us for a while. She wasn't in the IRA. We just got her in to do typing and stuff, typical fucking sexist pigs that we were. She was away in London or somewhere for a weekend and she brought me back an apron; she knew that I liked cooking. It was one of those funny aprons that had a pair of boobs on it. Morrison came up the stairs first. I says, what do you think of that, Danny? He fucking took a wobbler. Then Tom Hartley came in and I tried it on him and he took a wobbler: shouting, angry. "There's press people about here and we're releasing the women's part of the manifesto today."

'Then Adams came in. I thought I'd nothing to lose, put it on, and he started laughing, said come here, put the arm round me, took me into the room where they were all meeting for their strategy meeting and says, "Look at this."'

O'Rawe says that is the Adams he knew. 'He had a sense of humour. He'd have had the confidence to pull off something like that. He wouldn't have been led. He didn't have to look over his shoulder and wonder, what's Gerry thinking? Because he was Gerry. So it's all right for him to bring Hodgy in with the big tits, then it's so funny. Right? But the rest of them are wondering first, what will Gerry think of this? That's the reality.'

Chapter 16

Adams won the West Belfast seat in the 1983 Westminster general election but he was arrested the night before the vote. Standing as a senior republican put him in danger from loyalists, who would kill him if they got the chance, and drew the interest and close scrutiny of the British army and the police.

He had been canvassing in north Belfast and flying an Irish tricolour from the car and had been stopped and charged with obstructing the police and with disorderly behaviour. Though the flying of the flag was itself illegal in Northern Ireland then, he was not charged with breaking that particular law. He would have been able to make rich political capital out of it if he had.

But it wasn't just the police and the courts he had to fear. Republican strength was always limited to the local area and Adams's security was compromised when he had to travel to and from Belfast Magistrate's Court for the hearing in March 1984. The case was heard by Resident Magistrate Tom Travers.

Travers was a south Belfast middle-class Catholic, of a type sneered at by republicans, a person with working-class roots who had left school at fourteen and was now employed by the state to defend its laws and structures. He and Adams, meeting in court, would each have felt the contempt in which the other held him. Travers was challenged to be an impartial judge because he was already familiar with the name of Gerry Adams. Adams's whole political vision told him that an Irishman in the North should not be serving the state but seeking to destroy it, not sitting in power over him under the emblem and authority of the British Crown.

The magistrate heard the case in the morning then told Adams and his co-defendants that he would make his ruling after lunch. This was awkward for Adams and the republicans charged alongside him for they had to be on guard against the danger of attack. Adams asked permission for them to stay in the court building over the lunch break for their own safety but was refused it. He and his co-defendants then opted to drive up Howard Street, towards the Falls Road, agreeing en route to stop at Long's Fish and Chip shop for lunch.

Two cars were trying to tail them.

In one was a group of British soldiers. In the other a loyalist paramilitary hit team. The loyalists got to Adams first, drawing alongside his car and strafing it. It isn't a good way to get a clear steady shot at a target, but if a gunman gets enough bullets into the target car there is every prospect of a kill for there is not much the others can do to defend themselves. For a time they may not even know what is happening. Adams didn't, not at first. 'Then the car came in around me. I felt the thumps and thuds as the bullets struck home. The crack of gunfire came after.'[1] A later effort to recall the shooting put events in a different order. 'Then there was a terrific sound of gunfire very close up and the window came in around me.'[2]

Adams was hit four times but retained consciousness. He prayed for himself, he says. 'Jesus, Mary and Joseph, I give you my heart and my soul.'[3] Then he crouched by one of the wounded men beside him and recited the Act of Contrition into his ear. That is what the Church advises Catholics to do for those close to death who might not have sufficient breath to repent unaided.

His driver accelerated away from the loyalists. Adams ordered him to go straight to the Royal Victoria Hospital and there, with four bullets in his body, he was able to walk into Accident and Emergency. His wife Colette arrived at the hospital with journalist Eamonn Mallie. Mallie says there was a commotion around the door of the room in which Adams was being treated. The door opened from the inside, and Adams appeared, demanding that his wife be allowed in. He was able to give Mallie a recorded interview from the bed, which was broadcast before the police even confirmed to the media that he had been shot.

Critics of Adams in the IRA make much of the fact that he wasn't 'an operator' but it is hard to make the case that he was physically a coward when he was able to get up from a bed and argue with the police while being treated for four bullet wounds.

The shooting of Gerry Adams drew him little sympathy outside republican circles. Gerry Fitt, himself ideologically a republican and the SDLP member from whom Adams took the West Belfast seat, said, 'Mr Adams has become a victim of a war in which he believes.'[4]

This was not very different from the statement by Ian Paisley on the other extreme of the political divide: 'it's the natural law that you reap what you sow. That is God's law and that cannot be escaped.'

Still, Adams had escaped. One bullet had passed through his neck without touching his spine, and might have left him paralysed. Another passed close to his heart. If being shot at can be said to have a lucky outcome, Adams had had one. But after recuperating he had to return to hospital with pain in his arm only to have another bullet removed. Surgeons had failed to find it the first time.

There are conflicting conspiracy theories about the ambush itself. The simple account that seems sufficient at first sight is that the UDA (whose paramilitary arm, the UFF, claimed the shooting) was always looking for an opportunity to shoot members of the IRA. It knew about Adams as a senior republican because he was an elected representative. The fact that he was appearing in court was not a secret. There was an obvious route from the courthouse back to the Falls Road.

Yet parking was restricted in the city and vehicles coming in were routinely searched, so the gunmen could not have just sat parked near the court and waited for Adams to come out. They must have had a better plan than that.

The gunmen were seized by British soldiers immediately after the attack. Adams says he believes the soldiers were monitoring his movements and stepped back to allow the UDA a clear shot at him, then moved in afterwards. That assumes that the army wanted him dead.

Another theory says that a close army presence was there for the protection of Adams and the other republicans but slipped up. Further, this theory has it that the guns used by the loyalists had been interfered with to limit the damage they could do. Whichever, if either, of these theories is credible, soldiers were at hand to intercept and arrest the attackers. The army lied repeatedly about who those soldiers were, maintaining a cover story that they were off-duty military police and an Ulster Defence Regiment soldier who just happened to be at the scene, only changing it to say that they had been on duty after all, though in tasks unrelated to the movements of Gerry Adams.

Mark Urban in *Big Boys' Rules*[5] claims to have been told by intelligence operatives that the army had had an agent inside the UDA, who told them to expect an attack on Adams, without being specific about the probable location, though anyone might have guessed that they would want to kill him and that he was more exposed on his day in court.

A former army intelligence officer, using the pseudonym Martin Ingram, has claimed that army intelligence had doctored the ammunition used in this ambush, a claim that the Police Ombudsman says it found no evidence of.[6]

Gerry Brannigan recalls visiting Sean Keenan, one of those injured in the Adams car, and seeing him with a bullet wound at the bridge of his nose. 'I said to him, "How are you not dead, Sean?" My take on it is that that bullet was going slow.'

And a 'slow bullet' might account for one loyalist in the car being accidentally shot with an automatic rifle, just inches from him, and yet surviving.

David Sharrock and Mark Devenport say in their unauthorised biography of Adams, *Man of War, Man of Peace?*, that the soldiers were part of an SAS team charged with shadowing and protecting Adams. Urban reasons that the army had not actually set up the attack, a point that republicans accept. None of the loyalists made any claim in their defence that they were working for the state. But he says it is harder to argue that the army did not wish to allow the attack to go ahead. If they were tasked with stopping it and they were in the area and they were armed, surely they could have done more.

Urban also believes the soldiers were more gentle with the loyalists than they would normally have been with republicans. '. . . from 1976 to 1987 the RUC and Army only ever killed republican terrorists with their undercover units. Loyalists, although responsible for many scores of killings, during the same period, have never been subjected to an ambush.'[7]

Two men arrested for the attack on Gerry Adams were remanded to the same wing in Crumlin Road Gaol that housed young Dominic Adams, who was awaiting trial for a plot to murder a policeman. Dominic wrote in *Faoi Ghlas* that he had been warned by his IRA Officer Commanding on the wing not to get provoked by them. But he got a closer look at them than they had at Gerry. He described John Gregg's tattoos, including one of a rabbit running down his back.

The other, Gerard Walsh, would nod at Dominic as he passed him and once sat beside him in the visiting area when he was meeting two of his sisters.[8]

Gerry Adams was under constant surveillance at this time. The diary of Ian Phoenix, a Special Branch officer, notes that police intelligence worked to a list of key suspects to be monitored. Gerry Adams was Number 1 on the list.[9]

The magistrate Tom Travers, who had heard the case in the morning and was reserving his judgment until he had had lunch, went home to eat with his fifteen-year-old daughter Ann. She says that she and her father talked about the case and that he told her he intended to send Gerry Adams to jail for three months, finding him guilty of the charges against him.

Travers never got to impose that sentence. The adjournment was extended because Adams was in hospital recovering from bullet wounds.

A month later, Travers was leaving mass in St Brigid's Church in south Belfast with his wife and his daughter Mary, a twenty-three-year-old teacher. Another young woman called Mary McArdle was rushing to meet them. It was a warm spring morning but she was wearing heavy surgical tights under her skirt. McArdle was able to find a sheltered spot in which to hoist her skirt, delve into her tights and withdraw two pistols and hand them over to two IRA men waiting for the Travers family.

As the family group approached, the men took aim but one of the guns jammed. Tom Travers took six bullets into his body. In what he thought were his dying moments he saw one of the IRA gunmen hold a pistol to his distraught wife's head and pull the trigger. That gun jammed again. Mary took a single bullet in her back and fell into the arms of her mother and the two went down together. Mary died.

The plan apparently had been to kill all three.

Ten years later, Tom Travers recalled the attack in a letter to the *Irish Times*:

May I say that on the day my lovely daughter was murdered her killer tried to murder my darling wife also. At that time Mary lay dying on her mum's breast, her gentle heart pouring its pure blood on to a dusty street in Belfast. The murderer's gun, which was pointed at my wife's head, misfired twice. Another gunman shot me six times. As he prepared to fire the first shot I saw the look of hatred on his face, a face I will never forget.

Ann, the sister who was not there, says, 'The case [against Gerry Adams] was due to be reheard on 12 April and dad was shot on Sunday 8 April. Had he not been shot, my father would have sent

Adams to jail four days later. When he went back to work months after that, he discovered that the case had been dropped.'

Had Adams gone to jail at that time, while steering the broader republican movement towards prioritising politics over revolutionary violence, he would have lost that top-table influence that he had earlier used to end the feud with the Officials. The prospects of a peace process developing might have been reduced.

Only one person was convicted of the attack on the Travers family and that was nineteen-year-old Mary McArdle, the girl who had delivered the guns to the hit men. One side-effect of the case against Adams being inexplicably dropped was that he was spared a jail sentence. If he was, as some claim, a member of the IRA army council at that time, he would have lost that ranking on imprisonment. But Adams always denied that he was a member of the IRA and the only time he was charged the case was thrown out.

Chapter 17

Ken Livingstone saw a demure civility in Gerry Adams. Livingstone was the left-wing Labour leader of the Greater London Council at the time and himself a figure vilified in the media for his radical ideas. The tabloids called him Red Ken. He had never been to Dublin to watch the Sinn Féin delegates gather in a dusty hall for their annual conference, their Ard Fheis, usually with detectives monitoring their comings and goings. But he had been told that Adams would queue like others at the microphone for a turn to speak and if somebody in front of him made the point that he wanted to make he would leave the queue and go back to his seat. 'There are few male politicians who would behave in that way,' wrote Livingstone.[1] English left-wing male politicians usually felt that no issue had been properly dealt with until they had had their say. This civility observed in Adams was proof that he was an authentic democrat. He understood that things can't be changed by individuals but that a politician with popular support doesn't have to shout to make a point.

This overlooked the fact that Adams was happy for the IRA to use bombs to make these points.

Some say this was Adams exercising a technique for manipulating a group, to let others speak for him and then to gently signal his approval. This way, ideas could be discussed with a sense among everyone that Adams had endorsed them but without him having said anything. And he could try out ideas for their impact and popularity before fully identifying himself with them. Another example of this detached management of ideas is that day in the prison when Gerry Brannigan argued that the Sinn Féin prisoners should recognise the court and Tom Hartley had argued against this. Adams's intervention: 'Let the man speak.'

This was the time when Gerry Adams was emerging as a personality. He was electioneering but he was also writing and giving media interviews. He had said in the 1970s that he was deeply averse to being mentioned in the press but in the early 1980s he began to work on creating a public image. From the start, this persona was presented as wise and well grounded, civilised and gentle, the feminist man who loves children, the natural democrat. Whereas his friend Joe McCann had been depicted as a young warrior in media images, Adams, from the start of his work to create a celebrity republican, wanted to be seen as an elder. Though he was in his mid-thirties, he aspired to being a model of the experience of his community, to be known more for wisdom than anger, a man with organic links to west Belfast who presented basic republican principles as self-evident, at least in his own wise old young head.

He now wanted to present his republicanism as elementary common sense rather than as revolutionary communism. His first published book since the pamphlet *Peace in Ireland* was not a manifesto of political action or a vision of a free Ireland but a work of nostalgia for a simpler, more innocent time. At the start of *Falls Memories*, he returns to the Falls Road after a long time away. He had been in prison twice, most recently four years before the book was published and both times among other people from the streets where he grew up. He had been based in Dublin for a time while Vice President of Sinn Féin.

He actually hadn't been away long at all, just two years. His estrangement from the place is surely affected. He is shocked by the changes wrought by developers and the dismantling of the community he knew as a child. He remembers also that, when he was young, old people would say similar things to those he is saying now, lamenting change, and he wonders if he is now just like them. If this describes his feelings on his release after the failed IRA membership charge in 1977, then he made these observations when he was twenty-nine years old and did so in the tone of one who has returned in old age to the place where he spent his childhood. He is sentimental in this book, reproducing the language of the street so excessively that he parodies it, making an Irish joke of himself and the people there. Yet from the recorded interviews of that time it is clear that he did not, himself, talk in the patois that he expresses such affection for. He lost the city accent in his school elocution lessons or perhaps in the devices with which he overcame his childhood stammer. He has a distinctly lower and rounder tone than is characteristic of the Belfast accent of others in his family.

Many of his stories are about childhood and the adventures of gang fights among boys and 'slagging' about girls. Gerry's description of the chatter of women at a wake seems nostalgic and endearing. He tells us that, as boys, he and his friends would call at the wake houses of people they didn't know, just to see the dead body.

For Adams, the people of the Falls Road are heroic and stoical, noble and generous, bravely enduring British oppression and maintaining their wit. There is nothing else in his writing that suggests the black humour, the swearing, the caustic mannerisms and the hardship. You would think, reading this, that he had taken everything he knows of Belfast from vaudeville and most of what he knows of childhood from fiction. He told Anthony Clare, the psychiatrist broadcaster, that his childhood reading included *Just William* and *Jennings and Darbishire*, and it is the high-jinks of these fictional boys that his own stories draw on.

His political thinking was unpacked a little in 1982 for an interview with the BBC *Panorama* programme. Most interesting in this is the confidence he projects and the dexterity with which he evades and scoffs at questions he has no intention of answering.

He doesn't look like a working-class rebel, more like a school teacher, perhaps an intellectual revolutionary. There was a style at the time for republican street militants – leather or denim, a thick moustache. Adams wore tweeds and suits, woolly jumpers, and had a full but well-tended beard. In this interview, he is dapper and engaged and he pits himself against the broadcaster as a confident intellectual equal, or superior. He had a simple argument for dealing with unionism.

'They are not a different people,' he snaps. 'How are they a different people?'

He is smiling like someone who has decided to indulge the stupidity of the interviewer for a moment, give him a chance. This is the sort of combat that suits him.

His argument is that unionists do not have a different culture and a different set of values. They are as oppressed as the nationalists are. They do not even have different allegiances; their endorsement of Britain is conditional, as is made clear in the Orange oath. So, when Britain eventually decides to no longer meet the conditions by which unionism pledges loyalty, that is, supporting the Protestant ascendancy, the unionists will simply revert to being ordinary Irish people.

Adams had clearly thought this through and rehearsed these arguments in other groups, probably in the Long Kesh political discussions, and he had concluded that the Union with Britain was Britain's to dispose of. When a future government broke the Union, under pressure from the IRA, most Protestants would simply have no choice but to reconcile themselves to their neighbours in their common Irish identity. In the Anthony Clare interview he betrays more by his asides and evasions than by what he declares frankly. Surprisingly, Clare skirts the evident paradox that Adams's early reading included boyhood adventures in an English public school. Talking to Clare, Adams several times mentions his dropping out of 'college', though his education ended in a grammar school, St Mary's.

What we are getting now is an impression of a man who is

intelligent and eloquent, who speaks with a modulated accent, unlike the Belfast working-class tones that he reproduces in his characters. He is proud of himself and, rather than engage with contrary ideas, he feels entitled to mock them.

That same confident assertion is the tone of the political treatise he wrote in the mid-1980s. Even there, in *The Politics of Irish Freedom*, he identifies three strands of republicanism, any one of which may predominate at different times: an apolitical military tendency, a revolutionary tendency and a constitutional tendency. He is clearly trying to expand the base on which his republicanism is grounded and to include larger numbers of people within the swathe he claims support from.

He comes back to the fundamental premise that injustice in Northern Ireland is a necessary prop for partition and that when the injustice is removed partition will fail. Yet the evidence he provides for this theory is slight. He does tell us, however, that it was this basic insight that drew him away from the republicans around Billy McMillen who had thought progressive reform towards unification was possible. His analysis said that the refusal of justice was the bulwark against Irish unity and would be maintained regardless of protest and pleas for minor adjustments.

The main evidence that reform is simply impossible, he believes, is that the state attacked republicans and civil righters when they asked for justice. He never concedes that protesters themselves sometimes generate violence and provoke heavy policing. He gives a curiously slight example of the state's determination to preserve sectarianism and prevent cross-community activism.

A group of Protestant residents wanted a safety rail on a road corner to protect children from traffic. They had asked for it and nothing had been done. When they aligned themselves with local republicans the campaign succeeded. They got their safety rail. Adams says, however, that for him the instructive part of the experience was the anger of unionist politicians that Protestants had agitated alongside republicans. 'If the state would not allow

Catholics and Protestants to get a pedestrian crossing built together, it would hardly sit back and watch them organise the revolution together."[2]

But this argument doesn't work. The state had not refused the pedestrian crossing (or safety rail, whatever) but actually provided it. The grumbling about it had come from unionists who didn't want a rival political party to make gains on its patch. That's not evidence of state oppression but of normal inter-party competition of the kind that the British Labourites he was now aligning with would have fully understood. But it does seem to be the best argument that Adams can offer.

His evasion of the common questions about IRA bombings marks him out as a dissembler. He cannot plausibly pretend that he did not know that critics of the IRA worried about the killing of civilians. In *The Politics of Irish Freedom*, he dismisses much of this criticism as 'cynicism' by the British and dishonesty by peace campaigners, but he never takes time to explain why it was necessary to bomb pubs, shops, hotels. He never acknowledges that people might have decent humane reasons for not wanting to have bombs go off in their town.

He never explains what the strategic value was in the IRA campaign, how it was ever going to persuade the British to leave. He comes closest perhaps in describing it as 'armed propaganda', yet in the same paragraph he anticipates the day in which the IRA might expand into an army that can hold territory and eject the British army by superior force.

He describes an IRA that is organically interwoven with the nationalist community and that draws its legitimacy from the community endorsement, some of it secret, covert, 'sneaking regard'. He speaks of this community support as if it is extensive, ignoring the fact of it being rooted only in some Catholic working-class communities and rural areas. Adams accepts that there is 'war weariness' but does not interpret this as a lack of enthusiasm for the IRA's goals.

The point of 'armed struggle' as inferred from Adams's writing was to provide evidence of there being a constitutional problem in Ireland, definable as British occupation of the North. The violence of the IRA, in Adams's vision, was therefore symptomatic. This is the idea he aired first in *Peace in Ireland*. Peace could not be produced by a simple decision of the IRA to stop bombing and shooting, for even then the real cause of that violence would still persist. By this analysis, we were expected to believe that young men like Gerard Hodgins and Richard O'Rawe waged war because they fretted in their beds at night about the border and the British government. Gerry Adams gave no sociological explanation of why young men bonded together under arms, though he was in the best possible position to know.

But another republican writer, Eamon Collins, had a direct insight into why young men joined the IRA. He was part of the security department that interviewed them, and he lists the motives he heard from them in *Killing Rage*. The border was not one of them. He says the same simple reasons cropped up all the time. The British were killing people, the system was biased against Catholics and almost all had had experience of being harassed and intimidated by the British army.[3] Like Anthony McIntyre, they wanted to hit back. Without their experience of being abused by the British army they would not have been ideological republicans.

But many young IRA members misunderstood what the strategy was to be. Gerard Hodgins believed that the IRA was seeking to acquire a massive arsenal to equip it for a Tet type offensive. He believed that a day would come when the Provos would take territory and hold it against the British army. Arms and explosives were the tools with which republicans would physically curtail the options of the British; they were not just instruments of propaganda.

Hodgins would never get the battle he longed for. The IRA, as Gerry Brannigan said, was turning people away. It did not want to grow bigger or escalate the war.

Some republicans in the prisons broke away from the IRA because they did not accept that 'armed propaganda' was sufficient justification for killing people. Tommy McKearney, Oliver Corr and others set up a League of Communist Republicans (LCR) in 1986 and left Provo discipline precisely on this principle. They understood that the IRA in Tyrone was fighting for military advantages, was waging war in the conventional sense, as a test of arms against an enemy. It was blowing up police stations and depriving the British army of operational bases in order to expand its own freedom of movement. This might have been a strategy that would force the British to change tactics too, for instance to resort to helicopter gunships; it was never going to defeat them. But it was at least like war in the old-fashioned sense. There was, despite this, no plan to expand on possible gains, to enlarge the IRA into a tenable physical challenge to the British. This was a showcase war, an enactment or parody, not a serious pursuit of military victory.

The LCR argued that shooting people just to stay in the headlines was immoral. Tommy McKearney, one of the 1980 hunger strikers, summarises his attitude of the time: 'If you can't deliver a significant war, stop it. There is no justification for maintaining a war just to have a column in *Republican News*. If there is a purpose to your use of arms, let's hear it but if there isn't, call it off.'

He says that prisoners were excluded from IRA decision-making and from the serious debate at the centre of the movement. 'There were political arguments in the wings. What we didn't have was the ability to impact on the republican leadership. Possibly our views were being reported to the army council but we didn't have a chance to communicate with them and make our case.'

While Gerry Adams argued that the IRA was a democratic army representing the will of the people it actually excluded even its own members from discussion of its purposes. The prisoners were mostly people who had been armed activists yet they had no participation in meaningful discussion with the IRA about what the point of the armed campaign was.

Oliver Corr, one of the defectors to the LCR, says the men had to leave the IRA wing because they were being bullied and ostracised. 'Anybody who objected or started to question the orthodoxy of the leadership was sidelined. That was my feeling, if you questioned what was coming through you were gradually pushed out and made to feel more and more uncomfortable.'

Even when the IRA was dealing very heavy blows on the British, the purpose was largely propagandist, says Corr. In 1984 they had come close to killing the Prime Minister, Margaret Thatcher, by bombing the Grand Hotel in Brighton where the Conservative Party Conference was being held. 'If Thatcher had died, I don't think many of us in the prison would have been too upset about that. But it was all about the spectacular, the one-off big thing. What appealed to me was the logic that in order to effect major political change in Ireland you had to have a mass movement that wasn't dependent on a small group going out and pulling stunts. This wasn't about a mass movement, it was about small cadres of armed propagandists.'

McKearney doesn't believe that the entire IRA campaign was propaganda led. 'Hitting the financial centre of London is not simply propaganda but damages the economy. If propaganda accrues from that, OK, but there is a military logic in undermining your opponent's capacity.'

Nor does he think that the group inspired by Adams, which took effective control of the movement in the late 1970s and redirected it in the early 1980s, was entirely wrong to run down the armed campaign. 'The new emerging Belfast leadership was perfectly correct in some things. One problem was that too many republicans were content to let a small number run an armed campaign and they would act as supporters, an audience in the theatre, and for that reason it was necessary to have people engaged politically. That was correct. The recognition of the limitations of armed struggle are justified and you can't say that everything that came from that emerging leadership was wrong. A lot of it was an accurate analysis of the situation.'

The exclusion of prisoners from even political decision-making made it easier for Adams and his Sinn Féin leadership team to make policy changes, so long as they stayed out of jail themselves.

McKearney says, 'This is the problem with IRA-type organisations. You don't have debate within the organisation. The IRA operates very hierarchically, very much like the Catholic Church; the Pope has an idea, he tells the cardinals and the cardinals tell the faithful what they ought to believe.' An example of that constraint on debate was Adams telling delegates at the Sinn Féin Ard Fheis, on taking Dáil seats, that they had no choice but to vote on something that the IRA had already approved.[4]

This doesn't fit well with Ken Livingstone's vision of Adams as a natural democrat. It suited his style of leadership to have others promote his ideas and also to intimidate dissenters in the movement. That was how he managed the political movement but McKearney says he had also to placate the IRA.

'It would appear that from the early 1980s there was a constituency within the republican movement who believed that progress could only be made through electoral politics. But if you think like that then you have to appease those who have not come to the same realisation you have, and give them some toys to play with.'

Chapter 18

Gerry Adams was left sitting in the BBC green room with his minders while the programme presenter went off to argue with his producer. He sat on the sofa that doubled as a bed for overnight producers on the morning current affairs programme, *Good Morning Ulster*. He was brought tea and biscuits. He was now an MP and could expect to be in Belfast's Broadcasting House occasionally and to be received respectfully by the staff, but he was a worry. The security men downstairs were hired to be on guard against bombers and gunmen, but here was the most senior republican they had heard of and his attendants, and they had to let him in by the back door and trust that if they were armed they'd at least behave themselves.

The main problem that day was one of editorial judgement but Adams's paramilitary status was part of it, or at least the perception that he wasn't quite a constitutional politician. Brian Garrett, a lawyer and sometime radio presenter, was going to be interviewing him in a few minutes and if the other guest didn't turn up he was going to have to give Adams a full hour, live on air, and he was frankly refusing to do it. Garrett was a plummy, genteel man who had been a leading member of the Northern Irish Labour Party during its brief popularity in the 1960s. His programme, *Behind the Headlines*, was a once-weekly lunchtime political discussion, interspersed with a little music. Garrett's style was to give people time to answer, not to be too confrontational, to lead them towards the implications of the positions they took. He would have enjoyed doing that with Adams but not for the full programme. That would elevate him in importance and Garrett didn't want to be the one to do that. The producer was a different kind of man. Martin Dillon was untypical for the BBC. A Catholic from the Falls Road with a mischievous streak, he liked to break conventions.

But the fourth man in the drama would save them all. That was John Hume, leader of the SDLP, Sinn Féin's chief political rival. The SDLP took the majority of nationalist votes and that made it the most potent argument against the legitimacy of the IRA campaign. But it was typical of Hume to be late. He was one of the sharpest political thinkers in Ireland. He was a good old-fashioned glad-hander who remembered people's names and made contacts at high levels, especially in Dublin and Washington. But he still had the slouch of the tired old school teacher about him.

Adams didn't like Hume, who took more votes from Catholics and stood in the way of his own political progress. If most Catholics were content with reform, of the kind Hume wanted, then it was impossible to argue that only Irish unity would free them. Adams's riposte to that was to say that the SDLP were slow learners, not yet acquainted with the fundamental reality that the British would never allow reform anyway.

The SDLP represented mostly the professional and middle-class Catholics, teachers, publicans, civil servants, lawyers, the self-employed. These were people who identified themselves more as Irish than British but whose priority was a stable society in which they would work and prosper and raise families.

They were aspirationally nationalist but not urgent about it. In private, SDLP politicians could be the most scathing critics of Sinn Féin and the IRA, for they had the insight into how they operated in their neighbourhoods. In public they tended to shy away from naked confrontation and felt that they had votes to lose by appearing not to understand and sympathise with the motivations of republicans. A nationalist who was bluntly critical of the IRA was too easily accused of giving succour to the unionists and losing touch with the native community.

To Garrett's relief, Hume had arrived and the programme could go ahead as planned. Garrett settled himself facing his two guests, one of them looking tired and bored, as much with life as with politics, the other, young Adams, looking almost leonine and voracious. He was the one with something to gain, if only another chance to represent himself to a large audience as genial and thoughtful, not the insane terrorist many took him for.

Gerry Adams accepted in the discussion with Hume that there were contradictions between the armed struggle and political progress. Hume was accusing him of hypocrisy in seeking housing for west Belfast while supporting the bombing of factories and the killing of workers.

Adams offered talks between Sinn Féin and the SDLP but Hume said he did not accept that Sinn Féin was the real decision-maker in the republican movement. He said that Adams had already effectively acknowledged this when he conceded that the IRA would make its own decisions on how to conduct armed struggle and Sinn Féin could not criticise those decisions even when they impinged on electoral progress.

Hume said, 'If I am being asked to talk to the Provisional Republican Movement then it is the Provisional Republican Movement I want to talk to, and as I understand Sinn Féin are subject in all matters to the army council . . . if I am to talk to Provisional Republican Movement I want to talk to the people who are taking the decisions.'

It was a first for Adams, being accused in public of not being the leader of the IRA.

Adams did not deny or answer the claim that the IRA army council took decisions but sidestepped the issue, dismissing Hume's question as a 'long-winded fudge'. He was still trying to limit the discussion to Sinn Féin and the SDLP, suggesting they could come to agreements on 'pan-nationalist interests'.

Hume was determined to speak to the decision-makers.

His move into talks with Adams after this reflected his

understanding that Adams was indeed the decision-maker, that he could speak for both Sinn Féin and the army council. This started a dialogue or contest between Sinn Féin and the SDLP in which both risked losing credibility. Hume put himself in danger of being implicated in the IRA's justification of political violence. Adams, on the other hand risked being won over to constitutional nationalism. Often in his writings he sneered at the very prospect. In 1986, a year after the first contact with Hume, Adams wrote, 'No Irish nationalist could support any treaty which institutionalises British government claims to a part of Irish national territory.'[1]

Hume must have read that as a total rebuff to any thought of a settlement short of a united Ireland.

Yet Adams was electioneering now, trying to get Sinn Féin into local councils and to win seats at Westminster, and in an experimental Stormont assembly, though refusing to take them.

Adams made the calculation that if Sinn Féin was to have power again it would have to compromise on principle and start recognising some of the bodies it might be elected to sit in.

He wanted Sinn Féin not only to fight elections in the Irish Republic but to take seats there. Previously, the party reasoned that if partition was a crime against Ireland then parliaments on both sides of an illegitimate border were equally illegitimate.

Adams was at his manipulative best at the Ard Fheis in 1986, when he stood before the delegates and herded them the way he wanted them to go on the vote to end abstention from the Dáil. He bullied and cajoled them. He ensnared them in contradictory logic. He told them they were democrats and their opinions mattered then took all choice away from them. Having insisted in the media and to the electorate that a vote for Sinn Féin needn't be read as endorsement of the IRA, he told the delegates that the IRA had already made its mind up and that they could not dissent and still regard themselves as loyal supporters.

Up to that time, Provisionals had sneered at their rivals in the Official movement who had diluted their militarism with 'political opportunism'. Abstention was precisely the principle on which the movement had split in 1970, the reason why Gerry Adams had gone one way and his sister Margaret and Joe McCann had gone another. Then Adams had argued that abstention was a fundamental principle. A government in the North or South established by partition had no right to the allegiance of the people; it should be ignored. Now he simply reversed that principle and took nearly the whole party with him.

'Some of you may feel that a republican organisation making such a change can no longer call itself republican . . . I would remind you that another republican organisation has already done what you fear we are going to do tomorrow.' And he wasn't referring to the Stickies. He told delegates that they were not bound by decisions of the IRA. Then he said they were. 'The logic which would dictate withdrawal of support from Sinn Féin if decisions go against you means that you have already decided to withdraw solidarity and support from the IRA and the armed struggle.'

The implication of that was that you could hardly be presumed to be a good republican if you did not fully support the IRA, not just in its armed actions but in its political thinking. So Sinn Féin and the IRA were separate but they had to be fully aligned in their thinking with each other, that is, not separate. And it was the IRA that was taking the lead.

Adams is good at these ambiguities, affirming that you have a right to think what you like before explaining how you don't.

John Joe McGirl, a sixty-five-year-old veteran, next day clarified the distinction as he understood it. The Stickies had made their decision as an evasion of military responsibility. The Provisionals were doing no such thing: '. . . it was clear that the then leadership had abandoned Irish freedom but today we have an army that has been fighting for sixteen years and will continue to fight until British rule has ended.'[2]

If Gerry Adams thought differently, he didn't interject to clarify.

Bishop and Mallie in their history of the Provisional IRA concluded that the abstentionism vote provided no hope that the revolutionaries were morphing into mere radicals, content with political activism. They said that even if the leadership tired of the armed struggle, the ordinary rank and file would carry on 'if only as a monotonous act of revenge'.[3]

The real lesson of the vote was that Adams could coax the whole movement to waive fundamental doctrine. No matter how enthusiastic the IRA leadership appeared to be for war, it had made a decision that would direct its energies away from violence.

The vote was followed closely by the prisoners in Long Kesh, hundreds of IRA men and Sinn Féin members who had had no say in the discussion and whose views would likely have tilted the debate against Adams. Oliver Corr says the debate in the prison was lively, but that what prisoners thought of it was plainly irrelevant: 'Effectively the prisoners had been taken out of the discussion.'

Tommy McKearney emphasises that this was primarily an IRA decision rubber-stamped by Sinn Féin, and not even a decision taken democratically within the IRA. 'There is some sense in the prisoner not having influence over the movement in military decisions, but in a political decision like ending abstentionism, that was something we felt entitled to have a say on.' He says, 'Had the prisoners objected, I don't think it would have gone through as comfortably.'

The vote was a precursor to two splits in the Provisional movement.

Former Chief of Staff Ruairí Ó Brádaigh, and Adams's predecessor as party President, led a few purists out of the Ard Fheis to establish Republican Sinn Féin. And McKearney would later take thirty prisoners out of the Provo wings in Long Kesh into the League of Communist Republicans, averse to the management of the movement by a clique and the use of violence for propaganda. A major split in the IRA inside Long Kesh passed virtually unnoticed in the media.

The breakaway LCR in the prison chose not to align itself with Ó Brádaigh's Republican Sinn Féin. McKearney says there was 'something honourable in the old Fenian tradition' but that he had realised it was a cul-de-sac.

He was starting to see signs that the Provisionals were leaving the old Fenian tradition behind too. 'We were starting to get the local newspapers in and what caught my eye first was that constantly the Sinn Féin party was referring to the "nationalist population" and qualitatively that was a big change. There had been an actual parting of the ways between republicans and nationalists and republicans had traditionally had this scepticism about nationalism, and you can't marry the two. We were now electioneering to the broader Catholic community and the programme was going to be diluted.'

But the IRA showed no sense of anticipating its own decline as the movement shifted its energies further towards electioneering. A New Year's statement to prisoners was belligerent, written perhaps with a consciousness that some felt they had been unfairly excluded from the decision on abstention. 'Morale is the vital key to our success and the key to high morale is successful operations.'

The IRA was equipped for escalation and claimed to be eager.

While Adams was making overtures to John Hume, the IRA was talking to the Libyan dictator Colonel Gaddafi. It offered Gaddafi an opportunity to punish Britain, which had expelled diplomats after one of them had shot dead WPC Yvonne Fletcher from the embassy window in London while she was policing a protest there.

Gaddafi ordered tons of automatic weapons and explosives to be loaded onto commercial ships and sent through the Mediterranean and up to Ireland. And the IRA organised, at its end, convoys of lorries to receive the weapons by night at remote harbours and transport them to ready dumps.

So the IRA was preparing for war and following Gerry Adams towards political compromise at the same time.

Logically, these two approaches were incompatible with each other. The question is whether Gerry Adams understood that or had yet to learn it. Fighting elections only made sense if the party had ambitions to grow and extend its influence, yet while the armed campaign continued, elected representatives were harried by questions about the IRA's behaviour and exposed to danger of attack by loyalists and the SAS. Further, many potential voters were discouraged from supporting Sinn Féin while that support was being interpreted, by the party and others, as endorsement of the IRA campaign.

The Special Branch assessment, as set out in the diaries of Ian Phoenix,[4] was that there was a substantial overlap in the leadership of both Sinn Féin and the IRA. His files listed four members of the army council as holding prominent positions within Sinn Féin and these included Gerry Adams and Martin McGuinness, who both denied they were ever on the army council. Yet the military and political purposes of this single organisation were diverging and becoming a strain on one another.

Indeed, many of the IRA's violent actions in the following years damaged its standing in the Catholic community from which Sinn Féin sought votes. And Gerry Adams and his close associates repeatedly suffered the political embarrassment of having to rationalise or excuse atrocities like the bombing of a Remembrance Day service in Enniskillen, the murder of two corporals who strayed into the path of an IRA funeral, the bombing of a fish shop on the Shankill Road.

This was the decade of the long war, a persistent routine of bombing and shooting, never with the objective of expanding or escalating, just a steady attrition, killing between forty and fifty people a year, the IRA losing on average only three or four.

Adams had been elected President of Sinn Féin in 1983. Now an MP at Westminster, though refusing to take his seat, his energies were expended more in political than military concerns.

Yet this was also the period in which the IRA did acquire an arsenal. Colonel Gaddafi had given the Provisionals 1,200 Kalashnikovs, tons of Semtex plastic explosive and unusable SAM 7 missiles, apparently with components missing.

Gerard Hodgins says the new Kalashnikovs proved to be an embarrassment, that a promotional video to be used for fundraising in the US had to be remade on advice that 'commie weapons' wouldn't inspire rich Irish Americans to open their wallets. He was one of the Belfast IRA activists who were, he says, 'tickled pink that you were getting gear'. He says, 'For years we had been crying to the leadership for them to get us access to hardware and we'll finish it off.'

The new weaponry did change the profile of the IRA campaign a little. IRA engineers developed drogue bombs that could penetrate the armour on RUC vehicles, but then the police countered the new technology by reinforcing its vehicles. The IRA also developed barrack busters, mortars employing bombs inside gas canisters that could be propelled some distance through firing tubes. These tended mostly to impose on the state the expense of further reinforcing defences, by raising perimeter walls round police stations.

Ten officers killed in a mortar attack on Newry RUC station died when a device landed on a Portakabin they were using. Yet most of the missiles had failed to cause any appreciable damage.

There were other spectaculars that lifted republican spirits and helped them present themselves to the world momentarily as a viable army, like the bombings of the forensic laboratory in Belfast, the Baltic Exchange and Bishopsgate in the City of London and other enormously expensive attacks. Yet, even these were acts of armed propaganda, to use Adams's own term, with no prospect of tilting the balance of power between the IRA and Britain and with no such prospect really being sought. This was no longer an army at war seeking a military victory, if that means imposing on the enemy by force of arms the need to concede to demands.

A war that had no purpose other than propaganda would have to stop when it got in the way of Sinn Féin candidates being elected. Hume had wanted to talk to the organ grinder in the IRA rather than the political monkey, but soon found out that the monkey was the one to deal with, for he could tell the IRA organ grinder what tunes to play.

Chapter 19

In those days, Gerry Adams was chauffeured around in a black hackney, a taxi like the standard London cabs. That meant that he could move discreetly, there being so many others like it in west Belfast. One of the big changes since the start of the Troubles had been the growth of a Falls Taxi Association using old London cabs to run along bus routes into working-class areas with up to eight passengers at a time paying a fixed fare. There had never been as many English number plates on the Falls Road before. This service kept running, getting people home, even when there was violence that would discourage the bus companies.

Belfast was a bleak city at this time, and most city centre businesses simply closed down at six in the evening when the staff went home and the security gates across main streets closed. Most social life was confined to the suburbs.

Adams's car was armoured with heavy metal plating in the doors. Few people rode in it with him other than Eamon, his driver, and Peadar, his bodyguard. He told people that he no longer gave lifts to friends after the attack in 1984 because he did not want to put them at risk; the same reason he did not visit his mother in hospital in her last days. He was more exposed when electioneering, and in May 1987 another election was approaching and Adams had planned, as part of his campaign, to visit the office of the Housing Executive.

The UDA had plans to meet him there and to try once again to kill him.

The Ulster Defence Association had grown out of vigilante groups during the early Troubles and specialised in killing random Catholics. It was now infiltrated by British army intelligence, which was pointing it towards republican targets through an agent called Brian Nelson. Nelson had a contact in the Housing Executive who told him when Adams was expected. A sniper attack was set up and later aborted.

Research into Nelson's work has established that, though he was working for the state, the army's Force Research Unit (FRU), he was more interested in breaking the law than in protecting it. He was keen to kill members of the IRA whether his handlers approved or not.

Some in the army later offered a convoluted justification for using an illegal paramilitary group against the IRA. They said that plans to attack real activists rather than random Catholics would take longer to implement and would therefore be easier to intercept. This would also save the lives of the innocent Catholics that the UDA would otherwise be concentrating on.

The flaw in this plan is that interception almost never succeeded. The army's FRU was lax in gathering information from Nelson on UDA attack plans. It passed much of it on to the RUC Special Branch but Special Branch usually didn't bother passing on the warning to the person who was to be shot.

This laxity was revealed by the 2012 report of Sir Desmond de Silva QC into the murder of the Belfast solicitor Pat Finucane.[1] The report was commissioned by the Prime Minister, David Cameron, in an effort to meet demands from the Finucane family and their supporters for a public inquiry.

De Silva wrote:

My extensive research into the contemporary material leads me to the view that, when certain individuals were targeted, the reaction of the RUC SB [Special Branch] was also influenced to a significant extent by whether or not the individual under threat could be 'traced' as a paramilitary on either side of the sectarian divide. This theme is evident in documents from throughout the period . . . It was clear to me that steps were often not taken to secure the protection of those who were considered to be (as referred to in one intelligence document) 'a thorn in the side' of the security forces during this period of the Troubles.

De Silva found only two republicans who were actively protected from the UDA. One of them is given the codename T/o2. The other was Gerry Adams.

The agent, Brian Nelson himself, was to be Adams's assassin. He was equipped with a limpet mine. He was to drive alongside Adams's car on a motorbike and place the mine on the roof, which he believed was not armoured as thoroughly as the doors and windows.

Nelson's army handlers did not notify the police of the plan to kill Adams, apparently not trusting them to save him, but they had the threat dealt with at a higher level, through the army's own Tasking and Co-ordinating Group. TCG arranged for the area around the Housing Executive office to be flooded with security, forcing the UDA to abort the plan.

On the following day a senior Security Service officer in Northern Ireland sent a telegram to the London office outlining Nelson's role in the conspiracy to murder Gerry Adams. De Silva quotes the crucial section of this telegram:

We [Security Service officers] have discussed this extensively with ASP [Assistant Secretary Political] who shares our view that the operation threatens to get out of control. At the very least if [Nelson] is to be tasked by the UDA with a range of projects against high profile republican targets and is expected to take an active part in their execution he will inevitably be blown very quickly for precious little intelligence dividend and considerable expenditure of time and money by the Army. At the worst, if the attempt on Adams is to be repeated particularly before the general election and [Nelson's] involvement in . . . plus his links with the Army were to get into the public domain in some way . . . then British Intelligence and HMG [Her Majesty's Government] could face accusations of having conspired in the murder of a prospective MP with all the attendant adverse consequences.

So the logic for sparing Adams is that a successful attack on a high profile republican would raise suspicions of collusion and risk exposing Nelson as an agent before he had proven his value, and that it would be just too embarrassing for the army to be seen to have assisted in the assassination of a candidate in a general election. It would amount to a military interference in the democratic process. There would be 'adverse consequences'.

The UDA returned twice again to considering an attack on Adams. It met a week after the failed attack, but the army had now captured the limpet mine, and the UDA decided against an immediate ambush.

Adams around this time changed his armoured car to a Ford Granada, which was rumoured in west Belfast to have been bought from the London embassy of Saudi Arabia, though this may have been just a little myth that republicans enjoyed.

But two years later, in 1989, Nelson learnt that the UDA was hoping to strike against Adams again. This time it appears that someone in RUC Special Branch, which was not trusted to protect Adams in 1987, intervened to direct the hit man away from him. De Silva concluded that the intelligence which the UDA based its planning on was so similar to Special Branch filed information that it was probably drawn from it. The hit man for the operation this time was Ken Barrett. He would be convicted in 2004, after pleading guilty. Barrett concluded on the basis of intelligence he had access to that there was a much higher-value target available to him than Gerry Adams. He appears to have been persuaded that Adams wasn't important. The new target was the Belfast solicitor Pat Finucane. Finucane would take the bullet for Adams, or, in fact, fourteen bullets.

Special Branch intelligence said that Finucane was an intelligence officer for the IRA and that he laundered money for them. As evidence of his importance, passed to the UDA, Special Branch said he had been seen in a south Belfast hotel talking to Gerry Adams about Sinn Féin policy and the future direction of the republican campaign.

De Silva believes that the killing of Finucane went ahead because Nelson, who was their agent inside the UDA, did not relay back to the FRU the details that would have enabled them to stop it. He had been feeling uneasy in his double agent role. The plan to kill Adams in 1987 had obviously leaked out and that had brought him under suspicion of being an informer. The flooding of the area with security personnel had been a particularly gauche way of saving Adams and clearly advertised the army's prior knowledge of a planned attack in the area. But then the last time the army had been set the task of saving Adams, in 1984, the car had arrived too late.

Nelson did not want another attack to be scuppered in such a conspicuous way. That would lead the hard men in the UDA to suspect that he was an informer. De Silva also believes that Nelson preferred to kill republicans, not to save them, so he may have been happy to see Finucane killed.

A UDA team smashed in the front door at the home of Pat Finucane on a Sunday evening when the family was having dinner. Two gunmen shot Finucane fourteen times and wounded his wife while Barrett waited in the getaway car.

De Silva reported that the RUC Special Branch Daily Intelligence Book included the following note: '[L/28] claimed responsibility for Finnucane's [sic] murder . . . he was an I.O. [Intelligence Officer] and had been seen with G. Adams + other top PIRA at a meeting.'

The shooting of Pat Finucane has been one of the most discussed murders of the whole Troubles period. The family and several organisations have campaigned for an inquiry and the police have said that there was no evidence that he was a member of the IRA. De Silva's report was commissioned by Prime Minister David Cameron to concede something short of a full inquiry.

Brian Nelson explained to the journalist John Ware why he had been deflected from Adams to Finucane as the target. 'They were going for Adams but [L/28] was told – I don't know by whom – don't bother with Adams: Finucane is the man who really counts. He's the brains; he's the man who organises all the money to be laundered; he's the man who gives them advice. I assume that that came from the cops.'² Adams's political profile had made him an obvious target for the loyalist paramilitaries. It had also made him more accessible to them since he had to make public appearances while electioneering, but his candidacy in elections imposed an obligation on the state to protect him more carefully than it was protecting other members of the wider republican community.

The state had now to view Adams more as a politician than as a revolutionary pariah, and Adams had to consider how IRA actions would affect his vote. He convened a meeting in Divis Flats to discuss his strategy for the 1987 general election.

One of those in the inner circle was Gerard Hodgins who had recently been released from prison. Hodgins was PR officer for Sinn Féin in the West Belfast constituency and his job was to come up with ideas for attracting votes from people who did not support the IRA. Adams needed those votes. A lot of IRA members wouldn't vote at all because they didn't trust the political project, so even the support base couldn't be wholly relied on.

'It was an interesting brief,' says Hodgins. 'You were allowed to push against the parameters of strict republican theology. You could question more, make contact with people you wouldn't normally make contact with. Out of that I actually wrote a briefing paper for Gerry on the question of membership of the IRA, and gave him it, suggesting just that you're better acknowledging past membership, put it out of the way, put it to bed and it'll not come back to bite you again. The reaction was "No; thank you but no."'

Another Sinn Féin activist of that time, Alex Maskey, has said that he did not believe that briefing paper was written and, of course, Hodgins's account is at variance with Gerry Adams's repeated insistence that, while he would never disown the IRA, he was never a member.

Hodgins got to know Adams better in that period and says he had a 'saintly aura' about him because he 'didn't drink and didn't chase'. He says, 'He didn't do any of those things other men did; at least that's what we thought.'

This was a time of crises. This was also the period in which Adams first confronted his brother Liam about claims by Liam's daughter that he had sexually abused her. Adams had to deal with the rebound against Sinn Féin following the bombing of the Remembrance Day ceremony in Enniskillen in 1987 in which eleven people had been killed. Then there was the sequence of horrors following an SAS ambush that killed three members of an IRA bomb team in Gibraltar in March 1988.

Adams led the funeral cortege with the three coffins down the Falls Road, only a lone piper walking ahead of him, though he was informal in that position and even at one point left the middle of the road to chat with Martin Dillon, the BBC producer who had brought him face to face with John Hume. The police had kept a distance to ease the tension of a growing battle with republicans over the conduct of funerals so IRA members stewarded this one, even shifting parked cars off the road onto the pavement to clear the way, bouncing them on their springs to get a lift from the rebound. There was a carnival atmosphere almost until the funeral reached the cemetery. There it was attacked by a lone gunman. Loyalist Michael Stone had hoped to shoot Gerry Adams and Martin McGuinness. He was a narcissistic fantasist who was fixated on Adams. He later wrote that he was disappointed in the Sinn Féin President because he had not come out of the crowd to meet him like a man. Adams was calm under fire. With several shots being directed at him, he crouched and called practical instructions to those around him. Had Stone been as rash and brave as he had expected Adams to be, he could easily have got close enough to kill him but he put the blame for his failure on the target.

He killed three mourners before he was overcome while running from the cemetery.

Three days later, at the funeral of one of those killed by Stone, the IRA killed two soldiers who had apparently driven rashly into the path of the funeral. The funeral was passing Casement Park football ground when it met a silver Volkswagen coming in the other direction. The car rushed towards the funeral at first, perhaps trying to push a way past it, then reverse skidded to get back the way it had come. This alarmed the crowd and dozens of men swarmed round it. As they closed in they noticed that one of the men was armed with a drawn pistol. The driver fired a shot in the air to disperse the crowd. That merely escalated the crisis. IRA men dragged two men from the car, stripped them, beat them, then took them to waste ground and shot them dead. Much of this was televised.

The army would say the two men had lost their way while off-duty. But they did not have the short haircuts of ordinary corporals, which suggests that they were undercover.

For a Sinn Féin propaganda manager these were difficult days. Republicans had taken the moral advantage after the shootings in Gibraltar and depicted the British as the ruthless enemy who would gun down republicans on the street and finish them off, but now the IRA was seen acting savagely.

The IRA was also escalating its campaign of bombings of commercial property, though it had not advanced the plan to train a larger army and seize territory. Others were making their preparations just in case. The BBC established a secret studio from which it could continue broadcasting in the event of the IRA seizing Broadcasting House in Belfast.

The city had been spared big bombs for years but these became routine again, forcing the police to establish permanent checkpoints on all roads into the centre. These turned a campaign against property into a burden primarily on ordinary citizens trying to get to work. And that cost votes.

Adams would have to do something about that or the political prospects of Sinn Féin would decline. The balance between the IRA and Sinn Féin had to shift further from the militarists to the politically minded.

The contradiction between armed struggle and electoral politics didn't impose itself immediately on the republican movement because electoral successes were few. Adams had won the West Belfast constituency in the 1983 election and retained the seat in 1987. In the South where the party had expected early gains it got poor results that it found difficult to explain.

And it was around this time that Adams started sending his envoy, Father Alec Reid, to meet with government officials on both sides of the border to intimate that a peace deal might be possible.

Civil servants would receive handwritten and unsigned notes from Adams for the Secretary of State, Tom King.

And when delegates of the main parties met in Duisberg in October 1988 to try to negotiate a way out of political deadlock over the Anglo-Irish Agreement of 1985, after which unionists refused to meet ministers, Father Reid was at those talks too, as the eyes and ears of Gerry Adams.

Reality imposed itself after the 1992 election in which Gerry Adams lost West Belfast to the SDLP. Danny Morrison said that he had been defeated by the combined efforts of the SDLP and the UFF, the Ulster Freedom Fighters, as if Protestants voting tactically for the SDLP to oust Adams had no legitimacy; as if breaking out of their sectarian camp to vote for a social democrat against a republican was just a dirty trick. But the result prompted Morrison to offer an article to *An Phoblacht* from prison. He and Gerard Hodgins were serving sentences for convictions that have since been overturned.

Morrison argued that the IRA had either to escalate its campaign or consider ending it. Later he put the problem more plainly. 'The IRA will never overthrow the government or drive

out crown forces.' He had a freedom to air his doubts that few
others in the movement had previously enjoyed, though his
opinions were too strong for the paper he had edited until his
arrest and the article was 'banged'.[3]

Such 'liberated territory' as the IRA could claim was only 'in
the hearts and minds of a section of the nationalist people'. He
reflected on the logic behind the decision to develop the Sinn
Féin party. It was an acknowledgement that the purely military
struggle was being isolated and marginalised and could not win
on its own

In February 1992, a policeman who had had a mental breakdown
resolved to kill republicans. Allen Moore had been arrested firing
shots over a colleague's grave in Comber, County Down. He had
been allowed to leave Newtownards police station with a friend.
That night he phoned a friend in a distressed state of mind and
spoke of plans to kill republicans. The next day he travelled to
the Sinn Féin office in Divis Street with a shotgun. He shot five
people, killing three of them. The dead were Paddy Loughran,
a white-haired man who admitted callers to the building, Pat
McBride and Michael O'Dwyer.

Annie Adams, Gerry's mother, had been in the office that day,
delivering a package for prisoners in Long Kesh.

Adams was faced with a critical array of problems. Sinn Féin
could only function as a political party by making itself accessible
and thereby vulnerable. Where was the sense in maintaining an
IRA campaign that was costing the party votes anyway? His
mother had a stroke following the attack. People that he worked
with every day were dead. These were high prices to pay for an
IRA campaign that was failing to advance his political objectives.

Adams now understood that the IRA campaign had to stop if
Sinn Féin was to grow, and he started intimating to the Irish and
British governments that an end to violence was possible through
negotiation. He had been discussing with John Hume how the

core principles of republicanism might be rephrased to enable the IRA to stand aside and a political campaign to continue.

To this end he agreed with Hume that rights were accorded to people rather than territory; that is, the land of Ireland had no intrinsic right to be governed as a single jurisdiction if the people who lived on it chose otherwise. He also agreed that the 'armed struggle' was not a principle but a tactic.

And he developed the idea with which he had contested the Peace People in 1977, that the IRA campaign was a symptom rather than an initiative. If other parties took their share of responsibility for creating peace, then the IRA campaign could stop. This signal of changed thinking and the prospect of peace helped to open channels for discussions with the British and Irish governments. The United States helped by allowing Adams a visa to travel there and generate support for a peace process.

Gerard Hodgins got a postcard from Gerry Adams on his first trip to the United States. Adams wanted the prisoners to lobby for the negotiations. He wrote, 'Padraig Wilson, who is the best letter writer in Long Kesh, Bob Mor? Hodgey's start spreading the news. I'm leaving today, Gerry A.'

Hodgins came out of jail to a republican movement much changed from the one he had been part of before. He had Christmas parole in 1995. 'I went into The Felons [a drinking club] and Gerry was there with some guy over from South Africa, an ANC guy. "Come on over and say hello," he said. He asked me to come round to the house and say hello to Colette. And he got Eamon his driver to take me on wherever I wanted to go. They invited me down for dinner on Boxing Day but he wasn't there, he was away at meetings.'

Hodgins went back to work in the Press Centre but he didn't fit in as well now. The emphasis on politics and image had changed the culture.

'It wasn't called the Republican Press Centre any more, it was the Sinn Féin Press Centre. I was still in the old mode, pick the phone up, "Hello, Republican Press Centre". A couple of times Rita O'Hare phoned.' O'Hare was the General Secretary of Sinn Féin and avoided visiting the Belfast office for fear of arrest on an outstanding arms charge. Hodgins says, 'I remember her quite colourfully telling me that if I ever say Republican Press Centre again, she will come up from down south, take the chance, and hit me a good boot in the balls, honest to God.

'Plus, at that time you weren't allowed really to talk to a journalist. You were told if any questions come through, write them down, get a spokesperson. You had this thing called the peace process and you could bring it all crashing down if you said the wrong thing. So it wasn't really an enjoyable place to work. It was Stalinist.'

Part Three

Peace Processing

Chapter 20

Everyone of consequence in Ireland eventually had to meet Gay Byrne. Gay was the silvery-haired patrician talk-show host who had come to represent the conscience of the Irish people. His Friday night programme on RTE didn't just cover the historic turns in the evolution of Irish society, it was often a platform for the transformative events themselves.

So when Gerry Adams announced a ceasefire in August 1994 to cheering crowds outside the Sinn Féin headquarters at Connolly House, it became inevitable that he would soon be on Byrne's *Late Late Show*, explaining himself.

It was on the *Late Late* that a woman had shocked the nation by saying that she had slept naked with her husband on the first night of their honeymoon, and it was often by tracking similar changes in the Irish attitudes to God and sex that Byrne put his own programme into the history books. He handled these issues in the manner of a concerned and slightly bewildered grandfather, affecting to demonstrate that the core of the nation's values remained intact despite all these shocks and marvels.

But was he up to the job of patronising a hard-edged and combatively eloquent revolutionary from the streets of Belfast? He had had little chance to study Adams's ways of handling a hostile interview because Sinn Féin had been barred from the airwaves North and South during the later years of the Troubles.

The ceasefire had been an occasion for a family reunion. Rita Adams, the wife of Uncle Sean, who had left for Canada in 1952, came home to the Falls Road for the celebration and stayed at the home of Gerry's brother Dominic. Dominic remembered the event in his message of condolence to the family a few years later after her death. 'Sinn Féin had organised a huge peace rally in Dublin at the time and Aunt Rita travelled to Dublin with us and forty other Republicans on a bus. The craic was 90 [it was the best possible fun] and as the songs started Aunt Rita joined in and was soon singing away. In O'Connell Street she stood with the masses and cheered as Gerry told us it was time for Britain to leave Ireland.'

Yet Adams was in no better position to tell Britain to go than he had been with an armed campaign. His words were ambiguous. He had so far refused to say that the 'cessation' of violence was permanent, only that it was complete. Byrne felt obliged to give him limited respect, to handle him with care.

Adams was invited onto the programme for a one-on-one interview with Byrne to be followed by a confrontation with a panel of critics. RTE's main concern seems to have been to avoid a charge that it had gone easy on him. But faced with the toughest interviewer in the country and this panel of politicians and writers, Adams prevailed and he won the support of an audience that sensed the injustice of his disadvantaged position.

He had had little experience of the media before this. Where he had been interviewed, his voice had been silenced and lip-synced over, as a device for managing a ludicrous law that banned representatives of paramilitary organisations from being heard. But he had been trained in a few devices for protecting himself. One of these was to allow his critics to develop their points in full without interruption. Then, when given a chance to answer, he would launch on his own case, the critic would seek to butt in urgently to correct him, and he would stop and say, 'Did I interrupt you? Then have the courtesy to hear me out, the same courtesy I extended to you.'

This worked in silencing perfectly valid arguments and creating for Gerry Adams the space in which to develop his point, promote his propaganda, often founded on superficial and simplistic reasoning.

He was now making an evolutionary step in his thinking but he had a problem. He had to intimate to the governments, particularly to the British, that it might be possible to reach a peaceful settlement in Northern Ireland by negotiating with him, yet he could not state plainly to his own support base that the stated objective of a united Ireland was unattainable.

He had moved from being an idealist to being a pragmatist. He had had comrades who preferred to die rather than compromise, to demonstrate the intolerability of injustice by giving up their lives. These had been the most apolitically minded of people if politics is adaptation, the art of the possible.

In this major interview he positioned himself as one who could help to end conflict rather than as someone who was on one side and had decisions of his own to take, as a mediator rather than as a player.

'I come from within a situation where there has been conflict for seventy-five years. Now, if John Hume and I have done a service it has been to show that it doesn't have to be the way it was for the last twenty-five years.'

The IRA campaign was now to be presented as a by-product of bad politics and not as something for which he would accept individual responsibility or even for which he would accept that the IRA itself should be called to account.

Challenged on the violence of the IRA he adopted an approach he has used many times since.

'Let's not just zero in, in this interview, on the politics of the last atrocity. I mean, what happened in Enniskillen was wrong. I never defended what happened in Enniskillen and I've never tried, by the way, to distance myself or to dodge my responsibility on these issues.'

In saying he had not 'dodged my responsibility', he was doing precisely that, pushing the issue aside and moving on. He was never going to define what that responsibility was.

Asked if he supported the IRA, he insisted that he had done

only what the founders of the Irish state had done earlier.

'Because of a situation that existed, and let me repeat what I have said many times, that in a situation where people see no alternative, as it was here, seventy-five years ago in this city, where people went out and did exactly the same thing.'

Gay Byrne, the great defender of fundamental Irish decency, snapped at that. 'There is actually no comparison . . .'

But, of course, there is, in that in both cases a self-appointed army chose to represent the Irish people and to protest through murder and sabotage. The Easter Rising of 1916 and the campaign of the Provos are not comparable on the scale of military activity but they are, arguably, on the question of legitimacy. Each was instigated by small groups of armed people assuming the right to represent the Irish nation.

'Well now, I don't want to get into an argument,' said Adams, but actually this was one of the stronger points he could have made. If the Provisional IRA taking up arms without a democratic mandate was wrong, then so was the Easter Rising of 1916, a consideration that Byrne was unable to allow since the story of the courage and self-sacrifice of the leaders of the Rising is the founding myth of the Irish state.

Adams's basic argument, as in much of his writing, was that the British had denied civil rights to nationalists in Northern Ireland as a necessary measure towards preserving partition and that the army had been sent in to quell protest and to defend injustice. The alternative had been to allow that the protesters were right, grant them civil rights and watch partition fail. The denial of civil rights as a mechanism for keeping Ireland divided is a highly debatable point, but no one on the *Late Late* engaged him on that.

'Because the statelet couldn't afford to give the Catholics in the six counties the right to vote at local government elections and the British statelet couldn't afford to let that situation endure, so they moved in the British troops and we all of us got sucked into a cycle of ongoing conflict.'

Adams had not been 'sucked in'. Few in the republican movement who knew him saw his role in such passive terms. He had energetically supported the IRA campaign and worked to retrieve it from demoralisation in the mid-1970s. He had attacked the Peace People yet, in doing so, had begun to redefine the IRA's role as a symptom of injustice rather than as an active revolutionary initiative. He had, out of that thinking, developed the idea that the campaign was 'armed propaganda'.[1] In that, he had found a justification for the IRA maintaining its campaign at a low level of irritation rather than building towards a guerrilla war. And now he understood that it was an effective veto on political change. He would not get the united Ireland he had started out demanding, but he knew that no one else would get a political system they could work within either unless the IRA campaign stopped. That reality made him indispensable.

It quickly became obvious that Byrne and the panellists had thought that Gerry Adams would be easily vanquished by arguments that connected him to the IRA. The playwright Hugh Leonard, one of the panellists ranged against him, seemed to think that he could blame Gerry Adams for everything the IRA had done and that Adams would then be speechless and humiliated. It turned out the other way round. 'These people in their graves are crying out for retribution and it is not going to come any more,' Leonard said. 'You are morally responsible for that. You are a murderer, and now you add the extra dimension of saying you want peace and you are a hypocrite as well . . . If you lie down with dogs you're going to get up with fleas.'

To which Adams replied, 'I don't come here to be sanctimonious and to engage in theatrics. I want to see peace.'

Leonard held him responsible for the violence. Wasn't he responsible?

GA: No more than you are, and I have never dodged my responsibilities in any of this and unlike you I am prepared to the best of my ability to do something to bring that peace.

HL: I don't think I ever shot anyone. I don't think I was in charge of a brigade of the Provisional IRA.

GA: Nor I.

HL: Weren't you?

GA: No.

HL: You never sued for libel. Why?

GA: I might do after tonight.

But he would not sue, perhaps because the kind of evidence which Justice Lowry had decided in 1977 did not establish beyond reasonable doubt that Adams had been an IRA leader might well have been sufficient to succeed in a civil court with its lower burden of proof.

Another panellist was the former SDLP representative Austin Currie. Currie knew Adams. He had been part of the team led by John Hume that had met him in inter-party talks that would evolve into the peace process. Now Currie called him to account over punishment beatings, but Adams simply denied any responsibility for them.

'According to the RUC eleven people have been assaulted in nationalist areas. Eleven people in eight weeks. I'm sure there will be eleven people assaulted in Dublin tonight and tomorrow night as a result of drunken brawls and all sorts of other brawls.'

So it was all hardly worth worrying about. Yet he was opposed to punishment beatings, he said.

An eloquent playwright and a seasoned northern political activist had both challenged Adams and he had made them look trivial and picky and ill-informed. However, none of the people beaten in drunken brawls in Dublin that night would have bones broken systematically by IRA men wielding iron pipes.

Adams then said he had concerns of his own about the way in which the programme was structured, not primarily about the numbers lined up against him but about the fact that none of them were women.

Addressing the Dublin audience, he asked how many of them would want the British to come back and rule them, but Austin Currie scored one decent point when he interjected to ask, 'How many of you have been put off the idea of a united Ireland because of the activities of the Provisional IRA?' That interjection won immediate applause.

And Michael McDowell of the Progressive Democratic Party, another panellist, touched a raw nerve too. 'Why don't you level with your supporters and with the Irish people and say that Northern Ireland is going to remain part of the UK for the foreseeable future? And now let's talk about how it can be made into a just society.'

It was perhaps the most dangerous question of all. Adams might not have been able to preserve republican backing for the peace process if he had acknowledged at such an early stage that he had no hope of removing Northern Ireland from the UK and getting rid of the Irish border.

He said, 'A united Ireland is a very logical, honourable political view. Let us, when we sit down, make sure that everything is on the negotiating table. I'm not talking about the six counties joining the twenty-six counties and us coming into this situation. I'm talking about a new Ireland. I have used the term "to transform Irish society" to build a non-sexist, a just society, a new society in all of this island.'

One would have thought to listen to him that the IRA had been bombing city centres and had killed hundreds of people for women's rights.

He had not just learnt the trick of deflecting criticism; he had learnt also to be vague and general in defining his goals so that neither the constitutional nationalist beside him nor the ardent socialist republican behind him could be sure he was asking for too much or settling for too little.

Chapter 21

There are several theories for why Adams announced the cease-fire. The most pressing reality for him at the time was that Sinn Féin's growth had stopped and he had lost his West Belfast seat in 1992. That setback had forced a choice between political growth or continued armed propaganda. The new voters that Sinn Féin needed to attract were not IRA supporters and many of the core IRA supporters had little interest in voting at all. The two parts of the movement were now working against each other, competing for resources, getting in each other's way as never before.

'I'm glad,' says Richard O'Rawe, 'that Gerry Adams stopped the war and led the whole movement by the nose into the peace process. Somebody had to do it and he was the only one who could.'

If this reflects the private thinking of other former IRA men of Adams's generation, then it provides an explanation for their willingness to accept goals so unlike those they set out to achieve. Anthony McIntyre sees an uncanny docility in the republican movement, people who have, in his judgement, been conned and can't see that. He may be right, or it may be that these people are just relieved that they were spared further years of killing and getting nowhere.

Another theory is that the IRA had been so thoroughly infiltrated that its campaign could not continue. Adams, it became clear, was surrounded by spies. In May 2003, the IRA's head of security, Freddie Scappaticci, would be accused of being a British agent codenamed Stakeknife. He was allegedly being run by the British army while vetting all new IRA volunteers, which suggests you couldn't actually join the IRA without the approval of the enemy.

The Sinn Féin head of administration, Denis Donaldson, was a spy. Sinn Féin would itself later claim that Adams's driver, Roy McShane, had been a spy too.

Adams was being driven around in a bugged car and worked in a bugged office.

The peace process started in 1988, when Adams turned forty and his son was fifteen. He was of an age at which people reassess the direction of their lives and their achievements. And crises within his own family were adding to the pressure. His niece Aine had in 1986 gone to the police to tell them that her father, Liam Adams, Gerry's brother, had raped her when she was four years old and continued to abuse her sexually until she was ten. The child's mother had reported the rape to the police and then withdrawn the complaint.

Adams's mother died in 1992, and Adams, adapting lines by Pearse, acknowledged in his *Irish News* death notice that she had wept for him and that her heart had broken. 'Since I was little I have seen how you battle with your tears for me, and with a proud glad look, although your heart was breaking.'

The main reason for his seeking peace, as understood by John Hume, his ally in the beginnings of the process, and John Bruton, the Taoiseach through most of the first ceasefire, was simply that he wanted to get the IRA 'off the hook'. The IRA campaign had gone on too long and was unproductive. It had to be wound up but Adams had to have something to show for the sacrifices people had made.

John Bruton, as Taoiseach, had several meetings with Gerry Adams in 1995, the year of the first negotiations between the British and the republican leadership. Republicans then saw the Irish government as their sponsor within the peace process and took their complaints to officials and ministers. Bruton believes that Adams understood that success required a complete end to the IRA campaign. He also believes that Adams was giving a different account of progress to the IRA, keeping alive its hopes that much more was achievable. Some of the ideas floated by Adams and his colleagues in the early stages included a proposal that members of the IRA would transfer to a new police force, holding the rank that they had held in the IRA. Bruton believes there was no chance they were ever going to get that.

Adams made a strong case that the British should be 'persuaders for Irish unity'. They refused this and maintained that refusal throughout.

The IRA resisted demands that it announce clearly that its 'complete cessation' in 1994 was a permanent end to violence.

Ed Moloney[1] says that the army council had only been narrowly won over to support for the cessation on the understanding that it was temporary and part of a new strategy by which armed actions could complement political progress. This was, he says, encapsulated in the acronym TUAS by which the strategy was described in internal IRA communications. Some had defined this clumsily as Totally Unarmed Strategy. Moloney more plausibly says it stood for Tactical Use of Armed Struggle.

Anthony McIntyre left the IRA after the Good Friday Agreement, regarding it as a sell-out of the campaign he had participated in, and he critiqued it in a series of articles for *The Blanket* website. He predicted that the IRA would eventually decommission its weapons, asking, 'Who do you think Adams is lying to; to Clinton and Blair or to the base?' But perhaps Adams always hoped that political agreement would be possible without the IRA having to decommission, yet realised in the fullness of negotiations that this was not achievable.

Sinn Féin and the IRA were, by one view, wooed into a political process in which they would fail in most of their demands and be reduced from a revolutionary socialist movement to a constitutional nationalist one. Then, potentially, they would be direct rivals of the SDLP and would be swept away by the more experienced party. Yet in this same period Sinn Féin grew rapidly.

Adams left behind some republican purists who could not accept that the IRA had lost and who viewed the switch to party politics as a surrender of principle. Among these were the pure militarists who, while in the IRA, had always distrusted politics and participated little in Sinn Féin's growth. There were others, like Anthony McIntyre and Tommy McKearney, who were the intellectual critics. They accepted that the IRA campaign had failed but they argued that Sinn Féin could be a revolutionary party; it could hold to the left instead of shifting to the centre to attract votes.

Yet even in shifting to the centre, Adams was still fighting to exact the greatest possible concessions.

The chief device by which the IRA prolonged the peace process and changed the political map was through the refusal of the decommissioning of weapons. Ironically, the demand for decommissioning, as coined by the British Secretary of State, Sir Patrick Mayhew, in 1995, was intended as a concession to the IRA, an assurance that no actual surrender was demanded of it.

There are no official statements of how much weaponry it had other than the assessment of the Independent International Commission on Decommissioning whose records are still secret. The IRA had received a couple of tons of Semtex in the mid-1980s but the estimated lifespan of that explosive is twenty years, which suggests that the consignment provided by Libya would have been close to useless by the time of final decommissioning in 2005. It had stocks of automatic rifles. These had more symbolic than practical value in the kind of campaign the IRA was engaged in, which avoided direct combat. It had wanted pistols but was apparently short of them until it opened a channel to a dealer in the US.

Mayhew's plan was that the IRA could merely get rid of its weapons themselves, agree a method of doing so and demonstrate that it worked by making a start. Though republicans and others responded as if this was an unreasonable demand, it could have been viewed as generous and even foolhardy given that it relied so much on the honesty of the paramilitaries who held the arms.

John Bruton, who was Taoiseach at the time, says now that he thinks there would have been no demand for decommissioning at all if the IRA had brought its campaign to a complete end, as had been required in a Joint Declaration by the two governments in December 1993 as a precursor to talks.

Adams told the governments that decommissioning was an impossible demand but he made political advances out of the deadlock between the demand and the refusal.

The IRA had also continued with killings and maimings. Republicans seemed to think they could get away with their vigilante work if they injured victims a little more discreetly than they'd done before. Instead of shooting joyriders they now broke their arms and legs with metal piping. There was anxiety around one case in Ardoyne in which a boy appeared to have a bullet hole in his arm but doctors affirmed that it had been caused by a screwdriver. The media then eased up on its speculation that the ceasefire had been broken.

Further testing its limits, the IRA started killing drug dealers but claimed the killings under the title Direct Action Against Drugs, DAAD. This was a group of IRA men from the Markets area of Belfast.

The governments weren't ready to close down the peace process in response to these actions, and this taught Adams that the IRA had latitude, that no one was going to crash the whole prospect of peace in reaction to one misdemeanour. And comforted by that insight, the IRA refused decommissioning and urged people not to co-operate with the police.

Adams was intimating to Bruton in 1995 that decommissioning was attainable, but conceding nothing. He met Bruton on 17 February to recruit his support in protesting against British army searches for weapons in South Armagh. Bruton says Adams 'seemed to think that normal security operations should

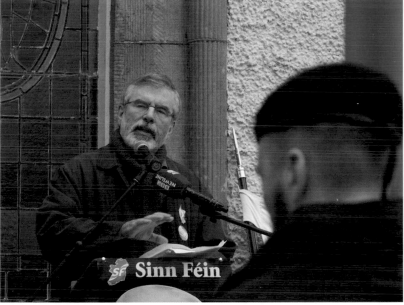

This shop stands on the site of the Adams family house in Ballymurphy, now demolished.

Gerry Adams addresses an Easter Rising commemoration in Roslea with uniformed IRA men in attendance.

Ann Travers, whose sister Mary was shot dead by the IRA, is now a campaigner for justice for victims.

Anthony McIntyre was a teenage scout for Joe McCann on the day he was killed. He later joined the Provisional IRA and served a life sentence for murder. He is now a critic of Gerry Adams.

Old republicans and members of D Company, the IRA unit once led by Brendan 'Darkie' Hughes, conduct a flag-lowering ceremony on the Falls Road, to remember their dead.

An Orange band honours a loyalist brigadier killed by the IRA. The parades have often been the focus of unrest.

Austin Stack's father was a prison officer, murdered by the IRA. Gerry Adams brought him to meet a senior IRA man, who read him a statement accepting responsibility for the killing. Stack is still critical of Adams and accuses him of withholding the name of the IRA contact from police investigating the killing.

A wreath to Gerry Adams's old friend Joe McCann is hung every year at the corner of Joy Street in Belfast on the anniversary of the day he was shot dead by British paratroopers in April 1972. A bullet strike is still clear in the brickwork below it.

Mairia Cahill worked with Sinn Féin in her teens and was raped by an IRA man. She claims that the IRA terrorised her.

Mairia Cahill crosses the Upper Springfield Road, past graffiti which appeared after reports that the IRA had investigated her rape by one of their members.

Michael Donnelly was a senior IRA man in Derry and knew Gerry Adams in Long Kesh during internment.

Richard O'Rawe was the press officer for the IRA hunger strikers in the Maze prison and accuses Gerry Adams of prolonging the protest.

Tommy McKearney was an IRA hunger striker.

Gerard Hodgins was the last of the IRA hunger strikers. He now accuses Gerry Adams of prolonging the hunger strike for political advantage.

A mural dedicated to Gerry Adams, erected on the Falls Road when he was arrested in May 2014. When he was released he asked for it to be removed.

Graffiti on the Falls Road on the day after Gerry Adams appeared on television reflecting on the life of Jesus.

be suspended'. Adams's case to Bruton was that 'harassment' of the IRA in South Armagh would make decommissioning more difficult. He called the raids 'gratuitous actions of the British'.

'I listened to him,' says Bruton, but he says he didn't phone the British Prime Minister, John Major, and ask him to call off the army. 'Adams constantly urged that the Irish government would be co-opted into a nationalist front including the Irish government, Sinn Féin and Irish America, to push the British and the unionists to do what this front wanted. I was never willing to do that because I was the head of the government of a state and a state shouldn't be part of a front with anybody. But that was the notion that seemed to underlie the Hume–Adams thinking, that if you could create a front it would be a kind of umbrella on which the IRA could get off the hook of their own making, the hook of the utterly futile use of violence.'

Bruton says Adams was difficult to deal with. He never dealt with him on an informal or personal basis. 'There was this wall which made that very difficult. It isn't conducive to full-faith negotiation. I contrast my dealings with John Major. He's English and he's different from me but I always felt if you scratched John Major he would bleed. You would know if you were going too far and you'd back off or you'd know there was a bit more give and you'd continue. You'd understand where the conversation was going, even on the phone. That wouldn't be a sense you'd ever get in dealing with Gerry Adams.'

He says Adams was 'delphic' and remote.

'I have a feeling that Gerry Adams wasn't necessarily communicating the realities of the situation to people in the IRA, that while he was trying to lead them in a particular direction, he wasn't being fully frank with them as he took them along the road. That lack of frankness internally within the republican movement imposed unnecessary and unfair burdens on other people. It would have been better if he had levelled with the IRA earlier on.'

The argument against that is that he might have split the IRA more deeply and left a rump that could have maintained the campaign at a high level and one of whose first targets might have been Adams himself.

'We might have avoided all that foot dragging that we had to cope with in getting talks going, dealing with the weapons issue, dealing with the threats, dealing with the fact that there is no halfway house between force and non-force. I don't think he exercised a proper leadership role in terms of the communication of reality being one of the responsibilities of leadership.'

By this view, holding out on decommissioning was not a considered strategy but a by-product of poor communication within the IRA about what the process required. 'By not being frank he created a difficulty for himself. After all, he was pushing other people to do things that they didn't want to do so he had a responsibility to push his own. I don't think he did that to the degree that was necessary and I think that explains that low-level violence continued and eventually they went back to full-scale violence.'

Despite his obduracy, Adams was elevated into global importance as a peacemaker when US President Bill Clinton visited Belfast in November 1995 and staged a casual encounter with him in a doorway on the Falls Road to shake his hand when unionists were still refusing to.

And though Bruton saw only coldness in him, Adams was capable of stunning flashes of humour and charm with others. At an on-street press conference behind the BBC's Broadcasting House in Belfast in 1997, reporter Eamonn Mallie tried to get him to acknowledge that he had already had a meeting with the new Prime Minister, Tony Blair. Often surly and disgruntled under pressure, Adams's impulse went the other way this time. He chuckled and said, 'Oh Eamonn, let me kiss you on the nose.' And he cupped the reporter's cheeks in his hands, lowered his face to him and neutralised the question with a playful peck.

The IRA ended its first 'cessation' in February 1996 when a South Armagh unit bombed Canary Wharf in east London in protest against what it saw as British obduracy, quaintly accusing John Major of ditching the Mitchell Principles, a set of preconditions for talks drawn up by US Senator George Mitchell. These principles chiefly governed the need to end violence and decommission weapons. Major had accepted the principles but angered Sinn Féin by announcing elections to a new Northern Ireland Forum that would facilitate the entry of a wider range of parties into the talks, including parties representing loyalist paramilitaries, the Northern Ireland Women's Coalition and Labour.

Ed Moloney provides an account of the growing dissent within the IRA and claims that a majority on the IRA Executive, which had been excluded from the decision-making, wanted a return to the armed campaign. Shortly before the Canary Wharf bomb went off, Adams phoned the White House to say that he was 'hearing some very disturbing news'. Moloney says that Adams was positioning himself as a frustrated peacemaker caught between IRA hardliners and the obdurate British. He says, 'It was a convenient cover story, but it was not too far from the truth.'[2]

The massive bomb caused huge damage to property and took two lives. John Bruton says, 'I was horrified by the murder of John Jeffries and Inan Bashir.' The man who was Taoiseach at the time says he had been given no indication that this was coming. 'I was aware that there were difficulties in the republican movement but Canary Wharf was something that had to have been planned for months. The idea that it was contingent on something that happened the week before the bomb went off is not credible.'

Yet even with the return to the armed campaign Sinn Féin's vote rose to 15 per cent in elections to the Northern Ireland Forum.

The IRA then carried out several spectacular attacks, devastating the centre of Manchester, causing £700m worth of damage, and bombing inside the British army's Thiepval

Barracks in Lisburn. But the lower-level activity in Belfast was evidently less competent and effective than similar actions had been before the ceasefire and some in the media speculated that the IRA was fighting a 'phoney war' with little intention of causing real damage inside Northern Ireland.

The objectives of the attacks in that period were different from those of the armed struggle that had ended in August 1994. That had been a campaign to propagandise through violence the demand for a united Ireland. This was an effort to wrest concessions in negotiations from the British government, primarily a fixed start date and duration for the coming talks and a relaxation of the demand for decommissioning of IRA weapons as a precondition of Sinn Féin's participation. Ruairí Ó Brádaigh, the Republican Sinn Féin leader who broke away from the Adams-led movement in 1986, objecting to the dropping of its abstention policy, now pointed up another fundamental republican principle that was being violated. He said that the IRA was only entitled to take life in pursuit of the Republic and not to advance political negotiations on a settlement short of the republican goals.

The IRA killed eight people in that year of the return to war, one officer of the Gardai (the Irish police force), two RUC men, two soldiers and three civilians. Most of the Troubles-related killing in that period was done by loyalist groups and the feuding Irish National Liberation Army (INLA), but their violence had less political relevance. The key political challenge for the government was to stop the IRA and get Sinn Féin into talks. The new Labour government led by Tony Blair was ready to concede that the decommissioning of IRA weapons might run concurrently with talks.

One of the last atrocities of that period, the shooting dead of two policemen in Lurgan, coincided with Adams signing his new book in a bookshop in Dublin.

Two gunmen ran up behind Constables John Graham and David Johnston in Church Walk, near their station, and shot them. Their bodies lay on the road for hours, covered by a sheet, in view of the passing shoppers and people bringing wreaths to the police station gate. In Dublin the queue of people wanting their copy of *Before the Dawn* signed by Gerry Adams stretched out into the street and round the corner.

It was Bloomsday and Paul Durcan marked the occasion with a poem that began: 'Not even you, Gerry Adams, deserve to be murdered'.

What appalled Durcan was that the book signing diluted media focus on the murders. Adams was asked to comment and said, 'Any death in this situation diminishes all of us.'

The ceasefire was restored in time for formal talks called by Tony Blair.

Whether by coincidence or someone's perverse numerological management, the resumed campaign had lasted exactly as long as the ceasefire that preceded it, 527 days. In April 1997, Blair visited Hillsborough Castle, which is more a mansion than a castle, and said this wasn't the time for soundbites but that he felt 'the hand of history' on his shoulder. He had decided to present the negotiations as being of global and historic significance. Much of the world's media went along with this, though the task was simply to establish devolved government in Northern Ireland and formally end the IRA and loyalist paramilitary campaigns.

Senator George Mitchell chaired the talks between the political parties while the international media waited outside for months, reporters often interviewing each other as experts when they couldn't get a politician to come out and tell them what was going on.

There were two loyalist parties in the talks: the Ulster Democratic Party representing the UDA, and the Progressive Unionist Party representing the UVF. Yet, representation is a concept these parties and Sinn Féin disputed. Adams always denied that he spoke on behalf of the IRA but continued to say that he would consult it on the talks. The SDLP still represented more nationalists than the republicans did. There was the Alliance Party, which saw itself as cross-community, the Women's Coalition and a Labour Party and others. The deal would be mainly done between the two big parties of the separate, estranged Catholic/nationalist and Protestant/unionist communities, the SDLP and the Ulster Unionist Party. The Democratic Unionist Party was refusing to attend.

The British and Irish governments negotiated with each other on their own relations and on cross-border bodies.

Blair was determined that the talks would work. President Clinton followed them closely and when they went into their hothouse phase, crashing their 9 April deadline, and had to end so that Mitchell could go home for Easter, he called the party leaders and urged them over the line.

What they came up with was a devolved assembly with a power-sharing cross-community executive, an understanding that all weapons would be decommissioned and an early release scheme for paramilitary prisoners.

Even after what was called the Good Friday Agreement, poet Paul Durcan was venomous in his contempt.

'The stomach of my soul seizes up and I wonder if the neighbours can hear me as I retch,' he said on the Pat Kenny show in 2002, '. . . all those hundreds and hundreds of unique, individual human beings murdered, many of them much more interesting and decent people than you or I, Gerry Adams. All of them dumped into the trashcan of history, their rotting arms and legs hanging out of bins everywhere, on estates and on seashores and on derelict bogs.'

Nor was the agreement the end of the process. The negotiations were framed on a principle that nothing was agreed until everything was agreed, yet the big hard questions around policing and demilitarisation were unanswered. That this was an agreement at all is questionable, given the contrasting interpretations. An opportunity for a trade-off between prisoners and weapons was squandered by letting the prisoners out without a clear commitment from the paramilitaries to disarm. The formula arrived at said that all parties agreed that weapons should be decommissioned within two years. The unionists saw the refusal to disarm as a breach of faith with the agreement by Sinn Féin, but Gerry Adams argued that the clause was aspirational and had no meaning because the IRA was not a party to the agreement anyway.

The Ulster Unionist Party leader, David Trimble, then refused to form an executive with Sinn Féin until decommissioning started.

The talks chair, George Mitchell, when asked if the agreement had, as he understood it, obliged Sinn Féin to secure IRA decommissioning, said he would not like to get into 'that level of specificity'.

Like Blair and Adams, Mitchell, too, believed in creative ambiguity, and found prospects for change in the gaps in understanding.

Chapter 22

Experience told republicans that most bombs killed nobody and the worst bombs, at Enniskillen and La Mon, killed under a dozen. Then on 15 August 1998 the pattern broke and Sinn Féin's routine equivocation about the legitimacy of continued violence became untenable. A rump of the Provisionals had carried on with a bombing campaign, styling itself the Real IRA. Others called them dissidents but they regarded themselves as purists who had not compromised as Adams had done. Adams, for his part, declined when pressed by the media to condemn their actions. Logically he couldn't. They were former allies who had made the same decision as himself, to endorse armed revolution against British governance in Ireland.

A bomb team from South Armagh, affiliated to the Real IRA, parked a car in Omagh High Street on a sunny Saturday afternoon when the town was crowded with shoppers and tourists. The group had bombed other towns in the previous months in the same way and with few casualties. This time the warning phoned in was misunderstood. The car was left on a street that led up to the courthouse. The police, taking the courthouse for the target, guided people down the street towards the car. The blast killed twenty-nine people, one of them pregnant with twins.

The surgeon from the local hospital heard the bomb and saw the smoke from the golf course. The dead included young and old, Protestant and Catholic, male and female, tourists and locals.

The mayor of Omagh, Sean Clarke, was a Sinn Féin councillor. He was about to fall into the gap between his party's assent to peace and its squeamishness about condemning republican paramilitaries who were doing what the Provisionals had been doing themselves. He was confronted with the need to make a press statement on behalf of the council. One of those council officials who checked the first draft sent it back to him. He argued that the council had no choice but to condemn the bombing. But Sinn Féin locally would not approve the condemnation of the bomb; clearance for that had to come from higher up.

The scale of the calamity was such that no evasion was possible for Adams and Sinn Féin's chief negotiator, Martin McGuinness, if they were to remain credible partners in the peace process. But this obliged them to distinguish themselves clearly from the armed tradition of republicanism. It bounced them over a line they had hoped not to cross.

Adams said what he had to say. 'I am totally horrified by this action. I condemn it without any equivocation whatsoever.'

He was claiming now to speak for the only legitimate republican tradition and saying that no dissenters from his position had the right to bomb or kill for Ireland. He had brought that militant tradition to an end. This was much more than he had conceded on Good Friday.

The poet Paul Durcan saw only hypocrisy in it. In the poem 'Omagh' he adopts the voice of the Omagh Quartermaster sending a memo to GHQ, saying 'Gerry, *a chara*, I am vexed with you.'

The Quartermaster says it is lucky for Gerry that he didn't go beyond his unequivocal condemnation of the bomb to sound off about the sanctity of life or apologising for the past. That would have been too much to take.

Adams was dealing with serious family problems now as well. This is the time, according to a later family statement to the BBC, that he first realised that members of his family had been sexually abused by their father so he had more to think about than war and peace. He could see now that the enemy that had harmed his family most was not the British imperialist but the thug in the corner, the old man who had urged him to join the IRA when he was the same age his own son was now. And if he had been a fraudulent father, feigning love for his children in order to have sex with them, how real was his republicanism? Adams must have asked himself that question. How much else in his life was founded on lies?

He travelled to Canada to meet his father's brother Sean, who had known him as a baby. When they had lived on the Shore Road, Sean and his girlfriend Rita had cycled out to visit them and babysit. Adams discovered a large family in Toronto, Sean and Rita's children, all grown up and still carrying on the resilient republican culture. And they received him like a hero.

His cousin Sean junior's website shows him partying with them. These are the most informal pictures of Gerry Adams in the public domain, taken at a time when he was anticipating having to disclose to the media that his father had been an abuser, also anticipating the likely arrest some day of his brother for child abuse.

Back home the violence had subsided but not stopped.

The Provisionals would continue to kill and to carry out huge robberies and Gerry Adams and the other Sinn Féin leaders would continue to make excuses for them. The following summer the IRA shot and killed Charlie Bennett in north Belfast but the Secretary of State, Mo Mowlam, worked hard to keep a review of the Good Friday Agreement on track and stood by Martin McGuinness. One reporter asked, 'Martin, if you shot me would that be a breach of the ceasefire or wouldn't it?' In response, McGuinness's press officer complained to the BBC and the *Scotsman* newspaper that this was an inappropriate question to put to a public representative.

This was a period of tragedy in the Adams family itself. Two sons of Margaret and Micky McCorry, Liam and Michael, died in a car crash on the Falls Road in November 1999. Their mother was a sister of Gerry Adams. A son-in-law of the McCorrys, Terry Enright, was shot dead by loyalists while working as a doorman at a club in Talbot Street just two years earlier.

Adams was determined through the peace process to defend the legitimacy of the IRA campaign as having been pursued by committed and decent people and supported by the communities from which they emerged. He continued to deny that he was ever a member of the IRA, though on occasions he put himself forward to apologise on its behalf. He became, in effect, a lightning rod for criticism of the IRA, such a target of frustration with his ambiguities and evasions that his comrades were spared.

For years, he was the only direct mediator of IRA thinking that other parties and heads of government would meet. He met many times with the Prime Minister, Tony Blair, and more often with his Chief of Staff, Jonathan Powell. He would come to them and explain why it was difficult to persuade the IRA to decommission weapons. He would never acknowledge that he was a party to that decision. And Blair and others went along with this. Adams had accepted the Good Friday Agreement, which required the IRA to decommission within two years, and yet he argued afterwards that the clause did not bind him because he was not a member of the IRA and did not bind the IRA because it was not a party to the agreement.

In the years of the peace process the biggest question hanging over Gerry Adams was whether he was playing fair. Did he really want peace or was he dragging out the process and procrastinating for political advantage, perhaps even holding in reserve the option of reviving the 'armed struggle'?

Jonathan Powell's account of his mediation between Adams and Tony Blair shows that Adams was often able to extract concessions by reminding Powell of a danger that the IRA would return to violence or be difficult to persuade. This can be viewed benignly as pragmatism, but was viewed more cynically by some as a protection racket. Republicans worked the conceit that the IRA and Sinn Féin were separate organisations, though the two governments regarded them as sharing the same leadership structures, whatever the division of labour on the ground. Adams's position was that he could influence the IRA to end its campaign but that he could not take that decision himself or be held answerable for the IRA's refusal or hesitation. For a time, this division between the party and the army had suited the governments and other parties too. It had allowed them to meet with Sinn Féin leaders and to imagine that they were not talking to terrorists, and so had not surrendered a vital democratic principle.

It had also allowed the peace process to continue even when the ceasefires were breached. Gerry Adams was usually understood to be doing his best.

Sometimes the timing of killings by the IRA seemed chosen to test latitude at the most politically sensitive times. In May 2002, having held out against decommissioning of weapons until the deadline had passed, the IRA conceded that its dumps could be inspected by independent outsiders, Cyril Ramaphosa, former Secretary-General of the ANC, and Martti Ahtisaari, former President of Finland. That enabled David Trimble to get the endorsement of his Ulster Unionist Council for restoring devolution on the understanding that the IRA's war was over. On the very next day, 29 May, Edmund McCoy was shot dead in a bar in Dunmurry. Perhaps alert to the political sensibilities, the police said only that they believed the killers were 'republicans' and even the Ulster Unionist Party, having struggled so far for a political deal, chose not to question seriously if the IRA was responsible.

The *Guardian* reported that McCoy had been suspected of drug dealing and that the prime suspects were indeed the Provisionals.

So, during the peace process, the vigilante beatings and shootings had two values for the IRA. Each attack tested the limits of what it would get away with. And when negotiations proceeded despite these vaguely deniable breaches of the ceasefire, greater infractions were tried, including robberies and murders, coming to a head with the massive £26 million robbery of the Northern Bank in 2004, followed two months later by the grotesque knifing of a young man called Robert McCartney by IRA members in a pub in Belfast.

The second value for the IRA was that attacking offenders was armed propaganda too; it could be popular with aggrieved victims of crime and that popularity could be presented as evidence that a policing vacuum existed. This enabled Sinn Féin to hold out on its refusal to accept policing reform and to recommend that its followers support the new service devised under the Patten Commission on policing in Northern Ireland.

Killings also provided evidence that a restive IRA might require further placating through the peace process if worse was not to follow. The IRA had tested its room for manoeuvre from the start of the first ceasefire. Less than two weeks after Adams had stood outside Connolly House in August 1994 and challenged the British to be as magnanimous as the IRA had been, five IRA men tried to break out of Whitemoor Prison. Follow-up searches uncovered explosives. And in the third month of the ceasefire, the IRA shot and killed Frank Kerr, a postal worker, in a sorting office in Newry during a robbery. The IRA command accepted that its members had been responsible but argued that the killing had not been sanctioned by the army council. This was one of many robberies during ceasefires, so, parsing the language used by the IRA, one might allow that the robbery had been sanctioned but the killing not. If the ceasefire and peace process could survive 'unsanctioned' operations, then there would be more of them, as indeed there were.

During the first ceasefire the IRA killed four men it said were drug dealers and claimed the killings under the title DAAD, Direct Action Against Drugs. It also continued with the maiming of young delinquents, though, in a concession to the rules of the ceasefire, by beating them with iron bars to break bones instead of shooting them. This seemed to reassure the governments and other parties that the IRA was making an effort to change its ways.

Challenged on this by a journalist, Adams's PR assistant, Richard McAuley, said, 'Keep your eye on the big picture.' He believed that no sane politician would squander the prospects of a new deal in defence of young hoodlums. He was right.

The IRA over-reached its indulged latitude twice in two months, in late 2004 and early 2005. Negotiations with Ian Paisley's DUP had broken down over the IRA's continuing refusal to decommission weapons and to endorse the Police Service of Northern Ireland (PSNI). Paisley had stupidly made this refusal easier for the IRA by demanding that the decommissioning be photographed and that republicans show repentance, in 'sackcloth and ashes'.

The robbery at the Northern Bank was backed up by two kidnappings used to blackmail staff into removing money and assisting an armed gang to load sacks of cash into a van. These are called Tiger kidnappings. A family member of a bank employee is held hostage. The employee is told by the kidnappers to go to work as normal, say nothing and remove cash for them. The first million was delivered in a sports bag to an IRA messenger at a bus stop in the afternoon. Later that evening a van came for another £25.5 million. The Chief Constable, Hugh Orde, said plainly that the IRA had carried out the robbery. In an effort to devalue the takings, the Northern Bank reissued its notes under a new colour and declared the older notes no longer to be legal tender, but that will have affected only about half of the haul.

The IRA had got away with other robberies with little political damage and even with the police and the media declining to point the finger. Anthony McIntyre, who had left the IRA in response to the Good Friday Agreement, speculated on his blog *The Blanket*[1] that the IRA was behind the robbery. Jonathan Powell, Blair's mediator, confronted Adams and McGuinness. 'I said I hadn't believed their denials of IRA membership down the years.'[2]

McIntyre wrote that many were cautious about blaming the IRA because the robbery seemed inimical to the aims of the peace process: '. . . the final stages of the operation were being put into effect while the negotiations that collapsed earlier this month were taking place.'

McIntyre reasoned that, had the robbery gone ahead after a deal with the DUP, 'the DUP would have been under serious external pressure not to buckle the institutions. London and Dublin would have pulled out the stops in a bid to persuade Paisley's party that it was the work of former paramilitaries beyond mainstream control.'

What McIntyre had not anticipated was that the DUP would have been willing to accept the rationalisation and the excuses as David Trimble's Ulster Unionist Party had been after the killing of Edmund McCoy.

The negotiations in 2004 had failed, McIntyre argued, because Adams was not getting the opportunity he was after. 'The only way that Sinn Féin was signing up for that deal was on the basis that it would sneak the IRA into government.'

The version preferred by much of the media said that the IRA was unable to enter the deal because of the humiliation that Paisley demanded.

This view that Adams knew or should have known about IRA criminal adventures was held also by one of his sternest critics, the man who was Minister for Justice in the Irish Republic at the time, Michael McDowell. In an article in the *Sunday Independent*, ten years later, on 26 October 2014, McDowell dismissed Adams's claim that he was never in the IRA by describing him as 'a pathological liar'. When in office McDowell had sat across the table from Gerry Adams at several meetings, 'and stared down his flinty glare as he denied to my face matters which I knew to be true. I remember well his expression as he told me that the IRA had nothing to do with the Northern Bank robbery, the Makro robbery and the Dublin port robberies. All of those events in this decade were, he told me . . . inventions of "securocrats" who wanted to damage the peace process.'

McDowell, now a senator, was often dismissed by Sinn Féin as an unreasonable critic motivated by political rivalry. He had been on that hostile panel that confronted Gerry Adams on the *Late Late Show* after the first ceasefire. But he was also for a time a minister. His later view that Adams was lying rather than merely deluded in attributing a list of crimes to 'securocrats' derived from his reading of intelligence briefings.

This is another example of the widespread perception that Gerry Adams was an IRA leader despite his emphatic denials.

Yet Adams and those around him tried to create an image of a cabal of senior soldiers and police officers conspiring to discredit him by carrying out robberies and killings that would be attributed to the IRA. Many of his followers may have believed that but no evidence of the existence of this conspiracy was ever produced.

Former Taoiseach Bertie Ahern, writing in the *Mail on Sunday* says that President Bush told him, in 2001, that he had been briefed that Gerry Adams was 'a murdering thief'. 'I had to work hard to explain to him that yes, Gerry Adams had a past that was to do with the conflict and the IRA. But that we were making a lot of progress and there were a lot of reasons for that.'[3] Another who believed that Adams was lying to him at that time was Jonathan Powell, the emissary of the Prime Minister, Tony Blair. Powell was on his way to a meeting with Gerry Adams and Martin McGuinness when he heard news of the Northern Bank robbery. The negotiations with the Democratic Unionist Party to form a power-sharing government in Belfast had collapsed and Blair had been contemplating proceeding through further negotiations with Sinn Féin alone. Adams and McGuinness were arguing for a plan to create an all-Ireland policing body.

Powell wrote that the robbery was 'a huge betrayal of trust', and that he 'felt like a complete idiot' realising that the IRA had been planning the robbery while he was in negotiations with the Sinn Féin leaders.

Powell gave it straight to Adams and McGuinness. He told them that he had never believed their denials of IRA membership. Adams tried to persuade him to continue with a policy of holding the IRA together and not making moves that would split the movement. 'He said that we did not understand how serious it would be if we left a vestige of the IRA in place.'[4]

The IRA might have got away with the Northern Bank robbery without crippling political damage being sustained by Sinn Féin but for the other shocking crime of two months later, the murder of Robert McCartney.

McCartney had been drinking in Magennis's Bar in Belfast, near the law courts, when a fight broke out between another man and a group of republicans. Several Sinn Féin and IRA members were in the bar at the time, including Gerard 'Jock' Davison who ran DAAD, the IRA gang that killed drug dealers. They had come back from the annual Bloody Sunday commemoration in Derry.

McCartney and another man were pursued from the bar by men with knives taken from the kitchen. Brendan Devine was stabbed and badly wounded. Robert McCartney was virtually disembowelled and died a few hours later. On the morning news next day, the Sinn Féin Member of the Northern Ireland Assembly for South Belfast, Alex Maskey, bemoaned the spread of 'knife crime'. He did not say that an IRA man had ordered the killing or that an IRA team had entered the bar later to clean away forensic traces. The IRA denied the murder but no one believed it. And Adams found himself confronted by a formidable team of critics: the sisters of Robert McCartney and his partner.

Gerry Adams told the sisters that he was away at the time of the killing. The momentum of protest and media interest was still building and he arranged to meet them. St Patrick's Day was approaching and Adams foresaw the danger that, having failed to secure a deal with the DUP, having refused to assent to policing, and the IRA having carried out the biggest bank robbery in UK history at that time and then a grotesque murder, he would not get his usual St Patrick's Day invitation to the White House, or a visa to allow him to raise money for the movement.

He visited the sisters. He presented himself to them as a concerned politician offering to find out what he could about the killing of Robert. He wrote down the names of the people the sisters held responsible and said he would make inquiries.

After the meeting the sisters received a call from an IRA representative asking to meet them at Clonard Monastery, the Redemptorist Order house that had hosted previous negotiations, to settle feuds or advance the peace process.

There, IRA representatives outlined their investigation into the killing, though in terms that absolved Jock Davison, the man who was chief suspect in the minds of the sisters. The IRA as a corporate body was declining responsibility for the killing and presenting it as the work of rogue members. No one believed that the IRA had set out to kill Robert McCartney that night, but there was premeditation in the response when members were despatched to the bar to clean up the forensic traces. The IRA could not seriously disown that operation as unsanctioned.

The sisters continued to meet Gerry Adams, sometimes tetchily. On one occasion they were spotted by a television crew and they accused Adams of having invited it. Adams then sent his press man, Richard McAuley, to ask the crew to keep a distance and allow them privacy.

Adams had meetings with Tony Blair that month. Jonathan Powell let him and Martin McGuinness into the side entrance of 10 Downing Street so that the media wouldn't spot them. Powell says Adams looked 'physically shrunken'.[5] He wrote, 'Tony tried to give him some hope.'

Powell met Adams and McGuinness again in Dublin before the party Ard Fheis of March 2005. There McGuinness said that the IRA would not give up weapons to the government or to the unionists; it would only give them up to Gerry Adams. Powell says Adams then argued for the IRA to be given the chance to 'dump arms', but Powell insisted on them continuing with the agreed arrangements for the formal decommissioning process and McGuinness backed him on that, he says.

Jonathan Powell describes a meeting at which Adams confronted him with, 'The thing I like about you, Jonathan, is that you always blush when you lie.' Powell's colleague Bill Jeffrey retorted, 'Unlike you, Gerry.'

Powell says that around the time of the Ard Fheis, Adams had seemed, to him, 'shrunken' and 'shell-shocked'. Others who saw him at the Ard Fheis that same afternoon describe him as 'ebullient and charming'. Powell had other interesting observations about Adams and his behaviour. He says that he always expected to be fed at negotiations and frequently complained about the quality of food he was served. This observation resonates with the frequent references to prison food in his memoirs.

Powell also says that Adams would sometimes get angry, 'one element of his negotiating repertoire that I found particularly tiresome.'

As part of the Sinn Féin propaganda endeavour, Gerry Adams had invited the McCartney sisters to attend that Ard Fheis. This was a potential trap for them. They would have lost much of their support if they had been seen as having been won over by Sinn Féin. This was an opportunity for Adams to present himself as an ally in their search for justice.

His political dilemma at this time was that he was still negotiating with Powell the terms on which Sinn Féin would assent to the reformed policing service of Northern Ireland, yet he was under pressure now from the media and the governments to urge those who had witnessed Robert McCartney's killing to come forward and give evidence. An *Irish Times* report on 14 February 2005 said, 'Mr Adams said those who have no faith in the PSNI should contact the family. He also launched a scathing attack on those who carried out the stabbing and stressed that his party supported the victim's family in their search for justice.'

He did not specifically say that witnesses should go to the police, presumably because Sinn Féin was still withholding assent to the legitimacy of the PSNI. Several members of Sinn Féin had been in the bar at the time and made statements claiming that they had been in the toilets at the time of the killing.[6]

Mitchell Reiss, the American special envoy, wanted to use the pressure on Sinn Féin at that time to push them over the line into accepting the police and taking a big step towards completing the deal with the Democratic Unionist Party that would allow devolution to proceed. The party leadership still resolutely held out against policing and would do so for another two years.

The sisters went to the Ard Fheis. They didn't want their presence to be read as an endorsement of Adams's efforts to help them, but the pictures going into the media at home and in the US would make it look like that.

When they arrived, the Sinn Féin stewards seated party member Caitríona Ruane between Catherine and Paula McCartney, to hold that seat for Adams. To counter the impression that an Adams sidekick was their friend, the sisters decided not to clap any of the speakers, a decision that will have puzzled a guest from the ANC.

Catherine was sitting with a cup of coffee when Gerry Adams planted himself down beside her and lifted the cup out of her hand and drank from it. It looked matey, and that was the point.

When they got back to Belfast, the sisters were asked to another meeting with the IRA, this time at Holy Cross in Ardoyne, a church run by the order of the Cross and Passion. There had been no progress. But on the following day the IRA issued a statement saying that it had made an offer to the McCartneys. Just give the nod and we will kill Jock Davison, the man who had ordered the killing of Robert.

The media was fascinated by the bluntness of the offer to

murder, but overlooked a claim by the sisters that it had not actually been made to them at all. There was a sequence of statements from the IRA to suggest lost faith in the peace process and a readiness to return to the old ways. Republicans may have calculated that a veiled threat from the IRA, a reminder of its murderous inclinations, might prompt the Americans to shore up Gerry Adams again as the one person who could hold it in check.

This was old-fashioned 'good cop, bad cop'. Gerry Adams was routinely the good cop, saying in effect, 'Cut me some slack and I might be able to hold the bad cop back.'

Jonathan Powell's interpretation of the IRA statement attributed less tactical cleverness to the IRA. 'They were trying to demonstrate that they were serious about revenge, but instead they let everyone see that they still lived in the mafia twilight.'[7] So, though he often said that he saw Adams as an IRA leader, he also viewed the IRA, at times, as a separate entity that might be stupidly making life difficult for Adams.

Adams was now under intense pressure from the two governments and the Americans to stand down the IRA and complete the peace process. He got his visa for a US trip for St Patrick's Day but he was barred from fundraising for Sinn Féin. He did not get his usual invitation to the White House, though with George W. Bush in the presidency these annual celebrations of Irishness were low-key. The McCartney sisters went to America too and were received by Senators Hillary Clinton, Ted Kennedy and John McCain, all of whom demanded justice for Robert. They got to see Adams again there at a Friends of Ireland dinner where he took a drubbing from John McCain, laying down the terms of future American support; the violence must stop.

The audience applauded McCain. Adams had lost face and sat and took a couple of sips of his Guinness, smiling as if untouched.

The IRA now understood it had no friends and no room for manoeuvre if it did not formally end the campaign, disarm and free up the political prospects for Sinn Féin. Adams crafted a speech calling on the IRA to end its campaign and showed it to Jonathan Powell. He wanted him to promise that once decommissioning was verified, Blair would push the DUP into restoring devolution. The speech said that the IRA campaign had been justified and that Adams had supported it when the people were on their knees and had no alternative, but now an alternative route to a united Ireland was open and the people had Sinn Féin. What it did not do was commit republicans to supporting the police. What Adams was working for now was a place in the government of Northern Ireland for a party that did not endorse the right of the PSNI to investigate crime.

Blair would have gone along with that but the Democratic Unionists refused and so a further round of negotiations followed to achieve Sinn Féin endorsement of policing and further, at St Andrews in Scotland, to reshape the Good Friday Agreement to allow the leader of the largest party, rather than of the larger community, to appoint the First Minister. This was good for both Sinn Féin and the DUP for it gave nationalists and unionists an incentive to draw votes away from the smaller parties in their communities. This was a deal that would be good for sectarianism.

Then, even at the very completion of the process, after Sinn Féin had formed an executive in Stormont with the DUP and smaller parties, in October 2007 the IRA murdered twenty-one-year-old Paul Quinn, from Cullyhanna in South Armagh. While three of Quinn's friends were held hostage, a team of killers worked over his body with iron bars and nail-studded cudgels, breaking every major bone. Gerry Adams insisted that the IRA was innocent. He said that the killing arose out of a feud between rival gangs that smuggled fuel. This hurt the family because it branded their son as a criminal.

Sinn Féin Minister Conor Murphy denied that the IRA was to blame, said that he believed assurances the IRA had given him. Government ministers don't usually make determinations like this on the advice of illegal paramilitary organisations in democratic societies, but there was little criticism of Murphy for this, and the institutions survived.

Chapter 23

Two major television documentaries about Gerry Adams in recent years celebrated him as a peacemaker and as a thoughtful and genial person.

One of the striking things in both was his physical presence. A politician interviewed in a studio is seated and judged by facial expressions. At party conferences he or she may stand and walk about, but in a mannered, semi-formal way. The Gerry Adams of these films was lounging, running, rolling on the ground, squeezing himself into tunnels. He expressed himself through his body with extraordinary confidence. For someone who shields himself constantly in interviews, he seemed physically unself-conscious. In both programmes, for instance, he wore woolly hats that rounded the top of his head like an egg. People will have watched that and wondered if he has no one to tell him not to dress like a tramp or a clown.

He is like two different people, sometimes striding manfully or glad-handing the Clintons in his tuxedo, sometimes just gauche. He is what the Irish would call 'a big ganche' and yet he can be relaxed and charming, even a natural stand-up. The best available example of that is footage on YouTube of his address to IRA ex-prisoners and others in Ballymurphy at the unveiling of a mural to dead IRA men, Jim Bryson and his own brother-in-law, Patrick Mulvenna, shot by an undercover British soldier in 1973. Adams is standing before the assembled ranks of the Ballymurphy IRA dressed in white shirts. He chides them like no one else would dare: 'I also want to commend the colour party. Some of them are a bit geriatric [laughter] and I saw that

F Troop there went the wrong way [more laughter].'

As usual he paid special tribute to the women: 'I want to commend all the former POWs that have turned out. Of course, the struggle here wasn't conducted just by those who died and just those who have turned out in their white shirts, though it's great to see them all here. The women of this area were always the backbone of this area.'

Here Adams is comfortable among people who adore him, as is plain from the expressions on their faces, particularly in the enrapt smiling eyes of the women standing near him. He can comport himself here with the confidence that he will be viewed as the victorious leader and not be challenged.

And I have said at different times in public statements and in speeches that there are brave people in every side of a conflict. There are brave people in the RUC and brave people in the British army but we have the bravest of the brave. And here in B Company of the Second Battalion of the Irish Republican Army in this area, right across from New Barnsley into Moyard, Dermot Hill, down through Springhill into Westrock and the Whiterock, here in the Murph we have the bravest of the brave.

A former IRA man who was close to him in the early 1980s says that Gerry is not comfortable in his own skin. 'Watch the way he crouches sometimes as if he's afraid someone is going to hit him; watch the tightness of him.' Yet there are times when he has the verve and style of a sportsman or an actor. This has been remarked on before; Jonathan Powell noticed it. Sometimes it would not seem surprising if it were disclosed that this is two different men.

The TV documentaries sought to show us a Gerry Adams we had not seen before, one who was not the deft rebutter of difficult questions, sunk back in a studio chair scowling at the interviewer and batting back questions about his responsibility or guilt.

In Below the Radar's *Adams* he was filmed for the first time in his garden at home in Belfast surrounded by children's toys, potting seedlings and discussing his love of trees. The camera crew followed him across the grassy saddle of Black Mountain above Belfast competing in the Poc Fada, the Long Shot. This is a test of hurling skill in which the winner belts the ball as far as he can, picks it up, belts it again and sends it further than any of his rivals can reach. Adams didn't win but he looked fit and strong in his sixties and fell over laughing on the grass when the prize was given. This was a Gerry Adams who has time for pleasure and companionship, not the politician warrior. Yet he has lived a nomadic life, years of it on the run and years since travelling for his political work. Asked who really knows him, Adams says grandly that the people of his West Belfast constituency know him, conceding nothing to the suggestion that he is elusive and difficult to know. Jonathan Powell says that even after numerous meetings and negotiations he really doesn't feel he knows Adams, though Tony Blair now says he understands and likes him.[1]

This was TV journalism from recent times in which Adams seemed to be presenting himself as an elder whose work was done. In fact, he was entering on a new project of taking leadership of the Sinn Féin parliamentary party in the Dáil in Dublin and building its electoral prospects.

In an interview with Press TV in 2011 he looked tired and bored. He was not confronted with antagonistic questions but he looked like someone who has said the same things too often. He warmed up a little towards the end when asked to reflect on the life he would like to have outside politics.

I would like to be an opera singer, I would like to write more, I would like to cook more; I would like to garden more. I have volumes of books from all sorts of things from building stone walls to growing organic vegetables. I love planting trees; I would love to plant four or five forests in the time ahead. And I absolutely love music. I couldn't imagine life without music. So there's lots to be done but there's also lots of politics to be made and a struggle to be pursued and I consider myself very lucky. I remember Martin McGuinness saying one time in an interview he never thought he would live beyond twenty-five. And I never thought I would live beyond twenty-five, so it's good to be sixty-three; it's brilliant to be still able to run and walk and talk and enjoy yourself.

Another programme about this time that sought to reach the personal Adams was the fifth in a series of discussions about the Bible on Channel Four (*The Bible: A History*). Adams was the nominal presenter, occasionally cross-examined by the off-screen director. In this programme, he sets off to Israel and the Palestinian territories to find out what Jesus was like. He meets several theologians and historians and sees that the Jesus story is, in many ways, a constructed myth.

Helen Bond, a senior lecturer at Edinburgh University, tells him that she doubts that Jesus was born in Bethlehem and he jokes that she has just ruined Christmas. She takes Adams into interesting relevant territory. Our myths are constructions so, by unspoken implication, perhaps the story of the British oppression of Ireland is as questionable as the Gospels. She says that maybe Caiaphas was doing what was pragmatically necessary in condemning Jesus, if that would avoid a war in which thousands would die.

Gerry Adams says that elites always present their decisions as being in the best interests of the people.

Remembering that week in Jerusalem with him, Helen Bond says Gerry Adams instinctively saw things from the underdog's point of view. 'For him, anyone who worked with Rome in whatever way could only be called a "collaborator", there was no possibility of being a pious and even nationalistic Jew and also working with the oppressor. I thought that a rather one-sided and perhaps idealistic way of seeing things. If none of the chief priests had worked with Pilate, things would have been much worse for the Judaeans (and I very much doubt that independence would have been one of their options!).'

But she thinks he had valuable insights from that perspective.

'I did find his views on Judas useful, though he suggested that (as the only southerner) the authorities had somehow "got" to Judas' family, and were perhaps threatening them in some way. I have to admit I'd never thought of that, and while I doubt there was a threat of physical violence, the scenario wasn't entirely implausible.'

She says, 'I also found his reflections on how groups form and mobilise themselves to be a useful insight into Jesus and his followers.'

At the start of the programme, Adams is filmed praying in church and receiving communion. He tells us that he was one of the few to go to mass in Long Kesh.

The programme includes a clip of the interview he gave to *Panorama* in 1982. 'Each one of us knows that which they are responsible for, and each one of us at some period in time is going to meet God and I am happy enough that I have tried to live by my standards.' He fails to notice that operating by his own lights is not always equivalent to being a good Christian.

Asked now in the Bible documentary if he has blood on his hands, he says, 'I feel I have done my best by my own lights [always his own lights, not those of Jesus] but I don't for one second step back from my responsibilities as a leader of a struggle that has caused both hurt and damage to other human beings. I don't walk away from that.'

It is one of those answers of the kind he specialises in. He uses the same rhetorical device over and over again to admit and deny, or deny and admit, in the same line.

This management of key questions recurs throughout his writing. In his book *A Farther Shore* he writes, 'Whether the people in the nationalist areas agreed or disagreed with the IRA and all its actions, they recognised it as their army.'[2] But people could not have seen the IRA as representing them if they disagreed with its methods and objectives.

'While loyalists or unionist paramilitaries have their own

agenda and not all of them act as dupes, they are in effect an arm of British military operations.[3] It is hard to see how loyalists could be viewed as both independent and manipulated.

His repertoire of devices for avoiding the pointing finger and turning it back on its owner is limited but effective and familiar and has enabled him to survive the best journalists in the world.

In the programme he wants to explore the Christian message of forgiveness and apply it to his own experience.

But, 'You can't really begin to understand a person's story, or a nation's, unless you see it in its proper context.' If there were no 'proper context' for understanding the Troubles and the IRA campaign, he would have to ask himself simply why a united Ireland is so urgent that people had to be killed for it when no other political movement in the country was similarly anxious for its implementation.

Adams enjoys the trip and perhaps also the respect given to him as a thinker, though there appears some uneasiness among those he meets when he jokes in a tomb about Sinn Féin having been 'an underground movement' or compares the cramped space to a 'Long Kesh tunnel'. The viewer is probably beginning to wonder how such a good-natured and civil man can be dismissed by many as an evil terrorist. We begin to see how many might have been persuaded by him that the IRA had a point, to believe that, since he is obviously not vicious and brutal, his cause must have some merit. Helen Bond, the academic theologian, tries to say that there is still a lot for Christians in these traditions, they just don't have to take them as literally true. This is the position of the modern republican like Gerry Adams who has reshaped his tradition away from the endorsement of present and future violence while celebrating the heroism of the killers of the past. But the modern Irish republican does not admit to having changed any more than the Church does. Adams has often pointed to the revisionist as the enemy, the one who supplants the republican narrative with readings of the past that suit other political agendas.

Then he is led towards reflecting on forgiveness, the central message of Jesus. The 'proper context' here, a Christian would say, is God's law: you will be forgiven if you forgive others.

Adams says he has forgiven people. 'Bad things have been done to me. I have forgiven those who did it. I did it in the first instance for me; I didn't do it for them. I did it for me because I didn't want to become corroded.'

He has been shot and beaten and he has lost uncountable friends to violence. He was interned and then imprisoned for trying to escape from internment. He lived much of his life under threat of death and is entitled to be surprised that he made it to his sixties in relative good health and comfort. He appears not to suffer the bitterness and grief that spoil the lives of other victims. He helped negotiate the Good Friday Agreement that brought about the early release of the men who had shot him. He could have withdrawn from it and left them in jail, though he would have been condemning his own republican comrades in the same stroke.

He says his forgiveness has limits. 'I don't forgive and I haven't come to terms and I still have a sense of outrage about the conditions that were created by those in powerful positions, who put one side against the other, who sectarianised it, who exploited the differences, who brought in all of their technology and so on, much like those who actively had to take a conscious decision to construct the cross.'

This is the 'proper context' again. He believes that to understand republicanism you have to see that the sectarian division in Northern Ireland was manufactured by people in power to preserve and extend their power, that there is a better, more natural Ireland within reach.

But, asks the director, what about the hundreds of civilians who were killed by the IRA? The IRA did most of the killing during the Troubles. It's time for another one of those ambiguous answers.

'I don't attempt to justify the actions. In fact, I've been very critical of some of the actions. But I do believe that it was legitimate to resort to armed actions and that was politically defensible and I haven't changed my mind on that.'

He says, in effect, I don't justify but I do defend. He never allows his reservations about IRA violence to be unqualified. And he insists that the IRA had no choice. 'I would love that there had been another way but I don't live in that world. I live in the practical world and I was part of that constituency which put together another way.' His problem there is that only a minority in Ireland, or even in Northern Ireland, agreed with him at the time that they had 'no choice' but to arm themselves and shoot soldiers and bomb pubs, shops and factories. The only way to contend with his assertion that he had no choice is to engage him in a historical argument, but then that would be a different programme, so understandably the director leaves it at that. He hasn't got all day.

But these convoluted statements are never unpacked. When was he 'very critical of some of the actions'? Not often. What was 'practical' about bombing pubs to drive the British out of Ireland?

He says, 'I am not a pacifist. I don't believe that non-violent resistance was an option for us forty years ago. The war is over but we are all still on a journey to freedom. And after decades of violent conflict, all of us have plenty to forgive and to be forgiven for.'

Towards the end of the programme, two of those who might forgive him are in the room with him. One is Alan McBride whose wife was killed in the IRA bombing of Frizzell's fish shop on the Shankill Road in October 1993, an attempt to kill the UDA leaders who were thought to be meeting upstairs. Had that operation worked it might have been one of the easier attacks to justify in terms of the logic of war. In its failure, however, it killed only innocent civilians and one of the bombers.

The other man there from whom Gerry Adams might have

sought forgiveness was the cameraman, Eugene McVeigh, whose brother Columba was among the disappeared, killed by the IRA and secretly buried. Adams knew that the cameraman was the brother of one of the disappeared. The director of the programme, Dan Reid, did not know this.

McVeigh maintained the 'invisible line' between real life and the story, did his job and did not interject.

Adams, who was trying to show us the more human and quizzical side of his nature, had been maintaining an invisible line too, denying real personal contact even to the production crew and to Helen Bond, the theologian with whom he had discussed ideas.

Helen says that 'his press officer was there the whole time, watching what was going on and what was being said. I felt a wariness from their point of view towards the production team, and by extension towards me. Overall, and on a superficial level, Gerry Adams came over as a kindly granddad, a definite family man; I had to remind myself of his past (I'd read his autobiography prior to going over to Israel so I knew at least some of his story) and had no real sense of what made him tick.'

She didn't get to know him in private between recordings because Adams never shared his private self.

So television, which sought to present the personal side of Gerry Adams, became, with its formal structures and professional routines, a means by which people who had personal stories to tell each other could hold those stories back. And when the cameras and microphones were switched off and those people might have talked more frankly to each other, as often happens in television production, the people did not engage.

Eugene McVeigh didn't seek to step forward because he didn't want his own grief to be part of the story. Yet he might have presented more of a challenge to Gerry Adams than Alan McBride could. Adams was trying to concede some limited regret to Alan McBride about a bomb of nearly twenty years earlier. The story of Columba's murder and disappearance was still unfinished, for the body had not yet been found.

Eugene says, 'I was there in a room in the monastery and it was all ready. I remember Dan making great presence about how this was such a seminal event in this film, and these two men were going to meet and this was going to be a special moment. I had a moment within the moment, even as Dan was talking. It was only afterwards when I was driving away that I started to internalise and reflect on what was happening.'

His professional responsibility on the day was to serve the needs of the documentary, to record the conversation between Alan McBride and Gerry Adams. Adams had carried the coffin of Thomas Begley, one of the bombers, who had died in the fish shop attack.

'It was very moody, almost confession box like in the way I had lit it. And I remember looking through the camera and saying, this is the confession box, what are you going to say? How do you justify what was done?'

As a current affairs camera operator, Eugene McVeigh had seen Adams protect himself from many probing journalists before. This time he would go further in criticising that bombing and would even hint at an acknowledgement that he was indeed the top man in the IRA.

He tells Dan Reid, the director, that the bombing of the fish shop was 'a stupid operation'. He says, 'It didn't take into account the safety of the civilians and of course Thomas gets the blame for this and clearly the blame is one which has to be shared. It was an operation which was just fundamentally flawed and fundamentally wrong.'

In that he acknowledged it as such, it was an exception.

Adams would have been taking his share of that wider blame if he had acknowledged that he had been on the army council of the IRA at the time the operation was planned and approved. He says, 'This was a corporate IRA responsibility. It wasn't just these two relatively young IRA volunteers who had been sent out obviously to do what they did.'

Alan McBride, in his turn, acknowledges that the mother of the dead bomber had suffered a grievous loss and deserved sympathy. He would not forgive the other bomber, the one who survived, preferred not to think about him. But the two men had inched towards each other, each allowing that the other deserved respect and consideration. Eugene McVeigh shot the scene as he had planned it, with Reid, the director, asking the questions that would elicit the frank statements.

Adams thanks McBride for 'the example you are giving people like me'.

Gerry Adams positions himself, not among the aggressors but among the aggrieved.

He says, 'There were times when I was afraid my heart would break. I mean, I can be as angry and as ruthless and as focused and as deliberate in terms of what I have to do as anyone else, but I have a fairly logical mind. So even though I could be angry at something that was done, either through the stupidity of the side that I supported or by those who were opposing us, I never felt entirely brutalised by what was going on.'

Here is more ambiguity. So which is he reminding us of, his ruthlessness or his capacity for reason? And if it is reason rather than compassion that preserves him against being brutalised, then how sensitive is he really?

He is saying that he is a good man still.

And in the end he appeared to signal in a gesture that he had been an IRA commander.

'It needs generals to make peace, OK?' And he raised his eyebrow. The gesture, the use of the word 'general', looked like a strong hint that he was referring to himself as a military leader.

And it is that peacemaking and that vision of a wider context that enables Eugene McVeigh to preserve his respect for Gerry Adams. 'I have known Gerry Adams a long time and I suppose he didn't always know who I was or the connection to my brother Columba.'

Eugene's name had featured in media reports around the creation of a commission for the recovery of victims' remains and again shortly after his mother died. She had appealed on television for information about the hiding of the body and said that she could die happy if first she could give Columba a Christian burial.

'Martin McGuinness and Gerry Adams got in touch with me and asked me if I would be prepared to meet them. I did meet them at Sinn Féin headquarters on the Falls Road and it was a very strange meeting, walking in without a camera to talk to them about my brother. Both of them did apologise to me. I assumed that when I was in a room with Martin McGuinness and Gerry Adams that's good enough.'

He says he didn't see much point in parsing the apology to evaluate its sincerity. Neither man was saying that Columba should not have been killed but they were saying that they would do everything they could to help find the body.

'We stood in a room and I looked Adams in the face and he said sorry to me. Well, blessed are the peacemakers, what do you do?'

Eugene does not blame the IRA alone for the killing. 'Columba McVeigh at nineteen years old, a young man who would be classed now as having learning difficulties, had been used by intelligence agents in 1975 to gather information about the IRA in Donaghmore. It was always in my head that though someone in Adams's organisation squeezed the trigger that took my brother's life, the state had some responsibility too.

'I don't dislike Gerry Adams,' he says. 'We have always been well enough disposed to each other in the same space. Even in the middle of that I never let much of my own internal thoughts get in the way of the work. I think he appreciated that. He did say to me, "I didn't know, you didn't tell me; it's hard to comprehend."

I told him why but I also pointed the finger. McGuinness said, "Look, we can take it on the chin from you; that is what we are here for."'

And he thinks at times that death isn't necessarily 'the unkindest cut'.

'When I look at his life and the things he has admitted about his own father; I have never had to own up to my father being a child molester; I have never had to see my brother going to jail for being a paedophile. That's a living torture as much as anything else. He has dealt with it. He has got it out there. I would think that all of that makes him the person he is, for good or bad.'

Which means that perpetually avoiding the direct question of his responsibility for the IRA campaign has not spared him disclosures that are just as difficult to make. That he led the IRA, is widely believed. Few accept his denials.

Another secret was not even suspected by most people. Even the police say it came as a surprise to learn that Gerry Adams senior was a violent paedophile. A former head of crime said, 'Usually there is gossip in the street; there was nothing.'

On the morning after the broadcast showing Adams in the Holy Land, walking in the footsteps of Jesus, the graffiti on a wall at the corner of the Grosvenor Road and Falls Road passed judgement without being specific about what part of the programme was most offensive. 'Gerry Adams what a wanker.'

Chapter 24

Two brothers stroll side by side along a beach in Donegal. They are talking quietly or they are arguing; much depends on whose version you believe. The taller one is Gerry Adams. Physically he looks like a Hannaway. His brother Liam beside him has the shorter, thicker-set look of the Adamses.

Gerry Adams has come to Buncrana to talk to his brother about Liam's daughter Aine. It is March 1987. The ceasefire is seven years away. It is chilly, though it is spring, but in the Swilly estuary they are sheltered from the raw Atlantic breeze. They are sheltered too from the routine dangers of Belfast, where Gerry Adams could not walk in casual conversation without protection. Yet this was not the part of Donegal he identified with; that was the rugged north-west that he had known first as a schoolchild, sent to the Gaeltacht for immersion in an Irish-speaking rural community. Buncrana was a seaside holiday resort for people from Derry. And the Swilly estuary was the play area of those who could afford yachts.

Aine at ten years old had told her mother that her father had been coming into her bed. The child's story was that, from the age of four, Liam Adams had subjected her to different types of sexual intrusion. She had now also shared the same story with her uncle Gerry.

By Gerry Adams's account, the conversation with his brother on the beach was the start of a 'process'. This was a family matter. It could be settled. There could be reconciliations. By Liam's account, his daughter's allegations were simply untrue and Gerry had come to say that if it was true that Liam had raped the little girl he would hit him over the head with a hammer. Gerry denies he threatened his brother. By his account they went back to Liam's house and had tea and biscuits. He couldn't remember if Liam's new partner, Brona, was there. These are details that emerged in Liam's trial decades later.

Gerry Adams first heard the rape allegation in 1984 when the girl's mother told him that she had reported it to the police. After speaking to him she withdrew her complaint. He says he had no part in persuading her to do that, though he was urging party followers at the time not to use the police.

Social services records in Belfast show that back in January 1986, more than a year before the conversation on Buncrana beach, Gerry Adams had himself used state services. The records quoted in the trial of Liam Adams say that Gerry Adams reported that his sister-in-law, the abused child's mother, was keeping an untidy house, that her children had lice. He has also said he doesn't remember making that complaint.

On the day after the conversation with his brother, on his return to Belfast, Gerry Adams visited the abused child's home. A social worker called Sheila Brannigan was there when he called. Since his complaint about the state of the house, social workers had maintained a close interest in the estranged wife and children of Liam Adams.

Whether or not the brothers had argued in Buncrana and threats had been issued during that walk on the beach, the brothers stayed friendly.

Four years later, in 1991, Gerry and Liam were pictured together in the Mansion House in Dublin with Martin McGuinness. Liam's little girl in his second family with Brona was hugging her granda, Gerry Adams senior.

In February 1994 Gerry Adams signed a photograph of himself addressing the Sinn Féin Ard Fheis: 'To Liam, Bronagh [sic] and Clare XOXOX Gerry.'

In 1996 Liam married Brona, and Gerry was pictured with his

arm around him in the company of his other brothers, Paddy, Sean and Dominic.

And in 1997, Gerry Adams attended the christening of Liam's second daughter with Brona. Later that year, Liam Adams stood for a Sinn Féin election candidature in Dundalk, though Gerry Adams says he asked him not to.

That was ten years after the conversation in Buncrana.

It was also around this time that, he says, Gerry Adams first learnt that his father was a paedophile and that some of his own siblings had been the old man's victims.

Ten years later still, Aine, now thirty-four years old, at last made a statement reporting the abuse to the police. That was in 2007, the year that Sinn Féin policy on policing changed and people in nationalist communities could now report offenders without fear of the IRA.

After Aine's complaint the police sought a statement from Gerry Adams and asked him to help them locate Liam. Gerry Adams replied that he was too busy to go to a police station but arranged to meet detectives at his solicitor's office and to make a statement. There followed an extradition process to bring Liam Adams back to the North to face trial. Eventually, in 2011, Liam Adams was charged in Belfast with the sexual abuse of his daughter, twenty-four years after Gerry Adams had first confronted him.

Liam Adams was tried twice. The first trial collapsed on a legal technicality. Gerry Adams was cross-examined at that first failed trial but not at the second.

Throughout his cross-examination he tried several times to explain the wider context of the Adams family difficulties, his own shock at the news his father had abused children and the nature of the 'process' he was involved in with Aine, to try to get her to meet Liam.

The court repeatedly reminded him that this was all irrelevant. It had already asked him to rewrite a convoluted statement and to focus on the core points. It was in that statement, written in the court precincts with his press officer, Richard McAuley, in a private room, that he claimed for the first time that Liam had actually admitted his guilt to him on another walk, in another border town, in Dundalk in the rain, in 2000. Liam, he said in the statement, had told him that he had only once abused his daughter. That admission, by Gerry's account, was made thirteen years after the conversation in Buncrana. It was a further thirteen years after that conversation that Gerry Adams conceded that it had been made. He had now given evidence that might incriminate his brother but did little to affirm Aine's complaint of sexual abuse of varied kinds over a period of six years.

His statement that he did not get an admission from Liam Adams until 2000 spares Gerry Adams the suspicion that he had recklessly endangered children himself by allowing Liam to work with them before that time, in his constituency. As a local MP, his advice to community organisations not to employ Liam would have been taken seriously. But if he wasn't persuaded till then that Liam really was an abuser, it follows that he had not believed Aine's claim that she had been raped and been made to perform fellatio on her father several times before the age of ten. Gerry had said, up to that point, including on a television documentary, that he *had* believed Aine.

In the years that Gerry Adams was meeting Jonathan Powell to advance the peace process, as he saw it, either resisting demands for IRA decommissioning and Sinn Féin assent to policing, or trying to concede them on the best terms attainable, he was also meeting regularly with Aine in that other 'process'.

The cross-examination of Gerry Adams by defence counsel, after he had taken time to rewrite his cluttered statement, exposed the Sinn Féin President to the closest scrutiny he had ever received in public. This was not a media interview that he could manage through time wasting and deflections, though he tried. Here his ambiguities could be tested for actual meaning. And the result was an insight into the personality and family of Gerry Adams that was fascinating and bewildering.

He told the court that one of his greatest regrets was that he had drawn such an affectionate picture of his father in his books. If he had known that he might one day have to disclose that his father was a child abuser, he would not have included a description of the man drying him after his bath and giving him this advice: 'keep your wee man clean and stay away from bad women'.[1]

Counsel took him back over the whole twenty-six years since the walk with his brother Liam in Buncrana and asked him to explain the anomalies in the story, the withdrawal of the complaint from the police, the continuing friendship with Liam.

He said that Aine's mother had withdrawn co-operation with the police, on her own initiative, because she realised that they were more interested in using the intelligence about Liam Adams in their war on the IRA. That may be true. But republicans would have wanted her to stay away from the police anyway. They killed people who reported republicans to the police and Liam Adams was a member of the movement. Ten years after her first report to the police, for instance, the IRA murdered a young Falls Road mother, Caroline Moreland, for passing information to the police about the IRA. Aine's mother had to consider the danger to herself.

What is striking is how poorly Gerry Adams had prepared himself for cross-examination in the case against his brother. He was asked if he had spoken to Liam's partner, Brona, and warned her that Liam Adams might be a danger to her daughters. Adams said he had but he could not remember where or when; he thought he had seen her in their house in Andersonstown, but they didn't live there until ten years after the walk in Buncrana.

It was an embarrassing day in the witness stand for Gerry Adams and many of his previous claims to have had little association with Liam, for several years, were picked apart.

Liam's counsel produced photographs of those Adams family

occasions that showed Liam and Gerry in close and affectionate proximity through the years after he had first confronted Liam with Aine's story. Curiously, the pictures became a focus of a side drama. When the court adjourned for lunch, Gerry Adams asked what he should do with them.

GA: Your Honour, I have documents here which aren't mine.

JUDGE PHILPOTT: Just leave those there, they will remain, no one will touch them. They will remain there.

GA: Okay. Am I free to go?

JUDGE PHILPOTT: Yes, you are free to go.

After lunch, there was a bizarre scene in which the judge, Corinne Philpott, and the defence counsel Eilis McDermott looked for the pictures again and couldn't find them.

JUDGE PHILPOTT: I just want to confirm, you didn't take these photographs out.

GA: Yeah, I have them in my briefcase here.

JUDGE PHILPOTT: You have them?

GA: Yeah, yeah.

JUDGE PHILPOTT: Well, could you get them back?

GA: I will surely, yes.

The court was adjourned again to allow Gerry Adams to retrieve the photographs from his briefcase.

The court tried to get a sense of just how close the brothers had been in the years after Aine had told her uncle Gerry Adams that she had been raped by her father. Was it true that Liam had actually lived with Gerry for six weeks in 1998, when he came to Belfast to work with a youth club at Clonard Monastery? Gerry said he didn't remember.

Liam Adams had worked for five years at Clonard Youth Club,

in his brother's constituency, and moved then to The Blackie Centre, in Beechmount, also in the constituency. He worked with young people there but he left after a year. Gerry Adams told the court that he had persuaded Liam Adams to give up his job with children out of consideration for Aine. Officially, Liam had left the job because a frozen shoulder made it difficult for him to continue.

In court, Gerry Adams offered no political explanation for his dilatory dealings with the police. He argued that he had done his best and that he always wanted Aine to report her father. If that was true, then he had been exempting her from the general call to his community through those years not to bring complaints to the police.

In 1995 Gerry Adams, still insisting that republicans should not resort to the police, came under severe criticism from two doctors who held senior positions in rival political parties, the SDLP and Alliance. GP Joe Hendron and psychiatrist Philip McGarry criticised him for advising people not to report cases of child abuse to the police. The *Irish Times* reported that he had told a meeting in north Belfast that there were bona fide and trained counsellors who could help.

Gerry Adams accepted in court that his own first statement to the police in 2009 had been incomplete. One police officer involved in the case has said that Adams was 'helpful up to the point of actually being any use'.

And by the time he made that statement, UTV had told him that it was preparing a documentary about Liam and Aine. He told the court that he did not accept that the timing of a TV programme influenced his decision to make a statement. But he would have been vulnerable to serious criticism on the programme if the presenter had been able to report that the police were seeking to interview Gerry Adams but that he was still not making himself available to them.

In the autumn of that year Adams travelled again to Canada

and met his four cousins, the children of his uncle Sean. This family was his refuge from his worries at this time.

Counsel for Liam Adams accused Gerry Adams directly of having withheld information that would have helped in a prosecution. But Gerry Adams said frankly that his priority in dealing with Liam was not to get him arrested. He claimed that he had been working with the wider family to help Liam and to reconcile him to his abused daughter.

Peter Sheridan, former Head of Crime in the PSNI, said, 'We tried for some time to get Liam and were unsuccessful. And then I had some contact with Gerry to try and help us to do that. I can only assume that he was doing his genuine best. I spoke to him on several occasions about it, to explain to him why we needed to talk to Liam. I didn't get any sense that he wasn't willing to help. This was before the story broke on UTV. I assume that he was doing his best.'

He said, 'As I understand it they were pretty close as brothers. It must have been horrifying and shocking for him, recognising abuse in your own home then handing in your brother. Not an easy decision, even though you know they have done wrong.' He was surprised to learn later that Gerry had had such close contact with Liam through a 'process' of trying to bring him face to face with Aine. He didn't think, however, that this crossed the line into illegal behaviour.

'There was no evidence that Gerry was an accessory or helping a fugitive. If there had been we would have handed him a charge sheet. He would have been interviewed about it if he had been complicit or helping him to avoid arrest.'

The counsel for Liam Adams more bluntly stated that she thought Gerry Adams's first statement, in 2009, was self-serving. It came twenty-two years after the conversation on the beach in Buncrana and two years after Adams and Sinn Féin had accepted the PSNI.

EILIS MCDERMOTT: I want to suggest to you in clear terms that the reason that you made this statement to the police on the 21st of October 2009 was to save your political skin?

GA: If I had been interested in saving my political skin I would not have got involved in this process at the beginning and tried to fulfil my responsibility as an uncle for a young woman who I am very fond of and I have a large family and I would not have tried to do my best to resolve this the way that I have outlined to you earlier. This is above politics and saving my political skin is no consideration whatsoever in any of these matters.

The 'process' that Gerry Adams had 'got involved in' was an effort to bring Aine face to face with the man she accused of raping and demanding fellatio of her between the ages of four and ten.

That process entailed several meetings with Aine.

Adams said in court, 'I was involved in the process of trying to keep, in so far as I could, my family together but also deal with this issue that Aine had alleged about her father. So you know, one tries in all of this to create circumstances where people can get their lives back together and so on and I dealt with this in a very forthright and honest way . . . I was trying my best to resolve these matters in a way which helped Aine, but also, if I may say so, in a way which allowed Liam to get rid of these demons.'

Liam Adams was given a sixteen-year sentence for abusing his daughter. During the period in which Aine was meeting her uncle and he was 'involved in a process' with her to persuade her to meet Liam, Gerry was also regularly meeting another rape victim, Máiría Cahill, as part of another 'process' to try to reconcile her to the republican movement that had protected her own rapist.

Chapter 25

The past would not lie down.

Gerry Adams was now a TD in the Irish parliament, the Dáil, representing County Louth, leaving Martin McGuinness to lead the assembly party in the North at Stormont.

The case against his brother Liam was drawing closer and he would be called to give evidence. He also knew that the story of his dealings with Máiría Cahill was about to break, how she had been raped by an IRA man, how the IRA had interrogated her and covered it up, how close Adams himself had been to these events.

His political enemies routinely challenged him to admit that he had been a leader of the Provisional IRA. He hated that stuff. He no longer thought of himself as the man who was 'a sender-outer', a general. He had boxed that all off in his mind. It was easier to do that while living in the South, though there were long memories of cruel killings there too. And sometimes all people wanted was a plain admission of IRA responsibility when Adams himself had been denying it. Even Gerry Adams could see that sometimes it was better to give people what they asked for.

He was being taunted by a prison officer called Austin Stack. This was a little ironic; the man had a famous republican name. There was a Gaelic Athletic Association club in Kerry named after the original Austin Stack, the revolutionary and politician. Stack and his brother Oliver wanted to meet Adams in his office to challenge him to admit that the IRA had killed their father, also a prison officer.

But the IRA wasn't supposed to kill state officials in the South, though it had done. Prisoners in Portlaoise had been planning an escape and Brian Stack was shot to stop him interfering in their plans and to send a message to other screws that the IRA men they supervised had a long reach on the outside.

Brian Stack had been to a boxing tournament in Dublin in March 1983. He had come out of the stadium with his friends, then remembered something and gone back. When he came out the second time he was alone and an easier target. A man had been standing in a doorway nearby, reading a newspaper. An Irish army officer had seen that man and was suspicious of him. The man dropped the paper, walked quickly up behind Brian Stack and shot him once behind the head, severing the spinal cord.

This was a gunman who had killed before and knew how it was done.

Then a motorbike sped up to stop near the slumped body and whisked the gunman away before Stack's friends fully grasped what had happened. There were doctors from Belfast at the tournament. Two came out of the stadium and saved Brian Stack's life for a time, though even some in his family would wonder afterwards if it would have been better if they hadn't.

Stack would last eighteen months, first in a coma, then awake but not as himself, more like a child. And then when the family had gone through the worst of adjusting to nursing a severely brain-damaged quadriplegic at home, he would die.

At first the Gardai suspected criminals. Brian Stack was a senior prison officer in Portlaoise Prison and he had dealt with and perhaps annoyed some hard men.

Austin Stack, who was fourteen at the time, would learn more about his father's murder than the police knew.

The Stack family were republicans aware of their history. They had supported Fianna Fáil, the party that had spent more time than any other in government in Dublin. Fianna Fáil had grown out of the IRA, which had fought for independence in 1919 and then fought and lost a civil war against the forces of Michael

Collins who had signed a compromise treaty with the British. Ten years after the civil war, the defeated leader Éamon de Valera, the Chief, took political power and shaped the independent Republic and defended it against future pretenders to the claim of a legitimate right to fight on.

The Irish often attribute change to the power of great men. Daniel O'Connell was the Liberator. They called Michael Collins the Big Fellow. De Valera was the Chief and Gerry Adams the Big Lad.

Brian Stack gave his children books about Wolfe Tone and Robert Emmet and told them that they were related through his mother to Emmet's fiancée, Sarah Curran.

As a prison officer, Stack guarded IRA prisoners in the 1970s and 1980s. They were smuggling in weapons and explosives and wanted him out of the way. They had identified him as the screw who would be most likely to obstruct them and they wanted to send a message to the other screws that if they monitored IRA prisoners too closely they could pay for it with their lives. That gave them a motive to kill him.

Austin Stack grew older and more curious and wary of the easy assumption that the IRA had had nothing to do with the killing of his father.

A journalist, Barry Cummins, was investigating it too. He procured the Garda file that showed evidential leads which the family had not been told about. The newspaper the gunman had been reading, the motorbike and the rider's helmet had all been recovered. A review of the case found flaws in the investigation but still didn't point to the IRA.

Austin Stack, now a prison officer himself, badgered Sinn Féin through media appearances demanding confirmation that it was the IRA that had killed his father. The Sinn Féin representatives denied it. Stack demanded a meeting with Gerry Adams. Adams agreed to talk to him.

Austin and Oliver Stack travelled to the Dáil with their

mother, though she stayed across the street in a hotel. The brothers met a media scrum outside the Dáil on their way to meet Adams. Austin told journalists that, in his understanding, Gerry Adams had only to speak to two senior Sinn Féiners who had been prisoners in Portlaoise at the time of the killing, to confirm that the IRA had shot his father. One of them, Martin Ferris, wrote a memoir in which he claimed that Brian Stack was unduly harsh with republican prisoners, though Ferris does not suggest that he had any insight into the killing or part in it.

Inside the Dáil building the two brothers were brought to a boardroom beside Adams's office. There was a round table for meetings, but ties on a coat-hanger suggested this was where Adams changed into and out of formal clothes. Adams was there with Richard McAuley.

Austin says, 'Adams looked at us. He said, "I want to thank you for coming in, you're awful brave men for coming in." You could take that as if he was trying to intimidate you or he was being condescending.'

Austin had prepared for the meeting. 'I had watched the interview he had done on RTE when he was denying the IRA had done this. I kept pausing and rewinding to see how he was answering questions.'

So he thought he could predict what Adams would say to him now.

'Adams tries to play the victim himself and it was the first thing he did. He sat back in the chair with his jacket open and he said, "Sure lads, we're all victims here." I was waiting for that. I'd said to Oliver, "When he says that, and he's going to say it, you keep your mouth shut and let me handle it."

'So I pounded the desk. I said, "You let me tell you fucking something." That's the way I spoke. "I'm telling you now the only victims in this room here are me and my brother Oliver, and my mother that's sitting in that hotel across the way that is terrified to come over here." I said, "We're the victims. And I'll tell you now what a victim is."'

His father would weep while he was shaving him, and Austin would weep too. He told Adams about that.

'I told him how my mother used to get up in the middle of the night when he called for her to come and scratch his nose. I said, "That's what a victim is and don't you come playing the victim with me."'

But he told Gerry Adams also that he was ready to trust him if he would undertake to help them. He did not believe IRA denials that it had killed his father.

Adams nodded to McAuley and they left the room. They sent in tea and sandwiches to the brothers. Oliver noticed that Adams had left his iPhone on the desk and they spoke warily, suspicious that he had left it there to record them. The news came on the television in the office and they watched themselves being interviewed on their arrival. Adams, they assumed, was watching it too in the other office. When Adams came back he said he would make an effort to help, couldn't promise anything but urged them not to be naming people in front of the media in the way they had just done.

'He said, "This is going to be a process, I will do what I can to help you and try and get some information for you."'

Adams met the Stack brothers several times over the following weeks, usually in hotels. A plan developed. Gerry Adams said he would take them to meet the IRA. At first the plan was to take the brothers across the border into the North. Adams asked them if they would be 'wired'. They said they wouldn't and that they would be happy to be frisked. Adams said that wouldn't be necessary. Then later they were told they wouldn't have to cross the border after all.

And a genial relationship evolved between Austin Stack and Gerry Adams. Many others who have dealt with Adams describe him as cold and distant. Stack's description is entirely different.

'At the last meeting we were talking about the Bill on the

abolition of the Seanad [the Irish Senate] and I knew Sinn Féin had two policies on it and they were caught between a rock and a hard place. And he was getting texts and calls on it while he was having a cup of coffee with me, and I said, "Gerry, what way are you going to go on this?" He says, "I don't know; we've two policies." I thought it was completely politically naive, you know. They actually ended up backing the wrong horse on that one.' But that very haplessness was endearing.

'I found him to be all right, personable. There was nothing not to like about him.'

On the day they were to get answers from the IRA, they arranged to meet Adams at 9 a.m. at the Regency Hotel at Dublin Airport.

'We were sitting in the lobby and Richard McAuley came in and said there has been a change of plan. I'd been expecting something like that to happen.' McAuley took them in his car and asked them to leave their mobile phones behind.

'We pulled into the City North Hotel up the M1 and Gerry was there standing by his own car. Gerry got in the passenger seat and Richard drove Gerry's car. We were shooting the breeze on the way up, talking about hurling.'

Further along the road, Adams checked his watch and said that they were too early for the contact, so directed McAuley to a pub. There, Adams went round the back to talk to the proprietor and they were all served tea and scones. Richard McAuley and Austin Stack were now discussing coffee machines and discovering a shared interest in one brand.

A little later they drove back onto the motorway and went on as far as Dundalk where they turned off and drove to an old cemetery where a van was waiting, guarded by a small middle-aged man who said nothing. Adams and McAuley got into the back with the brothers.

Oliver whispered to Austin, 'They really haven't gone away.' The van looked as if it had been fitted for surreptitious work, IRA operations. It was boarded on the inside to shield the driver from view and to block the windows. This was a vehicle that had been used before to transport things that people shouldn't see or people who shouldn't see out. So there was no need to blindfold them.

Adams and McAuley were both wearing strap sandals over bare feet and Austin wondered if this was the new uniform. He watched the close interaction between McAuley and Adams. McAuley was the runner and fetcher. He says, 'I think if Gerry left his underpants on the hotel room floor, McAuley would pick them up and put them in the basket.'

When they reached their destination, after just ten minutes, they stepped out of the van directly into the kitchen of a modern bungalow. They had drawn up alongside sliding doors that matched neatly those of the van. 'They had done it really well,' said Austin.

'A middle-aged guy was sitting there reading a newspaper. A school-teacherish kind of guy. He said that his name was John, "for the purposes of this meeting". John said he had played a senior leadership role in the IRA at the time of the ceasefire and all through the struggle he had had a leadership role.'

John had a prepared statement, written in response to questions the brothers had passed on to the IRA through Gerry Adams. He read it to them, then left them alone to transcribe it and to prepare follow-up questions for him, if they had any.

The statement accepted that the IRA had killed their father, that the attack had indeed been intended to kill, and that it had been part of the wider 'prison struggle'.

'They went on to say that the operation had been organised by an individual who didn't have sanction from the army council. While it was carried out by members of the IRA, they were acting on the assumption that the operation was sanctioned.' John's statement claimed that the army council of the IRA hadn't known for two years that the shooting had been organised and executed by its own men. It also said that the man who had ordered the shooting had been disciplined.

Austin says, 'They didn't say the word sorry but they went as far as they could in that regard. The guy expressed his own personal regret and remorse and he seemed very genuine when he did that.'

Austin Stack accepted most of the statement but rejected the claim that the shooting had been unsanctioned. 'I said to Adams that I didn't believe that the operation wasn't sanctioned and that it is not credible that for a number of years he didn't know who did this. He said it could have been the INLA or non-aligned republicans. I said that's bollocks. It's not credible that you woke up the following morning and didn't scratch your head and wonder, "Was it our boys did this?"'

The Stack brothers agreed to wait a week and think things over before making a statement to the media. Adams called Austin, after seeing a draft of the statement, urging him to include a line saying that the people responsible for the murder should not be arrested. Stack had said at the beginning of his talks with Adams that he was not seeking an arrest. But he says he refused to incorporate that point into his statement because he did not believe the IRA had been fully honest with him.

And despite that, for a while afterwards Adams would call Austin for friendly conversation. He would ask him how he was and he would inquire after his mother.

'Which I thought was nice of him. There was a lot going on in relation to his brother and his brother's trial. He kept referring to it as the little family matter. It would sound like he was trivialising it but I think it was more embarrassment. But I had a sense there was more to this and I thought that's what it was when the Máiría Cahill story came out.'

He says, 'I've met people that when you've looked them in the eye you can sense evil; you certainly don't get that from Adams. He looks more like guys that have organisational ability. I've spoken to convicted killers and you can sense from some of those guys that they got their hands dirty, that they actually did stuff. I get the feeling Adams was more the general in the armchair directing traffic.'

Chapter 26

The police in Antrim Serious Crime Suite phoned Mr Adams three times to discuss how he might be arrested. He took the calls and discussed the logistics from his car, as he was travelling north. He was a busy politician, leader of a party that was thriving in the polls and facing into two elections, one for the European Parliament on both sides of the Irish border and one for the new super councils created by local government reform in the North. He would really have preferred not to be arrested at all.

The police suggested that he drive into a car park in Antrim, near the station. A uniformed officer would then be on hand to meet him and formally place him under arrest on suspicion of having been a member of the IRA and having ordered the murder and disappearance of Jean McConville in 1972. (This was a case that the Public Prosecutor would later conclude there was insufficient evidence to pursue.)

Adams was having none of it.

But there was a technicality to be observed, said the police. If he just walked voluntarily into the station, they couldn't arrest him there. Adams had no time for their technical and legal considerations. They weren't his problem. He'd see them at the station.

The police had succeeded in securing several of the recorded interviews made by Anthony McIntyre for the Boston College Archives and they had arrested several suspects and would arrest more. At this stage, in April 2014, they had charged only Ivor Bell, a former member of the Belfast Brigade who had fallen out with Adams in the mid-1980s. Bell had suspected rightly that Adams was building a political challenge to armed struggle.

Anthony McIntyre had had no intention of gathering evidence against former comrades in the Provisional IRA when he interviewed them for the archive. He was an academic with no other work at the time. He had come out of jail in the early 1990s with a first-class degree in politics. He competed for the only funded place available at Queen's University to study for a PhD in the subject. His rival was the university's own top student, Joanne Murphy, then an activist for the SDLP. The Long Kesh boy beat the Queen's girl. But she went on to become an academic and he struggled to find work. His chances worsened when, as a campaigner against the peace process deal, he accused the Provisionals of murdering his friend and neighbour, Joe O'Connor, and, in response, Sinn Féin activists picketed his home.

Bobby Storey, then a senior IRA man who enforced compliance with the peace process within the movement, visited McIntyre with a sidekick to urge him to return to the party line. After the author reported this in the media, Storey put him up against a wall in the Felons Club and told him he was a slug.[1]

With the help of journalist Ed Moloney and his former PhD supervisor, Paul Bew (now Lord Bew), McIntyre was recruited as a researcher for Boston College to compile the oral archive. He accumulated some fascinating material. He interviewed Dolours Price, one of the 1973 London bombers. The promise that material would not be disclosed until after her death bound McIntyre to silence but it did not bind her, and she jeopardised the project by speaking to a journalist about her role in delivering Jean McConville to her execution. The police, assuming that a fuller account of this might be on her Boston College recording, moved to subpoena it.

The archive also included an interview with The Dark, Brendan Hughes. After Hughes died, Ed Moloney published extracts from his statement in a book, *Voices from the Grave*, naming Adams as the one who had ordered that Jean McConville be killed and that her body be hidden.

McIntyre and Moloney had believed in the assurances they had given interviewees and trusted Boston College to resist any attempts by the police to procure the recordings. They had also assumed at the time that, in the spirit of the peace process, the police in Northern Ireland would not want access to the evidence contained in them. Nor did it seem likely that such evidence was of much value unless corroborated.

At first it seemed that the main evidence against Adams at the time of his arrest was contained mostly in those interviews. Once the police had him in custody they set about trying to get other evidence. They went to Peter Rogers, one of the *Maidstone* prison ship escapees, who had spoken to the media about meeting Adams and McGuinness in Trinity College in 1981 to complain about the state of the gelignite they were sending him to England with, but Rogers refused to make a statement. And they went through Adams's published books and challenged him to admit that he must have been a member of the IRA when he was sent by the Belfast Brigade to negotiate truces with the Officials.

But the police suspected Adams of more than just having been a member of the IRA who had ordered a killing. Adams said after his release that detectives had put it to him that he had been a British intelligence agent for decades. 'They claimed I was turned by the Special Branch during interrogations in Palace Barracks in 1972 and that I became an MI5 agent!'

Had this been true, he would have been recruited before his meeting with Philip Woodfield to negotiate the 1972 ceasefire and, crucially, before his period on the run and his second period of internment.

If some in the police really believed that Gerry Adams was working for the British since 1972, then they were giving credence to an appalling scenario, one in which he was allowed to run the IRA, perhaps to contain it, for want of being able to close it down. If that was true, Adams might have run the hunger strikes for the purpose of killing off prime activists as much as for building a political alternative to the IRA. And it would mean that the IRA was managed directly by MI5.

The way in which Sinn Féin conducted its campaign for his release illustrates the party's style and principles. It argued immediately that the arrest was politically motivated and claimed that a 'dark side' of policing was trying to damage the peace process. It never conceded that there were any reasonable grounds for suspicion of Adams. And it elevated him above ordinary political activism to present him as a visionary leader, an Irish Mandela.

A republican youth group named after Mairéad Farrell, who was shot dead in Gibraltar in 1988 while planning a bomb attack, painted a new mural on the Falls Road, commemorating Adams as 'Peacemaker, Leader, Visionary'.

Bobby Storey led the speeches with a rant: 'That they would dare arrest our leader.' Martin McGuinness reinforced the claim that the arrest was driven by elements of the PSNI and the British government who were opposed to the peace process. But across the street from the protest an hour earlier a group of old IRA men opposed to the peace process had met for a flag-lowering ceremony in commemoration of Brendan Hughes's D Company, this being the fortieth anniversary of the death of one of the members, Volunteer Teddy Campbell.

Adams was detained for four days. Normally he would have had to be released after two days but the police sought and won an extension, after showing their evidence to a senior judge. This evidence appears to have largely been the transcripts of interviews for the Boston College Archives.

Sinn Féin maintained its vision of a conspiracy within the police against the peace process. The arrest warrant had been signed by Drew Harris, a police officer whose father was killed in 1989 by an IRA bomb. An officer close to the investigation, when asked if Adams had maintained the strict silence required of IRA volunteers, laughed as he said he had 'waxed lyrical'. But he did not give them the added evidence they needed to enable them to charge him. Apprehension grew when Adams was being put through thirty-three recorded interviews in Antrim Serious Crime Suite that he would come out to lead a robust challenge to the police and harden the party's position. He did the opposite.

The police had referred the case against Adams and others to the Public Prosecution Service, which would conclude that it was 'insufficient to provide a reasonable prospect of obtaining a conviction'.

On his release, Adams acknowledged that the party believed that there was a sinister dark side to policing, opposed to Sinn Féin, but he did so without the passion his supporters had shown and in the context of an endorsement of the police. He announced that Sinn Féin would continue on the path it was on. Its response to those who were trying to undermine or deflect it would be to hold fast to the current project, which is just what Sinn Féin would be doing if the sinister forces didn't exist.

'When I was leaving I commended the custody staff because I thought that they were decent in terms of how they were doing their job. I did make a formal complaint about one particular aspect of my interrogation and I want in due course to reflect on the structure within that holding centre. It's not up to the type of standards that one would expect, and the food in it is uneatable. I didn't eat for the first number of days because it just wasn't possible to digest it.'

But he would not concede that there could have been anything but a political reason for arresting him. Having been questioned for four days about his part in the IRA, he came out to say that his arrest had nothing to do with any reasonable suspicion that he had ever broken the law.

'I bear no animosity to anyone. I do not wish to be treated differently from anyone. I am an activist. This is my life and I am philosophical and I understand that I have detractors and opponents and I especially understand that there are sinister elements who are against the changes Sinn Féin and others are committed to achieving.'

He made no attempt to identify these imagined sinister elements nor to prescribe any campaign of action against them.

He said, 'Despite this I want to make it clear that I support the PSNI. I will continue to work with others to build a genuinely civic policing service. The old guard which is against change, whether in the PSNI leadership, within elements of unionism, or the far fringes of self-proclaimed but pseudo republicans, they can't win.'

Adams was presenting himself as the one political leader who understands the trend of Irish destiny. People are either for or against the peace process, and that process is now about more than settling sectarian differences in Northern Ireland; it is about achieving equality between citizens across the whole island. Those who do not see politics in those terms are diehards and throwbacks; what Adams is defending, by this vision, is not just himself and Sinn Féin but the proper order of politics. Dissent from the Sinn Féin vision is not just a divergence of opinion, as he sees it; it is error, the failure to grasp the truth of where Ireland is going; it is wilful opposition to progress. Perhaps because he was an ideological republican he can only be an ideological peacemaker, asserting that there is a firm narrative in place that must unfold. Perhaps because he has been a conspirator all his life he assumes that everyone who creates problems for him is also a conspirator. He attacked the Boston College oral archive as a concerted attack on the peace process and himself.

He said, 'Both Moloney and McIntyre are opponents of the Sinn Féin leadership and our peace strategy and have interviewed former republicans who are also hostile to me and other Sinn Féin leaders.'

He said that the allegation of conspiracy in the murder of Mrs McConville was based almost exclusively on 'hearsay from unnamed alleged Boston College interviewees but mostly from Dolours Price and Brendan Hughes'.

That these were people who had been close to him in the early days gave them no credibility that could not be undermined by pointing out that they were politically motivated to damage his good name.

Chapter 27

In the early stages of the peace process Gerry Adams was validated as a respected peacemaker by President Clinton's doorway handshake. He was not going to get that kind of endorsement from a British leader or a unionist in Northern Ireland. For them, he still had the taint of terrorism. Indeed the whole point of the project of making him respectable was to enable his enemies to trade with him, even to compel them. Another high-profile handshake came from the Irish President, Mary McAleese. McAleese had grown up in Ardoyne. Her father had owned the Long Bar in Leeson Street from which Adams's former comrades in the Official IRA had broadcast Radio Free Belfast.

McAleese may have seen her visit to her old grammar school, St Dominic's, on the Falls Road as an opportunity to contribute to the peace process by honouring Adams with a handshake. But the buzz around west Belfast afterwards was not about her. It was about Gerry himself and a schoolgirl called Máiría Cahill.

Adams had been clever. After meeting the President inside the school he let her leave before him. Outside, the hundreds of pupils were lined up to greet her. The greeting was warm and natural but when Gerry Adams emerged to smile and wave at the girls the cheers erupted.

'Ger-reee! Ger-reee!'

He then walked along the line of excited pupils until he recognised the niece of his co-founder of the Provisionals, Joe Cahill. He had known her as a child. When he had visited the Cahill home he was introduced to her as Uncle Gerry. He stopped and in front of the whole school gave her a warm hug.

Máiría says, 'It caused a bit of difficulty because some of the teachers weren't that enamoured of him.'

Máiría was born in 1981, the year of the hunger strike deaths, and though she came out of a strong republican lineage her parents steered her away from politics. In her teens she started working part-time, while still at school, on a community radio station that was a platform for republican messages. In the station she often met Adams and other prominent republicans and moved quickly from giving production support to taking the microphone herself. There is an insight into the complex nature of republican culture at that time in that she was reprimanded for playing a rebel song, having picked up the CD nearest to her, filling in without preparation for someone who had not turned up.

She says, 'It was all Ooo Ah, Up the 'Ra, and the place went ballistic.'

Máiría joined Ógra Shinn Féin, the party's youth movement, and was spotted as someone with talent who could take a senior position.

'In 1998 they had an annual congress which I didn't attend but somehow managed to get elected, without even knowing I was standing, into the National Secretary post. And I just accepted it. I was out in a bar with an older cousin of mine and Gerry Kelly and Bobby Storey were standing at the bar and they sent down a drink congratulating me for getting this position, and I thought it was a wind-up and it wasn't. So I ended up as National Secretary of a youth movement that was fairly radical and got itself into trouble. That was the squad that climbed the roof of the City Hall.

'They had a petrol bomb logo that caused a massive row at the time and they changed their logo and it was a glass bottle with an Easter lily coming out the top of it.'

Her childhood acquaintance with Adams left her less inclined than others to revere him.

She says, 'I wasn't nervous around him at all. But I would

293

have been aware that when he came in, for example to the radio station, that people fell over themselves to make him a cup of tea or whatever. And actually one of the earliest memories is of him coming into the radio and somebody saying, get up and make him a cup of tea and I said to him, "Can you not get up and make it yourself? I'm knackered." To be fair to him, I don't think he had a difficulty with that. He probably enjoyed the banter around it and did get up and make it.'

She says Adams had a reserve she didn't see in other senior republicans, even when good-humoured.

'He's almost childlike in a way at times. Possibly deliberately so. He has a good rapport with young people. He is happy and smiley most of the time he is in the office. Still there's, aloofness would probably be the wrong word, a reserve about him.

'There was a marked difference between Martin McGuinness coming into the station and laughing and joking and Gerry coming in and laughing and joking, because there still is that . . . And people do do that thing of "Oh My God, It's Gerry Adams!" I'm talking about women in their forties and fifties who would trip over themselves to please him.'

She could see how he enjoyed power. 'There was a press conference in Conway Mill and a journalist went for a wander and got locked in the third floor. And he just joked with Richard [McAuley], "Just leave him there and then we'll go and let him out." Somebody did eventually go and let the guy out.'

She says that, at that time, some of the prisoners getting released and other men around Sinn Féin and the radio station were quick to sound out their sexual prospects with her. 'Gerry Adams showed no sexual interest in me. Later, he would have said things like "I love you and we love you and you need to look after yourself" and he'd give me a hug. I certainly didn't take that as any kind of sexual interest. And his behaviour, I have to say, was remarkably different from other men his age at that time in relation to other women.'

It wasn't just Ógra Shinn Féin that recognised Máiría Cahill as someone worth recruiting. The IRA made four approaches to her, suggesting that she join. One of these approaches came from Denis Donaldson, a senior administrator in Sinn Féin, later exposed as a police agent.

Thinking about why she didn't join the IRA exposes a paradox in her family background; people in that family had been in the IRA and had done time in jail or been on the run. That was regarded as normal and even admirable; yet her parents retained a conception of respectability that clearly excluded the republican culture.

'I have never been able to work this out. You had the normal thing of other families' members having been in jail and you knew they had been in jail and it was almost accepted as normality, but the flip side of that is that I had parents who were both in good enough jobs, weren't involved in politics, never brought it into the house, so you had that kind of antithesis thing of respectability and non-respectability, normality and not normal, and they were hugely concerned at me going down the political route to the point where they actually barred me from going to Sinn Féin meetings and they didn't know until I appeared in one of the newspapers or someone saw an article and said, "Do you know that your daughter is running about with these people?"

'Why did I not join? I have no idea. Another time, maybe six months earlier, I may have considered it.'

Máiría Cahill's experience brought her to the point of being Adams's fiercest critic and perhaps most dangerous enemy.

She had been spending a lot of time in Ballymurphy while working with Sinn Féin and taking an interest in republican politics. She stayed most nights that summer of 1997 in a house in Ballymurphy Drive off Divismore Park where the Adamses had lived. She had relatives there.

An IRA man stayed there too. She says he had tried to groom her, impress or frighten her.

He raped and abused her several times while she was staying there. She would wake up to find the man groping her. She would pretend to be asleep while he raped her. She was only sixteen, raised no alarm. Nor did she stop going to the house. The man she accuses was a member of the IRA's Civil Administration, the section that carried out kneecappings, mostly of young men accused of stealing cars or dealing in drugs. Two other young women would later also accuse the same man of raping them in their early teens. In the year after the period of abuse, Máiría made no complaint against the man, either to the IRA or to the police, but she told friends who told others, and the IRA moved to detain and interrogate her, ostensibly to ascertain the truth about one of its volunteers, with a view to either punishing him or silencing the young woman who was maligning him.

The first approach from the IRA was through a woman volunteer. Máiría was told to be ready to meet her that night. She was picked up in a car and driven to a flat in west Belfast.

The IRA interrogators held several long meetings with her over a period of months. Sometimes when she was working in a café she would get a call with an order to meet them again in an hour at a designated location.

'I couldn't function. I would have got a phone call saying, be there in ten minutes. At one point I was working in a waitressing shift. Two girls came in for me and I had to arrange cover there and then. Everybody knew they were IRA and away you went. Or they would come into the radio when I was doing a show. I was a constant ball of nerves because I just never knew when the next one was coming. It was almost daily. In fact, it *was* daily at one point. And it went on for hours at a time. So when you are in that kind of situation it is about survival and you just clamp down any emotions that you have. I suppose the only thing that you have is trying to anticipate what their next step was going to be, having that or not having the knowledge of their internal structures and procedures; that only became clear some months in when somebody mentioned court martial. At that point I had to even ask what a court martial was. So there was a complete naivety around that kind of stuff for me.'

She lived for that period in intense anxiety, knowing that ultimately if the IRA decided not to believe her account of how one of its members had used her, it might draw on a repertoire of traditional sanctions against her. As a traumatised young woman she was poorly placed to reason that the IRA was unlikely to kill her, though it was down to killing very few people at that time. Nor perhaps was it likely to tar and feather her or do anything that would bring attention to the case. She wasn't likely to be able to work that out for herself either. Among other punishments that the IRA frequently imposed was exile, an order to leave the country. It would ultimately apply that one to the man she accused but only after the two other girls told their families that he had raped them as well.

Throughout the months of interrogation, Máiría Cahill says she was barred from telling her family about the process she was being put through. Towards the end of it, the IRA members brought her face to face with the man who had raped her, to see if they could judge better, from the interaction between them, which of them was lying. Then the IRA designated a member to inform her family that their findings were inconclusive.

She believes that Gerry Adams was probably kept informed about the IRA's investigation by her cousin Siobhán O'Hanlon who was his personal assistant.

'I think it would be inconceivable for him not to have known, considering the fact that the woman who was his advisor at the time knew about it from very early. I think she would have recognised at that point in time that it would potentially have caused a bit of difficulty for the republican movement, and certainly once the IRA got involved somebody would have had to have told him. When I had the first conversation with him it was clear to me that he knew the details of what had happened long before he claimed he did.'

That was in the first week of August 2000.

When the two other young women claimed that the same man had raped them the IRA investigation was reopened.

Máiría says, 'One of the other girls wanted to go to the police and we always had a thing where if one went we all went. My mistake was that I told someone that we were going to make a complaint and, of course, up would pop Adams. I was brought to a solicitor in the town by an IRA woman and the solicitor said this would be very beneficial to the security services and you would probably never get a conviction for it.

'One of the kids came out on 22 July 2000, and I was brought to a meeting the next day. The IRA said there was an army council directive that they couldn't speak to anybody under the age of eighteen and they wanted me to speak to her – she was around thirteen or fourteen at the time – to act as a go-between to get her details and I refused to do it. Bad enough living with your own details, never mind having that and doing their job, and that was not happening.

'And then the other child came back. She was on holiday. And the IRA did speak to her and her parents and then all hell broke loose, literally. The family went bugaloo and the IRA swept in and took the man out in the middle of my da squealing blue murder about going to the police.'

After this the IRA members accepted the man's guilt and consulted Máiría on what she expected them to do. They invited her to give a thumb down and have him killed.

'I was brought to Adams's office towards the tail end of their second stint, once the other two girls had come out, and one of the IRA women came in. Siobhán O'Hanlon opened Adams's door and the two of us went in. And she pointed at the light on the ceiling (to indicate a bug) and she wrote on a piece of paper, "What do you want to happen to him?" and pushed it across the table.

'So at that point I lost the head completely. I said, "How dare you? You have just put me through a year of forced investigation. It's not my responsibility. I think that is too easy an option." Meaning: "Don't even go down that road." I absolutely at that time couldn't have lived with that. And I mean that genuinely, I didn't want that on my conscience. I didn't know what was going to happen, to be quite honest. It was just an extremely mad time. And at that time, there was a discussion. I wanted him to stay in Ballymurphy because then everyone would know what he was. That's an indication of how naive I was.

'So you had this guy being held by the IRA. I didn't know where he was. Somebody got me to write a letter to him, which I did. I told him that he was a coward and that he should admit what he had done and that his children would grow up knowing that not only was he a child abuser but that he was a liar and a coward as well. And that he had caused an awful lot of personal damage to me and two other children. But I had already been through the process where I had been dragged into a room to confront him and he had completely denied it to my face, which was really really damaging.'

A Sunday newspaper carried the story without the names of the girls who had been attacked.

On the day the newspaper article appeared Máiría attended the opening of the West Belfast Festival, Féile an Phobail. She wanted to show those who knew about her that she wasn't going to hide away. Much of the gossip in the crowd was speculation about who the raped women might be.

'The festival parade was on that Sunday and I went to it almost like a "fuck you" kind of thing. I'm not going to hide away; people are going to know. Adams came over to me that night in the marquee, kissed me on the head. He could have taken me aside and said, are you all right? He literally walked over and kissed me right on the head.' It was a careless thing to do. 'And it did have the effect of everyone knowing that it was me because I then had people coming up and saying, "We didn't know." And then they knew.'

She says that nobody asked for the IRA to become involved in that second investigation. It confirmed for the IRA that her story was true, that the man had raped her and had raped others.

Adams asked Máiría to meet him in his Belfast office.

'I went in and he was sitting in his room. He was at one end of the desk. The gist of it would be, well, do you want answers, or are you looking for answers? And I said no, I got my answers.'

The IRA had told her it could do nothing about her rapist.

'And he flashed with anger like, for no more than a couple of seconds. And then he sat up. He had been doing this thing with his hands [bringing his fingertips together] almost like a priest. Then he got up from behind that table and came round and sat down beside me.'

Máiría met him several times over the following five years.

'I remember I was photocopying sheets one time and he walked into the office and took his shoes off and hopped across the sheets on the floor. There was only me and him in the room. I was just looking at him and thinking, if that had been anybody else you'd have said, "You're a dick!" I asked him, "What the fuck are you doing?" And he started laughing, you know. So there is that, where he just did it for the impishness of it. He just had to do something just to wind somebody up.'

She wonders still if his playfulness is motivated by a genuine sense of fun or a device for manipulating people. 'I think he is one of those people that can mess with your head from across the room without even projecting any sense that he is doing it.'

And they had regular conversations about the process the IRA had put her through, interrogating her about the details of her abuse and rape, forcing her to meet the man responsible. 'He did appear sympathetic at times. All that crap about "I love you" and "we love you and you need to look after yourself" would have been fine if it had not been in the context of everything else that was going on, which at times was me saying, "I'm going to go public about this and I'm not happy about this. This man has disappeared; he has access to kids; I can't live with this, I can't cope."

'The key times when he spoke to me were when I was thinking like this.'

Adams wanted to reintegrate her into the republican movement and to heal divisions with the Cahill family, to head off the danger of future disclosure. He also wanted to discourage her from going to the police.

He claims emphatically that this is not true, however, and that he urged her to go to the police. But in doing so he would have been making an exception from his routine urging of republicans at that time not to use the police.

'At times when I was threatening to go public or to the police a phone call would come through. On one particular occasion his secretary, Paula MacManus, rang a third person and I then rang her back after discussing it with the third person. And Paula apologised and said, "Oh I hope you don't mind. Gerry's concerned." I said, "If he's that concerned tell him he has my number and he can lift the phone and punch the fucking numbers in himself. I'll see him when I am ready to see him."

'And that would have been November 2005, and then around January 2006 I met Paula in the car park at Conway Mill and said, "I'm ready to see him now."'

Because of her grievance against Gerry Adams she is probably the person with most intimate knowledge of him to speak candidly.

'I've never seen him take a drink, though he does drink pints. I have never heard him swear. I think he is genuinely religious. I have sat in mass with him on three occasions. Once, when Tom Williams's body was brought back [19 January 2000].' Williams was an IRA man hanged for murder in 1942. He had been a comrade of her uncle Joe Cahill.

'I happened to be in between Gerry and Joe. I'm not religious so I don't do the praying and the kneeling stuff, but he was. He goes to mass every Sunday, or was going every Sunday. He kind of manoeuvred me out of the crowd when my cousin died. [Siobhán O'Hanlon died of breast cancer in 2006.] As people were lining in, he put his hand on my shoulder and I ended up between him and McGuinness while the family sat on the other side and I still don't know how that happened.'

She decided in 2009 to report everything to the police.

What clinched it for her after years of considering it and being talked out of it by Gerry Adams and republicans around him, was her discovery that Aine Adams, Gerry's niece, had been raped and that Aine's father, Gerry's brother Liam, was being sought. UTV had broadcast its documentary in which Gerry Adams had said that he believed Aine's allegation against her father and that he had been trying to bring them together.

'That was the reason I went public. I went ballistic after that programme. It was really really difficult. I cried most of the night. I had no idea because I had been told this has never happened to anybody and it will never happen again. That was the guarantee I wanted from Adams, that nobody else would be put through that. And I got that guarantee. I'd been told that this was a unique situation. This is what they were telling my da, Joe saying there was a fuck-up of the highest order in the movement. Then you find that they have literally been dancing Aine round.'

In fairness to Adams, it would arguably have been improper to divulge to Máiría that he was aware of another rape case.

Even at this stage, Máiría Cahill was not confident that she was safe from the IRA. 'When I gave my statement in 2010 I did something the police don't usually do. I did most of my video interviews back to back on the one day, I told them I wanted it all on record because I still thought I would be killed for naming people. That was still the degree of fear even in that year.

'I said to the police, after the statement, "I am not suicidal and the IRA isn't into shooting people, but if you find me dead at the end of the week with a load of pills in me, you know who has done it." I was seriously concerned that I would be killed. I don't think I was over-egging it either; I don't think anybody had any idea where it was going to go.'

The alleged rapist and the interrogators were arrested and charged, though reporting of their names was barred by the court until the cases collapsed. Martin Morris was charged with IRA membership and with rape. The alleged IRA interrogators were charged with IRA membership and conducting an illegal investigation. They were Seamus Finucane, Briege Wright, Maura McCrory and Padraic Wilson.

All were acquitted. After four years the cases all collapsed because Máiría and the two other women would not, in the end, give evidence. The Director of Public Prosecutions had decided that the defendants had first to be tried with IRA membership before the other charges could be heard. The prospects of a conviction there were low. Máiría Cahill saw little point in putting herself through an arduous and distressing trial that was likely to fail, a conclusion reached by many other raped women before her.

An investigation into the conduct of the case, commissioned by the Public Prosecution Service, confirmed that Máiría Cahill had been let down and she was given a formal apology.

Gerry Adams refused to concede that he or any other members of Sinn Féin had done anything but try to help Máiría. He said that he had urged her throughout to go to the police and that he had tried to get her uncle, Joe Cahill, to persuade her to report the abuse. Yet he was talking about a period in which Sinn Féin was refusing to acknowledge the legitimacy of the Police Service of Northern Ireland. Even his niece Aine had waited until after Sinn Féin had accepted the police before she made her complaint against her father, Liam Adams.

Máiría Cahill's story was huge. She met the leaders of all the major political parties in Northern Ireland and in the Irish Republic. She had also prepared the ground well for support and media attention by establishing relations with journalists and politicians in advance of the story breaking.

Adams was outraged by one detail. She said that when she first spoke to him about her abuse he had said that those who manipulate people are so clever that sometimes the victim enjoys the abuse.

She told the BBC: 'The most disturbing thing of that conversation for me was then he said: "Well, you know, Máiría, abusers can be extremely manipulative." And you know, he kind of put his hand on his chin and he sat forward a wee bit, and he said: "Sometimes they're that manipulative, that the people who have been abused actually enjoy it."

'I was absolutely horrified. And I, at that point, got very, very angry and said to him: "Well, I didn't enjoy it." And at that the meeting was over for me, there was no point.

'He apologised on behalf of the republican movement for what had happened to me.'

Adams insists he did not say this. He said in a statement:

When I learned of the allegation of abuse from Siobhán, she told me that Máiría was refusing to go to the RUC.

Siobhán and I met with Joe Cahill who was Máiría's uncle. We told Joe of the allegation and asked him to speak to Máiría about reporting this to the RUC. He did so. Máiría did not want to do this at that time.

I have contacted my solicitor with regard to the allegations made against me in the programme.

Adams insisted that members of Sinn Féin had sought only to help Máiría in her distress and that there had been no cover-up.

In a Dáil debate of 22 October 2014, the Taoiseach, Enda Kenny, wanted Gerry Adams to answer for the IRA's treatment of Máiría Cahill, and Adams, who has been batting back criticism for decades, held his nerve and made his case, concentrating only on defending members of Sinn Féin.

'All those from Sinn Féin who have met with Máiría Cahill accept and acknowledge that she was abused, accept that she was traumatised. She then puts a particular version of what occurred.'

The leader of Sinn Féin had just accused a rape victim of lying. There were not many politicians who would survive in office after doing that. He went further, to defend those who interrogated Máiría.

'These are not nameless anonymous people. These are decent people.' He was stabbing the air in front of himself for emphasis even as the Speaker sought to close the point. He continued, 'Will you meet with them and listen to their version of the story, and then make a judgement on these matters?'

Kenny then was back on his feet, to answer the shouting and air-stabbing of Adams with a soft, almost whispered, confident delivery. 'I find it absolutely unbelievable that you would come into this house of parliament and say that a man who raped a woman, who sexually abused her, is a decent person.'

Adams hadn't actually said that the rapist was decent, only that those republicans were decent who had put her through months of interrogation and then forced her to confront him.

'I did not say that.' Adams was shouting. Beside him sat his party colleague, Mary Lou McDonald. As a feminist radical, she was now having to support a party leader who was, effectively, accusing a rape victim of overplaying her grief to damage Sinn Féin. McDonald had previously been one of the most energetic critics of the Catholic Church and its own cover-ups of child abuse.

She is often at his side, inside and outside of parliament. Her respect and admiration for Adams are often evident in affectionate smiles and glances. Today she looked as if she was personally in pain, perhaps close to tears. She didn't enter politics to be at odds with rape victims.

'He did not say that,' she interjected from her seat beside Adams in a pleading tone, shaking her head, looking as if she wished this would all just stop.

Adams was up for fighting the point, demanding that the Speaker, the Ceann Comhairle, do his job. The other members were laughing and shouting at Adams, so keen to defend himself against misrepresentation, so righteous, so protective of his integrity and his dignity when they credited him with neither. And the Speaker refused to help him out.

Sinn Féin later briefed the media that he had not asked Kenny to meet the rapist or the IRA interrogators but that he had been talking about party members who had supported Máiría but who had not been part of the interrogation. While a substantial interview was required to clear this up, Adams was avoiding the media.

Where others might have been softened by sympathy for Máiría Cahill, Adams punched back hard to say emphatically that she was misrepresenting him and her experience. Just as, when faced with the outrage of the peace women in 1976, mothers and wives, appalled that the IRA campaign should lead to the deaths of children, Adams had stood firm and rebuked them for their tainted motives and their ignorance, he was blunt with those who rallied to support Máiría. He accused them of feigning sympathy with her in order to attack Sinn Féin. The real drive behind their anger was fear that the party was in the ascendant and had to be stopped. Conspiratorial at heart, Sinn Féin is incapable of allowing that others might have less devious motives for their actions.

There were times when Gerry Adams seemed not to be demonstrating the sort of political talent expected of a party leader with claims to govern. During the Troubles the defence had been, 'Look what you made me do.' After the violence stopped the case was basically, 'Why can't you be grateful it's over, and besides, you are more to blame than we are.'

Faced with the allegation that the IRA had interrogated a rape victim, he might have simply said that he knew nothing about it at first and then tried only to be helpful. Instead, he actually provided his critics with ammunition against him through his blog *Léargas*, where he acknowledged that the IRA had expelled sex offenders into other jurisdictions.

In some way, this was not a radical disclosure. Anyone familiar with the history of the Troubles knew about the punishment squads of the Civil Administration and knew that the Republican movement had been committed to undermining the police by erecting alternative structures. But a media now less familiar with the story than it should have been responded as if these were stark admissions of guilt.

On the one hand he could get away with propaganda. 'The conflict itself caused widespread hurt and suffering, but so too did the absence of the structures and institutions which are the norm in peaceful, democratic societies. These citizens never had a policing service.'[1]

In fact, at the time, the RUC's care units for rape victims were admired by the Rape Crisis Centre in Dublin, which was commending its procedures in the early 1990s to the Gardai.[2]

Adams described the work of the IRA's Civil Administration as filling a gap in policing rather than acknowledging that it was intrinsic to a strategy of undermining the state through imitation.

The bulk of this activity involved mediation between those in dispute, and went unreported.

However, the IRA often punished petty criminals, car thieves, burglars and drug dealers. The IRA, inevitably also made mistakes.

Despite the high standards and decency of the vast majority of IRA volunteers, IRA personnel were singularly ill-equipped to deal with these matters. This included very sensitive areas such as responding to demands to take action against rapists and child abusers. The IRA on occasion shot alleged sex offenders or expelled them.[3]

He had had no need to declare that the IRA had behaved like the Catholic Church in moving sex offenders to areas where they could find new people to abuse; he simply handed that information to his critics and deprived himself of the chance to say later, when challenged on this practice, that he simply knew nothing about it.

And he was writing to construct an argument that the IRA handled sex abuse cases where the victims had wanted them to, but that did not apply in Máiría Cahill's case, by her version anyway.

Then a blogger calling himself Ruaidrí Ua Conchobai posted a vigorous challenge to Máiría Cahill's credibility. He doubted not only her claim that her rape had been investigated by the IRA but that she had actually been raped at all. 'It's apparent, Ms Cahill is improperly seeking to retry her abandoned Court claims and such is a perversion of due process of law.'[4]

Republicans who had for decades been telling us that the courts were not to be trusted were insisting now that the acquittal of the accused was the final word on his guilt, even though the Director of Public Prosecutions had ordered a review of the case to see if it had been handled badly by his office, and would concede that it was.

The blog speculated further, 'was this possibly a year-long clandestine sexual relationship between these two people ignited by (what Ms Cahill described as) a "few cans of beer" evening, which ended with seduction by a silver-tongued, musically talented, IRA-powerful type of charmer whom many a 16 year old would likely fancy . . . it's possible but I don't know, do you?'

This blog was circulated by several Sinn Féin members, including prominent women who had campaigned on women's issues, posting links on their Facebook pages until Máiría Cahill challenged Mary Lou McDonald to condemn it, which she did.

A leaked memorandum to party representatives from Bobby Storey told them not to engage with Máiría Cahill on social media and to refer all press queries back to the party before making any statements about her experience of abuse. But other challenges were mounted against her.

The *Guardian* columnist Roy Greenslade attacked the BBC *Spotlight* programme and other journalists for omitting the detail that years after her rape and interrogation Máiría Cahill had joined the Republican Network for Unity (RNU), an umbrella group for republicans opposed to Sinn Féin. Membership of that group suggested that she did not support the police and that she is not credible when she says that she would have reported her rape to the police, eight years earlier, but for the IRA forbidding her to do so.

The solicitor representing the alleged members of the interrogation team published letters that Máiría Cahill had written to them. These letters seemed clear evidence that an IRA investigation had indeed taken place but disclosed Cahill's conflicted feelings about some of those who had participated in it. She had thanked one of her interrogators for her sympathy.

Máiría Cahill said that she had been a member of RNU 'for a period of a few hours in 2010'. Her emotional and rational inconsistencies were now fielded as evidence that she was deceitful, not as evidence that she had been confused and damaged. This has long been the standard weapon against abused and disturbed women.

And Gerry Adams may have insights into abuse. During the investigation into his brother Liam's abuse of Aine, he gave a media interview to reveal that his father had also sexually and physically abused children.

Neither Máiría Cahill nor Gerry Adams has told us much about what they talked about in six years of meetings to discuss her experience of rape and interrogation, but it may be reasonably assumed that Adams had empathy to share. Adams appears to have seen himself at this time as a healer or consoler of abused women. Máiría returned to him several times understanding that he could help.

She found him at times considerate and at times furious.

'He is pleasant and affable and all of the things that endear him to people. Affable, pleasant, jokey, childlike, and then moving into being spoilt childlike, when things aren't going his way. And that would be very clear to me. Particularly on a one-to-one basis, you know. That very jokey thing and then [she snaps her fingers] straight out of it if there's a challenge to him that he doesn't like. It is a bit like having a spoilt child around.'

Adams had exposed his party to enormous criticism and jeopardised support, particularly from women. He had implicated his southern colleagues in the defence of the IRA. He had moved south to strengthen the party there and had watched it grow progressively stronger through a period of economic collapse and recovery. New members untainted by the past had risen to prominence, perhaps imagining that the link to the IRA would not hold them back.

Máiría Cahill says, 'There is a cult following around Gerry Adams. I don't think there is any denial of that. Almost North Korean like and at the same time he tries to portray himself as some kind of humble figure that isn't like that.'

Speaking before the story broke, Máiría had predicted well how he would react. 'There is certainly an enigma about him. There is a folksy persona around him which is hard to work out. There are different sides of him obviously. I don't think even Gerry Adams knows who Gerry Adams is.'

Chapter 28

By the twentieth anniversary of the first ceasefire, Sinn Féin was in the political ascendant.

Adams had wanted his party, by then, to be closer than it was to creating a de facto unification in Ireland. He had hoped to have Sinn Féin governing in the North and in the Republic by another anniversary, the centenary of the Easter Rising of 1916.

That week-long battle against British forces had come to be thought of as the founding of the Irish state. That is acknowledged in the naming of barracks, railway stations and streets after the rebel leaders. It was reaffirmed in the character of the state-sponsored centenary memorial commemorations. Purist republicans see the Rising as more than the foundation of the state, they see it as unfinished business, the legitimation of their right to fight on for a united Ireland, beyond all the compromises agreed by Michael Collins in 1921 and by Gerry Adams in 1998.

That tradition had driven Gerry Adams and his brothers, but some of their contemporaries in the IRA had less regard for it. The IRA leader Martin McGuinness, as Deputy First Minister of Northern Ireland, said he had been motivated in his rebellion more by conditions in Derry than by the legacy of 1916. For Gerry Adams it was different; he was a republican activist before the Troubles started.

Had Adams been able to put Sinn Féin in government on both sides of the Irish border by 2016 he would have proven the success of his political project. He would have brought Ireland closer to meaningful unity than the militarists he had sidelined had ever had a chance of doing. He would also have had the opportunity to shape the commemoration of the Rising.

One of the discussion points in the Irish media at the time of the commemorations was the question of whether the campaign of the Provisional IRA had been as legitimate as the equally unmandated revolt in 1916 led by Patrick Pearse and James Connolly.

In the commemorations, modern Ireland was comfortably treating the 1916 Rising as brave and well warranted. It was struggling at times for a coherent way of explaining why the Provisionals had not had an equal right in 1970 to fight on to complete the project.

Pearse and Adams had responded to international developments they had not foreseen. Pearse's opportunity was created by global war; he sided with Germany.

Adams, pressing for the IRA to stand aside and allow him to progress politically, was aided by events abroad too.

The collapse of the Twin Towers in Manhattan in September 2001 had made it impossible for the IRA to force its point again in political deadlocks by trashing London skyscrapers, as it had often done in the late 1990s. Then the collapse of the market in sub-prime stocks, and the political expedient of putting the burden of banking debts on the poor through welfare cuts, opened huge opportunities for left-wing political parties across Europe.

Adams led Sinn Féin into a period of rapid growth in the Republic by attacking the austerity measures adopted by the Irish government to help clear its bailout debts to Europe. And even though he proved a cumbersome performer in debates about economics, he gathered talent round himself.

The party's ascent was slowed down by a number of factors.

One might have been that his support for Syriza, the Greek party that had presumed to stand up to Europe and was humbled, made him look dangerous to the Irish voter.

Another was the scandal around his management of Máiría Cahill and the widening story of sexual abuse in IRA safe houses.

Another was the apparent inconsistency between his argument against austerity in the Republic and the party's implementation of it in the North.

After the Sinn Féin Ard Fheis in Derry in 2015, Martin McGuinness returned to Belfast with instructions from Adams to say that he would not, after all, implement a deal agreed to manage welfare cuts imposed from London. That produced a political crisis.

Then guns returned briefly to the streets.

Jock Davison, an IRA man who had directed the killing of drug dealers in the 1990s and who had been implicated in the murder of Robert McCartney, was now a community worker on a salary. He walked from his home to his office in the morning.

After assassinations, the police would often issue a statement, or journalists would speculate, on whether it had the 'hallmarks' of a paramilitary or gangland attack. These 'hallmarks' are usually signs of planning. The IRA never sent individuals out to shoot someone but always had back-up teams, getaway cars, houses in which the killers might shower and change to get rid of forensic traces. The killer of Jock Davison simply walked up to him on the street and fired several shots into him and ran away. He might have had the cool demeanour of one who had killed before, but nothing suggested a team.

The killing of the chief suspect, Kevin McGuigan, weeks later was different.

Several people were involved. A team had staked out the area, watched his movements, even acquired a key to a security gate barring their way down an approach alley. The press speculation suggested that McGuigan had killed Davison and that the IRA had killed McGuigan in retaliation.

The police said members of the IRA had been involved. This did not necessarily mean that the IRA command had ordered it. Even so, Bobby Storey was arrested and questioned and released without charge.

This was politically damaging. Adams insisted that the IRA had 'gone away'. He avoided saying that it had disbanded or ceased to exist.

Storey, on his release, said that the IRA was now like a butterfly that had flown off.

A security report commissioned to inform a talks process through the political crisis that followed said that the IRA was still in existence and that members of the IRA believed that Sinn Féin was under the direction of the IRA army council. The report said, 'PIRA members believe that the PAC oversees both PIRA and Sinn Féin with an overarching strategy. We judge this strategy has a wholly political focus.'[1]

Another factor in the deceleration of Sinn Féin's growth may have been the character of the leader himself.

The party's achievement in the 2016 election to the Dáil, the parliament of the Republic, was outstanding by normal measures. The two larger parties, Fine Gael and Fianna Fáil, had failed to garner sufficient votes to govern or even to form a coalition without great difficulty. Neither would countenance a coalition with Sinn Féin, seeing it as tainted by its association with the IRA and worried that further scandals would emerge to damage Adams. And Sinn Féin said emphatically that it would not enter coalition with either of them. The past experience of junior coalition parties had been that they got swept up in the agenda of the senior partner and lost their distinctiveness and their support.

But Adams was being talked about now, ironically, as a liability to a party that was growing and garnering votes under his leadership.

A darker paradox presented itself with the question of who might follow him as leader and how the party then might fare. Sinn Féin was the party most committed to Irish unity but had secured its vote in the Republic through left-wing politics and in the North through its willingness to participate in a power-sharing executive and to make the pragmatic deals that would preserve it. Adams had sought to integrate the two wings of the party, by involving southern members in northern crisis talks, for instance, but the personnel and the priorities in Dublin and Belfast were different.

Only Adams himself really stood astride the border.

The irony is that when he goes, as some day he must, Sinn Féin may split and the border might run through the party. It would then become evidence itself of the organic reality of partition, the division it had committed itself to erasing.

Adams's vision of a country united, if not formally, at least by having Sinn Féin in power on both sides of the border, was in danger of being further divided by those separate wings of Sinn Féin seeking different agendas and requiring different leaders.

Now it was 2016, and the Easter Rising was commemorated in the Irish Republic as the foundation of the state. Ireland was not united, and the Republic seemed content to celebrate the anniversary of the Rising without fretting about the border.

Adams came into the republican movement around the time of the fiftieth anniversary of the Rising in 1966. A half-century of activism had followed. He had shown how he identified with Patrick Pearse, one of the leaders, by appropriating Pearse's poem to his mother, and reworking it for the memorial notice for his own.

He still insisted that the Proclamation of the Irish Republic remained a valid guide to how the nation should evolve, that is, as a thirty-two county republic in which the people owned the land.

He argued at his tribute to the 'patriot dead', which for him included the dead members of the Provisionals, that the execution of the leaders of the Rising had deprived Ireland of its most advanced and progressive thinkers and activists. A consequence of their loss was a counter-revolution that had conceded partition and led to the creation of 'two mean-spirited narrow-minded states'.

He said it might all have been so different.

'The people of the north were abandoned. The Free State was harsh on the poor, on women and on republicans or radicals of any kind. Our native language was devalued and subverted. Most, if not all of our renowned writers were banned. Censorship was rife. A false morality was imposed on our people. The scandals we witnessed recently emerged from this post-colonial condition.'

He blamed the great ills of both states on their inability to fuse into one state that he believed would have been more liberal and secular, having the 1916 Proclamation to guide it.

'It is a freedom charter for all the people of this island which guarantees religious and civil liberty and promotes equal rights and opportunities for all citizens. The Proclamation is also a declaration of social and economic intent for a rights-based society in which the people are sovereign.'

Chapter 29

Gregory Campbell is both intelligent and funny. He is a lean and edgy man with a Derry country accent. His chief instrument for making his point is his quirky humour. He used to set up a stall at Orange Order parades to sell trivia and memorabilia to marchers and their followers. These included Ulster flags, little caps with flag patterns on them. He had fun items like a baby's bib bearing the slogan 'Born to Walk the Garvaghy Road', a reference to a route from which Orange parades are banned.

It would be wrong to dismiss Campbell as a mere clown. He had been, for a time, a minister in the Northern Ireland Executive, and a good one, and he was in the top tier of leadership of the Democratic Unionist Party. He was frequently fielded by the party for panel debates on radio and television.

And Campbell's approach was always the same, to throw out remarks that were offensive, hurtful and often darkly funny and then to adamantly stand over them. He once described a republican politician as 'a failed hunger striker'.[1] He would use every occasion on which he was accused of being sectarian as an opportunity to rally a unionist argument that Protestants had also suffered discrimination, that the IRA was never legitimate, that Ulster was British and republicans would just have to learn to live with that.

He rattled Sinn Féin in the Stormont assembly by taunting them in November 2014 on their use of the Irish language.

Most Sinn Féin MLAs addressed the house almost exclusively in English but they would garnish their speeches with occasional Irish phrases, the most common being, *Go raibh maith agat*. Campbell parodied this with the vaguely phonetically similar phrase, 'Curry my yoghurt.' This was in a speech in which he criticised one of Gerry Adams's pet projects, a demand for an Irish Language Act. The St Andrews Agreement had provided for such an Act to give official recognition to Irish in Northern Ireland. Campbell enjoyed throwing the language back in the faces of the republicans.

But Adams had invested a lot of effort in trying to raise the status of the Irish language. When he first set out on his campaign against the British army, Irish was little spoken in Belfast. He used the English form of his name himself, as did all of the northern IRA leaders, unlike the southern ones, Ó Brádaigh, MacStíofáin and Ó Conaill.

But Irish had grown in importance since then for republicans. Many had learnt it in prison, coining a rougher dialect nicknamed Jailic. By the 1990s it was common to see Irish names on Falls Road bars and shop fronts. Even the local branch of the Bank of Ireland offered lodgement slips in Irish. A campaign to gaelicise street names had translated English names into Irish forms. And the Irish language became the visible expression of parts of Belfast being more Irish than British, though it was rare to hear it spoken and the market was not sufficiently strong to bear a single Irish-language newspaper.

Unionists see the Irish language as a badge of republicanism, despite the fact that their own forebears spoke a variant of it in Scotland.

In the nationalist community, even people who remembered little of what they learnt of Irish in school did not like to hear it parodied and insulted.

And perhaps the media and much of Northern Ireland thought this was no great problem. If old enemies were now fighting over the language rather than the territory, and merely mocking each other across the assembly chamber, this was what passed for progress in Northern Ireland.

Gerry Adams was confronted with a question about this deadlock and the acrimony in the assembly at a meeting in

Enniskillen in November 2014. What was the point in preserving a Northern Ireland Executive, in partnership with the DUP, if this was the way in which Sinn Féin concerns were dealt with?

Adams said, 'The point is to actually break these bastards – that's the point. And what's going to break them is equality. That's what's going to break them – equality. Who could be afraid of equality? Who could be afraid of treating somebody the way you want to be treated? That's what we need to keep the focus on – that's the Trojan horse of the entire republican strategy is to reach out to people on the basis of equality.'[2]

Adams was repeating an analysis he had made many times, that actual reform of Northern Ireland would not work, but the attempt would reveal the untenability of partition and the union between Britain and a separate Northern Irish state.

Unionists were annoyed.

They didn't consider the idea that he might have been trying harder to reassure his followers than to rattle them. They saw this as the tactless disclosure of a secret strategy. And perhaps that was what it was. On the other hand, maybe Adams was trying to convince republican doubters that some progress was still achievable in Stormont.

Some unionists argued that this proved that Sinn Féin was not committed to partnership but had a secret plan, through the equality agenda, to undermine them and advance the project of creating a united Ireland.

However, it appeared that Northern Ireland was working and that Sinn Féin Deputy First Minister Martin McGuinness wanted it to work, not to treat it as an experiment that would ultimately expose the unionists as the real obstacle to peace.

McGuinness had had an extraordinary career from being an IRA activist, a renowned dogmatic militarist, to being a reconciler. He succeeded more than Adams in persuading unionists of his good intentions.

Adams had tried but remained more caustically disliked. Once in a meeting with Protestant clergy, he had handed round sweets, like Love Hearts but with biblical references on them. But years on, he had not secured the indulgence of any significant unionists or Protestant church leaders, while McGuinness seemed almost, at times, forgiven.

McGuinness had formed a friendship with the Revd Ian Paisley, when he was made First Minister in 2007. The two men, who had been expected to hate each other, had come to be nicknamed the Chuckle Brothers because they so obviously enjoyed being together and shared a sense of humour. This was an embarrassment to the DUP, which ousted Paisley and replaced him with the colder Peter Robinson. If it had been equally embarrassing in republicanism, there was no public expression of that and no move was made against McGuinness.

McGuinness then worked with Robinson, and even met and shook hands with the Queen to demonstrate his willingness to end the old sectarian animosities. And the Queen had gone to Dublin and visited the graves of the republican rebels who had led the Easter Rising of 1916.

Then in 2015, a new First Minister was appointed to partner McGuinness. This was Arlene Foster.

Foster had made plain what she thought of Gerry Adams's 'Trojan horse' theory, that a push for equality between unionists and nationalists would ultimately 'break these bastards'. Adams's remarks had been made in her constituency and she had reacted angrily, saying his 'foul-mouthed abuse had been disrespectful to an entire community'.[3] She said, 'The hyperbole from republicans over recent days has been exposed as hypocrisy.'

She fully agreed with the view that the Irish language was a political instrument. 'Republicans use the Irish language as a weapon and tonight Gerry Adams confirms that they view equality as another weapon to attack unionists.'

Arlene Foster was married to a policeman and knew that the police assessment of Adams and McGuinness, going back to before she was born, was that they were dangerous terrorists.

McGuinness had already acknowledged that he was in the IRA in the early 1970s; Adams always denied that he was a member. Foster gave no credence to those denials. Her understanding of her position was that she was now sharing a political office with a former military commander of an organisation which had bombed her school bus, attempted to kill her father and bombed the war memorial in her home town, Enniskillen, in 1987, killing eleven people. A strong part of her appeal to her unionist base was that she had no illusions about Sinn Féin.

But this augured ill for relations between Foster and McGuinness. Her line was that she could work with him but was under no onus to like him. The problem was that such an attitude would not carry her through a crisis.

The crisis that fatally undermined their relationship was pure farce.

As Minister for Enterprise, Trade and Investment, Foster had introduced a scheme to subsidise the burning of wood pellets for heating. This was funded in part by the British Treasury for the purpose of encouraging the use of renewable fuels. But Foster's plan provided no cap on expenditure and overran the budget. This happened, at least in part, because her department had removed the caps on expenditure that were in the British version of the scheme. Under her scheme, people could profit by burning more fuel, because the subsidy was higher than the cost. The media nicknamed the scheme 'cash for ash' and 'burn to earn'.

Sinn Féin knew about this mess for months before a public outcry turned it into a threat to political stability, and did little but complain about it in committee meetings.

Then Adams returned to Belfast from Dublin to lead the party response. Sinn Féin initially chose to abstain from a no-confidence vote in Foster in December 2016, but this was seen by many followers as humiliating; the party should not be trying to save a First Minister who had botched up so badly and who, incidentally, was routinely contemptuous of Sinn Féin.

At this time, Gerry Adams was having difficulties of his own in Dublin where he was a member of the Dáil. This trouble followed on his efforts to help Austin Stack meet a senior IRA man to hear an admission that the IRA had murdered Austin's father, Brian, a prison officer. It emerged that Adams had written to the Garda Commissioner, the chief of police, before the 2016 Dáil election, and given her the names of four people who might have information about the killing of Brian Stack. Adams said that he had only been passing on names he had heard from Austin Stack, that he had not been divulging insights of his own. He insisted he had no actual information himself on the men named. It was an odd thing for Adams to do and exposed him to the charge that he was effectively informing on members of the IRA. This, in another time and from another republican, would have attracted a death sentence.

But Adams had been under pressure to demonstrate his commitment to legal procedures, especially after Máiría Cahill had accused the IRA of covering up her rape. He had also found himself pilloried in the media after describing Thomas 'Slab' Murphy, a tax dodger, as a 'good republican'. In 1998, Murphy had lost a libel action against the *Sunday Times* after the paper described him as a member of the IRA army council.[4]

Stack denied that he had given any names to Adams, though Adams stood by his account. Two charges against Adams came swiftly from the Dublin media and the rival political parties, Fianna Fáil and Fine Gael. The first was that he was lying when he said he had heard the names from Stack. Stack had in fact mentioned two of the names to the media before his first meeting with Adams and he had discussed those names with Adams during his meeting. Adams had asked him not to mention the names again. So this accusation was not as uncomplicated as it seemed.

The other charge, more serious, was that Adams was

withholding the name of the senior IRA man he had brought Austin Stack and his brother to meet. Adams defended that refusal as being consistent with the confidentialities expected of him during the peace process. He was mocked in the media for this. Miriam Lord in the *Irish Times* wrote, 'Gerry wanted to have it both ways – to look good in public by professing to do one thing while not doing it at all.'[5] An *Irish Times* editorial said, 'Adams has brought this latest crisis of credibility upon himself. It stems like the others that have dogged his career since Sinn Féin embraced parliamentary politics – from his one-time IRA membership . . .'[6]

Clearly the media had long moved beyond fearing that there were legal risks entailed in accusing Adams of having been a member of the IRA despite his denials. The *Irish Times* said that Adams's crisis of credibility '. . . arises from his personal decision, unlike party colleagues, not to fudge but to explicitly deny crucial parts of his history. They have caught up with him, as they inevitably would.'

While vilified in the South as a politician who was not fully committed to keeping the law of the land, Adams, by confronting Arlene Foster, was able to present himself in the North as a party leader and custodian of the peace process, making a stand for probity in government. He was needed in Belfast for another reason. Martin McGuinness was dying.

McGuinness's approach to Foster was initially conciliatory. He declined to back demands for a public inquiry into the ludicrously overfunded heating scheme. He refused to support the no-confidence vote in her. He pitched his demands as avuncular advice. She should stand aside to allow for a transparent investigation and resume office after the preliminary report.

There had been two precedents for such standing aside. The previous First Minister, Peter Robinson, had done so to allow an investigation into his financial dealings. Martin McGuinness had stood aside to contest the Irish presidency in 2012.

Foster seemed incapable of seeing any merit in a suggestion

coming from Sinn Féin and dug in. This was a mistake. The tension between the parties increased as the health of McGuinness declined and the role of Gerry Adams grew.

Addressing a rally in the Felons Club in west Belfast one Saturday afternoon in January 2017, Adams told his followers that if the DUP did not do what was required, Sinn Féin would pull down the Stormont institutions.

Two days later, on 9 January, a shrunken Martin McGuinness announced his resignation, crucially declaring that the problem now was much bigger than the heating scheme but covered a whole range of issues on which the DUP had resisted Sinn Féin, including the Irish Language Act.

'There will be no return to the status quo,' he said.

The Trojan horse was inside the gates. The clear demand of Sinn Féin now was that the DUP recognise Sinn Féin as an equal partner or it would have no partner at all.

The roles of First Minister and Deputy First Minister were linked. By resigning and announcing that the party would not nominate a replacement, McGuinness had effectively sacked Foster.

He and Gerry Adams appointed the Health Minister Michelle O'Neill to replace him, to lead Sinn Féin in the assembly executive, in the event of the party agreeing to restore it after an election.

That election result would stun unionism by bringing nationalism in the Assembly almost level with it. Most observers thought this could not happen for another decade or more.

Adams was back in the kind of politics he revelled in, not the tricky day-to-day management of routine problems but the big-picture critical negotiations around the very constitutional framework of Northern Ireland. He would have a wider range of issues in play than the Irish Language Act he sought, for Britain had pledged to leave the European Union, and the status and character of the Irish border would again be in question.

And this time, twenty-eight governments would have a say.

Chapter 30

Gerry Adams is one of the most successful politicians in the democratic world.

When he took over the presidency of Sinn Féin, Neil Kinnock had just been elected leader of the British Labour Party. Ronald Reagan was President of the United States. The Soviet Union appeared impregnable and inflexible under Yuri Andropov. The Ayatollah Khomeini was ruling Iran. Margaret Thatcher was enjoying a boost to her popularity following the war to retrieve the Falkland Islands from Argentine forces. He has looked David Cameron and Tony Blair in the eye with the knowledge that he knew their predecessors better than they did.

The first British government that he entered negotiations with was led by Edward Heath in 1972. He communicated with the officials of Margaret Thatcher in 1981 to try to woo her into talks. He negotiated also with John Major, Tony Blair, Gordon Brown and David Cameron.

Heads of government in three jurisdictions think that Gerry Adams is in no position to call them out on failings of integrity or judgement. Sometimes they and the media speak of him as politically naive and inept, but he goes home after such meetings to open a bottle of red wine and sit contented that he has wrestled with bigger and better politicians than those of this generation and outlasted them all.

He lives with the fact that the police in Northern Ireland still aspire to charging him, having come close to it, and the danger that the stories told about him in the Boston College Archives will spill out in a future trial or inquest.

Adams denies that he was ever a member of the Provisional IRA, the movement that sought to break the constitutional link between Britain and Northern Ireland through what he called 'armed struggle', that is, by bombing the commercial infrastructure of several British cities and by killing soldiers and police officers, by running vigilantes on housing estates and kneecapping young hoodlums.

His denial is accepted by those closest to him, formally at least. It is rejected by the intelligence services of Britain and Ireland, which have briefed that he was the top man. The strongest indication of his decisive influence over the IRA is that he led the republican movement into making peace with Britain and surrendering its armed campaign in return for prisoner releases, thereby creating political opportunities for Sinn Féin.

It is routinely said in the media and in political speeches that Gerry Adams was a leader of the IRA. He denies this and frequently impugns the sources of this claim. He is named as an IRA leader in several books, both by journalists and by academics, including J. Bowyer Bell, M. S. Smith, Peter Taylor and Ed Moloney, and he has never challenged any of these and other writers to bring evidence to court and defend an action for defamation.

Yet the sources are chiefly the security services and some of those republicans who have fallen out with him, like Dolours Price and Brendan Hughes and others, people who committed themselves to the IRA campaign and felt that they were betrayed when the centre of gravity in the republican movement shifted to the political wing, Sinn Féin.

It is worth, then, attempting to address through other sources the question of whether Adams was an IRA leader, setting aside those disaffected republicans and the security services, however much their statements are accepted and endorsed by other writers. Adams can always expect derision and accusations from such sources.

On the side of the argument that Adams was an IRA member are several statements in the public domain.

There is the story about Liam McParland, regarded as one of the first members of the Provisional IRA, who died before the split. He was killed in a car crash on the M1 into Belfast in 1969. The IRA's own record of its dead includes him and says he was 'on active service'.

Gerry Adams, by his own account in his books and blogs, was in the car with him. The fact that he was accompanying an IRA man on active service suggests that he was himself party to whatever operation he was engaged in, unless he had been deceived by McParland, but he has written several times about the accident and his admiration for the man, yet without explaining how he came to be accompanying an IRA man on active service.

In 1970, when feuding occurred between the separate wings of the IRA, Gerry Adams helped negotiate a truce with the Official IRA.[1] He also led negotiations with the Officials on several later occasions,[2] eventually succeeding in bringing all hostilities between the groups to an end in 1977.

Further evidence is that he was released from internment to meet British diplomats to negotiate the terms of the 1972 IRA ceasefire. One of those diplomats, in his report to the Secretary of State, William Whitelaw, described Adams and his colleague Dáithí Ó Conaill as 'prominent leaders' of the IRA campaign.

While it may be plausible that British sources would seek to taint Adams because they disagreed with his politics and his moral endorsement of the IRA, it seems unlikely that they would do so in secret correspondence.

Gerry Adams was a member of the IRA delegation that met William Whitelaw. If he was not an actual member of the IRA at that time, then he was the only member of that delegation, aside from the lawyer, who was not a member.

While he was in prison, sentenced for attempting to escape from internment, Adams was appointed Officer Commanding

Cage 11 in Long Kesh. There he had authority over several men who are acknowledged members of the IRA, including Bobby Sands and Danny Lennon. He could give them orders, discipline them. However, Lord Chief Justice Lowry later ruled that his having been seen there receiving a salute was not sufficient evidence to warrant him even being tried on a charge of IRA membership.

RUC Special Branch clearly thought he was a member of the IRA. That is clear from internal communications cited in the De Silva Report and in the diaries of Ian Phoenix.

During the hunger strikes of 1980–81, Adams was the contact person for the strikers and their leaders. All of them were members of the IRA, or the INLA, and all of those in the IRA deferred to him, which seems unlikely if he had not held office in the IRA himself.

In his book *Great Hatred, Little Room*, Tony Blair's envoy Jonathan Powell describes how he told Gerry Adams and Martin McGuinness that he frankly did not believe their claims not to be members of the IRA. Since then, McGuinness has died. His headstone honours him now as *oglach* – a soldier – Volunteer McGuinness. Then there is Adams's own reference to himself as one of the 'generals' who alone can make peace, in a television documentary based on his trip to Jerusalem.

The case in support of his denial that he was in the IRA includes that denial itself. There is also the plausibility of the claim that British and Irish security services who named him as a member of the IRA army council might have had secret motives for doing so.

And there is the strange remark of President Clinton in exchanges with Tony Blair that part of the problem was not knowing 'what the real deal is between [Gerry Adams] and the IRA', suggesting that he did not know whether Adams was or was not in the IRA.

George W. Bush also wondered about the Sinn Féin leader,

and asked Taoiseach Bertie Ahern on St Patrick's Day 2001, 'How about this guy Adams, my guy said he's a murdering thief.'[3]

More than three and a half thousand people died in thirty years of armed conflict in Northern Ireland. More of them were killed by the IRA than by any other organisation, an army that sought to make governing the region untenable for Britain. That army grew out of the Catholic population that saw itself as more Irish than British.

Defenders of the IRA argue that the war in Northern Ireland was a dirty war in which no one has clean hands, that there is no moral high ground from which anyone with integrity, and above all suspicion, can point the finger at Gerry Adams. Some see him as a demon and some see him as divine. He makes a point of reminding his followers, though they don't get it, that he is not personally important.

Father Alec Reid, his emissary to the Irish government at the start of the peace process, said, 'I would see Gerry Adams as a man sent by God. In other words, he was part of God's providence for peace in Ireland.'

Several people have remarked that Adams is like two different people.

One is the family man. This one is excited by the connections with his cousins in Canada. He has visited and partied into the night with them and invited them back to his Donegal home near Gortahork.

Another is the withdrawn thinker who climbs Mount Errigal with his dog, who wants to be alone.

One annual family duty now is to attend the Spring Bank Holiday hurling match established to honour Liam and Michael McCorry, the teenage nephews who died in a car crash in 1999. This brings together the Provo and Sticky wings of the family. That war at least is over and survives now only as a friendly sporting fixture.

He keeps fit and contends in the Poc Fada every year, a

challenge to belt a hurling ball, a sliotar, further than anyone else, and often he wins it. Cousin Frank now comes over from Canada occasionally to take part.

Adams seems both gregarious and withdrawn.

The novelist Edna O'Brien contrasted him with Michael Collins, the IRA leader of the war of independence who similarly settled terms on a compromise and on the prospect of his goals being achieved later by peaceful means.

Whereas Collins was outgoing and swashbuckling, Gerry Adams is thoughtful and reserved, a lithe, handsome man with a native formality that seems to confirm his remark that he has to be two people, a public and a private one. Given a different incarnation in a different century, one could imagine him as one of those monks transcribing the gospels into Gaelic.[4]

The withdrawn Adams is contemplating his political ambitions that are not yet fulfilled. There is one post that suits a man who sees himself as the embodiment of Irish destiny, who enjoys homage and the company of heads of states, and that is the Irish presidency, which becomes available again in 2018 when he will be seventy.

There are huge political hurdles to get over before that.

Having shifted his political focus to building the party in the Republic, he risks splitting it in two when he leaves. Without him the party is partitioned into a northern movement centred on Stormont and a southern one centred on the Dáil and the grasp for the presidency. Were he to stand down, Sinn Féin would ironically divide along the border that it fought to remove.

He has settled some of the anxiety about his IRA past, simply by conceding nothing to the claims made about him. The most appalling charge against him, that he ordered the disappearing of bodies, is at least partly undone by his help in having most of the bodies recovered.

Ironically, his arrest in May 2014, on suspicion of being or having been a member of the IRA, may have eased the pressure on him to explain his past to the media, for it made clear that self-incrimination could land him in jail. The arrest established that he has no immunity.

Much less of the blame for the IRA's crimes goes to Martin McGuinness, though McGuinness was, if anything, more of a militarist than Adams through the 1980s and 1990s. McGuinness only admitted to having been a member of the IRA for a short time in the early 1970s. He told the Saville Inquiry into Bloody Sunday that he had been second in command in Derry when British paratroopers opened fire on Civil Rights protesters, killing fourteen of them. Saville said McGuinness may have been armed with a Thompson submachine gun that day, though coining the observation so uncertainly that McGuinness could easily rebut it.

Both men and others who led the IRA use the same rhetorical devices to bat back any claims that they are answerable for death and destruction. They say that there was a war on, there was wrong done on all sides; they draw attention to the fact that they brought peace; and they deny any specific knowledge or direct connection to any event, whether the disappearing of Jean McConville, the bombing of Belfast on Bloody Friday or, though this is less often put to them, the lax security that allowed the movement to be infiltrated by informers.

Adams leads republicans in denial of the charge that the IRA was a prime initiator of the Troubles. Good people were caught up in tumultuous events and were left with no choice but to respond as they did.

The army of social media defenders of Adams, which emerged to discredit and tackle Máiría Cahill, acted as if trained, with the same devices and arguments, imputing political motivation to others even when they were the only ones actually serving the interests of a political party.

The litany of predictable media questions have their stock responses.

Did Sinn Féin cover up child abuse?

What about state-sponsored child abuse? Why do you direct more criticism at Sinn Féin than at the state? You must be biased.

Have you no compassion for a raped woman?

Yes, but you are using her for political ends, and she is not above being political herself.

Addressing party members in Belfast, Adams spoke more as if he was feeding them the approved line of argument rather than addressing possible doubts they might have had about his treatment of Máiría Cahill.

'While I am very mindful of the trauma she has suffered, I and the others she has named reject these allegations,' he said. 'These allegations have been seized upon in the most cynical, calculated and opportunistic way by our political opponents. Their aim has little to do with helping victims of abuse, but everything to do with furthering their own narrow political agendas.'

And the party held its nerve, even as Máiría Cahill's rape and the IRA investigation were debated in the Dáil and at Stormont. Adams had had the option of accepting her claim that the IRA had interrogated her and of disavowing responsibility for that. After all, he was denying still that he had ever been a member of the IRA. But, responding as he did, he instead implicated the wider party in the protection of the IRA.

Gerry Adams cannot move around Ireland without meeting people who despise him. He is good at coping with them. Mick Donnelly confronted him at a funeral in Belfast and Adams said he couldn't quite remember who he was.

Gerry Brannigan and Tommy Gorman have met him on Black Mountain on morning walks and he has always had a smile and a kind word for them.

Richard O'Rawe met him coming out of the courthouse with a group of supporters and immediately feared that he was about to be berated for having accused him of betraying the hopes of the hunger strikers. 'Risteárd, a chara,' said Gerry Adams, extending a hand.

Anthony McIntyre met him outside the Dáil when he was in conversation with a TD. 'Hello, Mackers.' And he was gone before McIntyre composed himself to snarl.

He has blanked Máiría Cahill, she says.

Gerard Hodgins says that he thinks he is now impervious to the Adams charm, that he has seen through him and would not be manipulated again. Others pour out their contempt on social media and Adams ignores them. Many, when they try to engage him on his Twitter feed, are blocked.

Adams occasionally retorts against a critic. When *Irish Times* columnist Fintan O'Toole reviewed the several obvious occasions on which Adams had been deceitful or contradicted himself, the Big Lad's reply was brief and sharp.

A chara, – I see from his column that Fintan O'Toole is now an expert on me. This on top of his other accomplishments.
– Is mise,
GERRY ADAMS, TD

This is not an answer but a jibe, not just against O'Toole's effort to nail Adams. He is saying, if you sneer at me I will sneer at you, and warning that he might be better at the game.

And he is saying, it took you a thousand words to smother me with blame but I have knifed you with two sentences. I don't have to explain myself to the likes of you. What other politician would get away with such cheek? In Ireland it makes him look clever, and he knows it.

Gerry Adams can take a verbal hammering from anyone and come back assertively. There are few people in public life anywhere who have braved so much abuse and criticism and survived as long. He conducts his life in parliament and out and about the towns and villages of Ireland in the knowledge that people have strong feelings about him and with the air of someone who can indulge their failure to appreciate him. Some regard him as a wheedling hypocrite, even a murderer, and others see him as a heroic self-sacrificing peacemaker and a champion of the poor. Few in Ireland can be indifferent to him.

His sense of self-esteem does not rely on political rivals. It relies on his achievements and his fame, and perhaps on more, an indefinable, inexplicable robustness of the ego. You can call Gerry Adams a murderer to his face and he will not be surprised and he will not crumble, not if the charge is coming from the toughest broadcast journalist or from the Taoiseach himself.

Sometimes he will seem to wilt a little, or stammer, as he did as a child. Sometimes he will snap in anger, but it is the anger of impatience with those who are distracting him with trivia, that's all. You will never see a flicker of self-doubt cross that face. How are we to explain the confident imperviousness of Gerry Adams?

Part of it relies on the fact that the worst things have already been said about him and he has survived. We can say that he was a leader of a murderous organisation, that he was party to the decisions to kill hundreds of people. But we knew that. There would have been no peace process if the two governments and the American President had not taken that all for granted and still trusted that this man, the Big Lad, was the one who could deliver a deal.

He broke all the political rules and most effectively the rule that says terrorists have nothing to offer and have no place in our political systems. From his own perspective, he is a good man who had no choice but to support the IRA. But he brought the armed campaign to an end and it wasn't easy and he believes he deserves some credit for that.

Notes

Many of the quotes in this book are from interviews with the author. The main sources for Adams's own anecdotes quoted here are his own publications, listed in the Bibliography.

Introduction

1 Dominic Adams, *Faoi Ghlas* (lulu.com, 2016), p. 4.
2 Gerry Adams, *A Farther Shore: Ireland's Long Road to Peace* (New York, 2003), p. 112.
3 David Sharrock and Mark Devenport, *Man of War, Man of Peace? The Unauthorised Biography of Gerry Adams* (London, 1997), p. 18.

Chapter 1

1 Gerry Adams, *Before the Dawn: An Autobiography* (London, 1996), p. xx.

Chapter 2

1 Sir John Hermon, *Holding the Line: An Autobiography* (Dublin, 1997).
2 Hermon, p. 58.
3 Adams, *Before the Dawn*, p. 51.
4 Gerry Adams, *Falls Memories* (Dingle, 1982), p. 133.
5 Brian Hanley and Scott Millar, *The Lost Revolution: The Story of the Official IRA and the Workers' Party* (London, 2009), p. 54.

Chapter 3

1 *Belfast Telegraph*, 4 October 1968.
2 Gerry Adams, *The Politics of Irish Freedom* (Dingle, 1986), p. 33.
3 Adams, *Before the Dawn*, p. 104.
4 Patrick Bishop and Eamonn Mallie, *The Provisional IRA* (London, 1987), pp. 110, 111.
5 Bishop and Mallie (1992 edn), p. 111.
6 Adams, *Before the Dawn*, p. 109.

Chapter 4

1 Adams, *Before the Dawn*, p. 128.

2 leargas.blogspot.co.uk, 16 November 2009.
3 Adams, *Before the Dawn*, p. 128.
4 Gerry Adams, *The Street and Other Stories* (Dingle, 1992) p. 45.
5 Hanley and Millar, p. 139.

Chapter 5

1 Adams, *Before the Dawn*, p. 135.
2 Adams, *Before the Dawn*, p. 136.
3 Adams, *Before the Dawn*, p. xx.
4 Hanley and Millar, p. 156.

Chapter 6

1 Ciaran de Baroid, *Ballymurphy and the Irish War* (London, 1989), p. 56.
2 Hanley and Millar, p. 162.
3 http://indiamond6.ulib.iupui.edu:81/charliehughes.html.
4 Paddy Devlin, *Straight Left: An Autobiography* (Belfast, 1993), p. 152.
5 Adams, *Before the Dawn*, p. 149.
6 Adams, *Before the Dawn*, p. 149.
7 Adams, *Before the Dawn*, p. 256.
8 Adams, *Before the Dawn*, p. 138.
9 De Baroid, p. 56.
10 Adams, *Before the Dawn*, p. 172.
11 Adams, *Before the Dawn*, p. 166.
12 John D. Cash, *Identity, Ideology and Conflict: The Structuration of Politics in Northern Ireland* (Cambridge, 1996), p. 158.
13 Adams, *Before the Dawn*, p. 172.
14 Adams, *Before the Dawn*, p. 188.

Chapter 7

1 Adams, *Before the Dawn*, p. 183.
2 Adams, *Before the Dawn*, p. 195.
3 *Rebel: The Story of Gerry Adams*, PressTV Documentaries (2013).
4 Devlin, p. 176.
5 Woodfield's report of the meeting to William Whitelaw, Secretary of State for Northern Ireland, is accessible through the CAIN website, cain.ulst. ac.uk. Document reference: PREM 15/1009 Top Secret Note of a Meeting With Representatives of the Provisional IRA.
6 Adams, *Before the Dawn*, p. 203.
7 Richard O'Rawe, *Blanketmen: An Untold Story of the H-Block Hunger Strike* (Dublin, 2005), p. 89.
8 Adams, *Before the Dawn*, p. 202.
9 Adams, *Before the Dawn*, p. 203.
10 Bishop and Mallie (1987), p. 227.
11 Adams, *Before the Dawn*, p. 206.

12 Interview with former IRA member Tommy Gorman.
13 Adams, *Before the Dawn*, p. 207.

Chapter 8

1   Adams, *Before the Dawn*, p. 210.
2   Ed Moloney, *Voices from the Grave: Two Men's War in Ireland* (London, 2011), p. 105.
3   https://thebrokenelbow.com/2015/06/17/the-tuzo-plan-1972-extirpate-the-ira-and-turn-a-blind-eye-to-uda-guns/ Sir Harry Tuzo's 9 July report is in the National Archives at Kew.
4   Adams, *Before the Dawn*, p. 212.
5   Ed Moloney, *A Secret History of the IRA* (London, 2003), p. 122.
6   Moloney, *Voices from the Grave*, p. 129.
7   *Irish News*, 12 February 2010.
8   *Guardian*, 21 December 2002.
9   Malachi O'Doherty, *The Telling Year* (Dublin, 2008), p. 146.
10 Tommy McKearney, *The Provisional IRA: From Insurrection to Parliament* (London, 2011), p. 105.
11 Maria McGuire, *To Take Arms: A Year in the Provisional IRA* (London, 1973), p. 75.
12 *Tirghrá* (Dublin, 2002), pp. 63–115.
13 Malcom Sutton, *Bear in Mind These Dead: An Index of Deaths from the Conflict in Ireland, 1969–1993* (Belfast, 1994).

Chapter 9

1   Hughes's account is in Moloney, *Voices from the Grave*, p. 152.
2   Adams's account is in *Before the Dawn*, p. 218.
3   Colm Keena, *Gerry Adams, A Biography* (Dublin, 1990), p. 57.
4   Moloney, *A Secret History of the IRA*, p. 134.
5   Adams, *Before the Dawn*, p. 183.
6   Sharrock and Devenport, p. 126.
7   Adams, *Before the Dawn*, p. 243.
8   Adams, *Before the Dawn*, p. 231.
9   Gerry Adams, *An Irish Eye* (Dingle, 2007).
10 William 'Plum' Smith, *Inside Man: Loyalists of Long Kesh – the Untold Story* (Newtownards, 2014), p. 95.
11 Gerry Adams, *Cage Eleven* (Dingle, 1990), p. 39.
12 Smith, p. 99.
13 Smith, p. 95.

Chapter 10

1   Adams, *Before the Dawn*, p. 243.
2   Hughes's account of this episode can be found in *Voices from the Grave*, pp. 187–92.

3 O'Rawe, *Blanketmen*, p. 71.

Chapter 11

1 Bill Rolston, *Children of the Revolution: The Lives of Sons and Daughters of Activists in Northern Ireland* (Derry, 2011), p. 122.
2 Rolston, p. 97.
3 Adams, *Before the Dawn*, p. 252.
4 Rolston, p. 122.
5 https://thebrokenelbow.com/2015/07/04/the-bryson-incident-a-misbelief-corrected-an-insight-into-early-ira-cells/.
6 Cited by Ed Moloney on *The Pensive Quill* website, 8 July 2015.
7 J. Bowyer Bell, *The Irish Troubles: A Generation of Violence 1967–1992* (Dublin, 1993), p. 538.

Chapter 12

1 David McKittrick et al., *Lost Lives: The Stories of the Men, Women and Children Who Died as a Result of the Northern Ireland Troubles* (Edinburgh, 1998), p. 746.
2 Adams, *Before the Dawn*, p. 265.
3 Adams, *Before the Dawn*, p. 268.
4 O'Rawe, *Blanketmen*, p. 25.
5 Dominic Adams, pp. 21–2.
6 Adams, *Before the Dawn*, p. 271.

Chapter 13

1 Adams, *Before the Dawn*, p. 281.
2 O'Rawe, *Blanketmen*, p. 32.
3 Liam Clarke, *Broadening the Battlefield: The H-Blocks and the Rise of Sinn Féin* (Dublin, 1987).
4 O'Rawe, *Blanketmen*, p. 107.
5 Bik McFarlane, June 2011, YouTube: sinnfeinlondon.

Chapter 14

1 Richard O'Rawe, *Afterlives: The Hunger Strike and the Secret Offer That Changed Irish History* (Dublin, 2010).
2 Thomas Hennessey, *Hunger Strike: Margaret Thatcher's Battle with the IRA: 1980–1981* (Sallins, 2014), p. 326.
3 Garret FitzGerald, *All in a Life* (Dublin, 1991), p. 370.
4 Hennessey, p. 312.
5 2011, YouTube: sinnfeinlondon.
6 David Beresford, *Ten Men Dead: The Story of the Irish Hunger Strike* (London, 1987), p. 297.
7 Hennessey, p. 329.
8 Beresford, p. 311.

9 Adams, *Before the Dawn*, p. 301.
10 O'Rawe, *Afterlives*, p. 199.
11 Beresford, p. 329.
12 Quoted in Beresford, p. 30.
13 *An Phoblacht*, 7 February 2002.
14 *Behind the Mask*, dir. Frank Martin, 1991.
15 Beresford, p. 162.
16 Beresford, p. 333.
17 Rogelio Alonso, *The IRA and Armed Struggle* (London, 2007).
18 Beresford, p. 337.
19 O'Rawe, *Afterlives*, p. 177.
20 Alonso, p. 114.
21 Beresford, pp. 336, 337.
22 Adams, *Politics of Irish Freedom*, p. 79.
23 Beresford, p. 216.
24 Adams, *Before the Dawn*, p. 306.
25 O'Rawe, *Afterlives*, p. 139.
26 Adams, *Before the Dawn*, p. 314.
27 Charles Moore, *Margaret Thatcher: The Authorised Biography* (London, 2013), p. 611.
28 *Daily Ireland*, 9 March 2005.

Chapter 15

1 Eamon Collins, *Killing Rage* (London, 1998).
2 Collins, p. 220.
3 Malachi O'Doherty, *The Trouble With Guns: Republican Strategy and the Provisional IRA* (Belfast, 1998), p. 145.

Chapter 16

1 Adams, *A Farther Shore*, p. 24.
2 Sharrock and Devenport, p. 221.
3 Adams, *A Farther Shore*, p. 24.
4 Sharrock and Devenport, p. 224.
5 Mark Urban, *Big Boys' Rules: The SAS and the Secret Struggle Against the IRA* (London, 1992), p. 181.
6 https://policeombudsman.org/getattachment/Investigation-Reports/Historical-Reports/%E2%80%98No-evidence-of-police-involvement-in-the-attempte/Public-Statement-The-Attempted-Murder-of-Gerry-Adams-on-14-March-1984.pdf.
7 Urban, p. 236.
8 Dominic Adams, p. 12.
9 Jack Holland and Susan Phoenix, *Phoenix: Policing the Shadows: The Secret War Against Terrorism in Northern Ireland* (London, 1996), p. 123.

Chapter 17

1 Adams, *Politics of Irish Freedom*, cited by Steve McDonagh in the introduction.
2 Adams, *Politics of Irish Freedom*, p. 15.
3 Collins, p. 238.
4 Bishop and Mallie (1992), p. 447.

Chapter 18

1 Adams, *Politics of Irish Freedom*, p. 112.
2 Bishop and Mallie (1987), p. 447.
3 Bishop and Mallie (1988), p. 449.
4 Holland and Phoenix, p. 303.

Chapter 19

1 The Rt Hon. Sir Desmond de Silva QC, The Report of the Patrick Finucane Review, December 2012, https://www.gov.uk/government/publications/the-report-of-the-patrick-finucane-review.
2 De Silva, p. 350, $19.51.
3 Danny Morrison, *Then the Walls Came Down: A Prison Journal* (Cork, 1999), p. 288.

Chapter 20

1 Adams, *Politics of Irish Freedom*, p. 64.

Chapter 21

1 Moloney, *A Secret History of the IRA*, p. 8.
2 Moloney, *A Secret History of the IRA*, p. 441.

Chapter 22

1 Anthony McIntyre, *Good Friday: The Death of Irish Republicanism* (New York, 2008), pp. 253–255.
2 Jonathan Powell, *Great Hatred, Little Room: Making Peace in Northern Ireland* (London, 2009), p. 264.
3 *Independent.ie*, 5 February 2017, http://www.independent.ie/irish-news/politics/bertie-ahern-reveals-george-bush-called-gerry-adams-a-murdering-thief-35424758.html.
4 Powell, p. 264.
5 Powell, p. 267.
6 *Guardian*, 27 June 2008, https://www.theguardian.com/uk/2008/jun/27/ukcrime.northernireland1.
7 Powell, p. 267.

Chapter 23

1 *The Late Late Show*, uploaded to YouTube 4 September 2010.
2 Adams, *A Farther Shore*, p. 35.
3 Adams, *A Farther Shore*, p. 27.

Chapter 24

1 Adams, *Before the Dawn*, p. 30.

Chapter 26

1 O'Doherty, *Trouble With Guns*, p. 1.

Chapter 27

1 leargas.blogspot.co.uk, 19 October 2014.
2 Interview with author.
3 lcargas.blogspot.co.uk, 19 October 2014.
4 belfast-child.blogspot.co.uk, 20 October 2014.

Chapter 28

1 Assessment on Paramilitary Groups in Northern Ireland (Northern Ireland Office and Theresa Villiers MP), 20 October 2015.

Chapter 29

1 *Derry Now*, 9 May 2016, https://www.derrynow.com/news/campbell-refuses-to-withdraw-disgusting-and-vile-hunger-striker-remarks/90931.
2 *Irish Times*, 26 November 2014, http://www.irishtimes.com/news/ireland/irish-news/gerry-adams-issues-qualified-apology-for-his-bastards-remark-1.2014987.
3 *RTE*, 25 November 2014, https://www.rte.ie/news/2014/1125/662258-gerry-adams/.
4 *Guardian*, 8 October 2015, https://www.theguardian.com/uk-news/2015/oct/08/thomas-slab-murphy-former-ira-commander-accused-tax-evasion.
5 *Irish Times*, 10 December 2016. http://www.irishtimes.com/news/politics/miriam-lord-s-week-gerry-adams-tries-to-have-it-both-ways-1.2900389.
6 *Irish Times*, 10 December 2016. http://www.irishtimes.com/opinion/editorial/the-killing-of-brian-stack-a-question-of-credibility-for-gerry-adams-1.2899949.

Chapter 30

1 Adams, *Before the Dawn*, p. 149.
2 Adams, *Before the Dawn*, p. 256.
3 *Mail on Sunday*, 5 February 2017.
4 *New York Times*, 1 February 1994.

Bibliography

Adams, Dominic, *Faoi Ghlas* (lulu.com, 2016)

Adams, Gerry, *A Farther Shore: Ireland's Long Road to Peace* (New York, 2003)

——, *An Irish Eye* (Dingle, 2007)

——, *Before the Dawn: An Autobiography* (London, 1996)

——, *Cage Eleven* (Dingle, 1990)

——, *Falls Memories* (Dingle, 1982)

——, *Peace in Ireland: A Broad Analysis of the Present Situation* (Belfast, 1976)

——, *The Politics of Irish Freedom* (Dingle, 1986)

——, *The Street and Other Stories* (Dingle, 1992)

Alonso, Rogelio, *The IRA and Armed Struggle* (London, 2007)

Beresford, David, *Ten Men Dead: The Story of the Irish Hunger Strike* (London, 1987)

Bishop, Patrick and Mallie, Eamonn, *The Provisional IRA* (London, 1987; 1988; 1992)

Bowyer Bell, J., *The Irish Troubles: A Generation of Violence 1967–1992* (Dublin, 1993)

Cash, John D., *Identity, Ideology and Conflict: The Structuration of Politics in Northern Ireland* (Cambridge, 1996)

Clarke, Liam, *Broadening the Battlefield: The H-Blocks and the Rise of Sinn Féin* (Dublin, 1987)

Collins, Eamon, *Killing Rage* (London, 1998)

De Baroid, Ciaran, *Ballymurphy and the Irish War* (London, 1989)

de Silva, the Rt Hon. Sir Desmond, QC, The Report of the Patrick Finucane Review, December 2012

Devlin, Paddy, *Straight Left: An Autobiography* (Belfast, 1993)

FitzGerald, Garret, *All in a Life* (Dublin, 1991)

Hanley, Brian and Millar, Scott, *The Lost Revolution: The Story of the Official IRA and the Workers' Party* (London, 2010)

Hennessey, Thomas, *Hunger Strike: Margaret Thatcher's Battle with the IRA: 1980–1981* (Sallins, 2014)

Hermon, Sir John, *Holding the Line: An Autobiography* (Dublin, 1997)

Holland, Jack and Phoenix, Susan, *Phoenix: Policing the Shadows: The Secret War Against Terrorism in Northern Ireland* (London, 1996)

Keena, Colm, *Gerry Adams, A Biography* (Dublin, 1990)

McGuire, Maria, *To Take Arms: A Year in the Provisional IRA* (London, 1973)

McKearney, Tommy, *The Provisional IRA: From Insurrection to Parliament* (London, 2011)

McKittrick, David et al., *Lost Lives: The Stories of the Men, Women and Children Who Died as a Result of the Northern Ireland Troubles* (Edinburgh, 1998)

Bibliography

McIntyre, Anthony, *Good Friday: The Death of Irish Republicanism* (New York, 2008)

Moloney, Ed, *A Secret History of the IRA* (London, 2003)

——, *Voices from the Grave: Two Men's War in Ireland* (London, 2011)

Moore, Charles, *Margaret Thatcher: The Authorised Biography* (London, 2013)

Morrison, Danny, *Then the Walls Came Down: A Prison Journal* (Cork, 1999)

O'Doherty, Malachi, *The Telling Year: Belfast 1972* (Dublin, 2008)

——, *The Trouble With Guns: Republican Strategy and the Provisional IRA* (Belfast, 1998)

O'Rawe, Richard, *Blanketmen: An Untold Story of the H-Block Hunger Strike* (Dublin, 2005)

——, *Afterlives: The Hunger Strike and the Secret Offer That Changed Irish History* (Dublin, 2010)

Powell, Jonathan, *Great Hatred, Little Room: Making Peace in Northern Ireland* (London, 2009)

Rolston, Bill, *Children of the Revolution: The Lives of Sons and Daughters of Activists in Northern Ireland* (Derry, 2011)

Sharrock, David and Devenport, Mark, *Man of War, Man of Peace? The Unauthorised Biography of Gerry Adams* (London, 1997)

Smith, William 'Plum', *Inside Man: Loyalists of Long Kesh – the Untold Story* (Newtownards, 2014)

Sutton, Malcolm, *Bear in Mind These Dead: An Index of Deaths from the Conflict in Ireland, 1969–1993* (Belfast, 1994)

Tírghrá (Dublin, 2002)

Urban, Mark, *Big Boys' Rules: The SAS and the Secret Struggle Against the IRA* (London, 1992)

Index

pl. refers to an illustration in the plates section.

Index

Robinson, Peter, 320, 323
Robinson, Samuel, 79
Rogers, Peter, 156–7, 287
Rolston, Bill, 122, 123
Rooney, Patrick, 39
Roy, Herbert, 40
RTE, 219, 220, 279
Ruane, Caitríona, 250
RUC (Royal Ulster Constabulary): armoured
  vehicles, 38, 202; Belfast rioting, 37–8;
  care units for rape victims, 307; casualties,
  78, 202, 234; Claudy car bombs, 92; GA's
  raincoat, 27, 30; IRA attacks, 202; Máiría
  Cahill case, 304, 307; relationship with
  loyalists, 52, 181; Special Branch, 181, 201,
  205, 207–8, 287, 328

St Andrews Agreement, 252, 318
St Finian's School, Falls Road, 15–16
St Mary's Christian Brothers' School,
  Barrack Street, 16–18, 24
Sands, Bobby: death, 148–9, 164; 'dirty
  protest', 140; hunger strike, 147, 148–9;
  hunger strike strategy, 145–6; internment,
  103; OC, 144, 145; parliamentary seat, 148,
  163, 164; relationship with GA, 103, 327–8
Saville Inquiry, 80, 331
Scappaticci, Freddie, 172, 226–7
Scotsman, 240
SDLP (Social Democratic and Labour
  Party): ceasefire policy, 72; child abuse
  reporting issue, 273; dialogue with
  Sinn Féin, 196–7, 224; founders, 32,
  61; Hillsborough Castle talks, 235–6;
  hunger strike issues, 161; leadership, 195;
  opposition to internment, 66; power-
  sharing negotiations, 113; relationship
  with Sinn Féin, 195–7; supporters, 66,
  195, 235–6; West Belfast seat, 179, 212;
  withdrawal from Stormont, 66
Semtex, 202, 229
Shane (dog), 68–9, 99
Shankill Butchers, 133
Sharrock, David, 101, 181
Sheridan, Peter, 274
Shevlin, Myles, 80
Shillington, Graham, 21
Shorland armoured cars ('whippets'), 38
Short, John, 126, 127
Short Strand violence, 54–5
Sinn Féin: abstention issue, 197–9, 234;
  Ard Fheis, 184; Ard Fheis (1970), 44, 47;

Ard Fheis (1977), 137; Ard Fheis (1986),
  197–9; Ard Fheis (1994), 268; Ard Fheis
  (2005), 248–50; Ard Fheis (2015), 313;
  Ballymurphy, 45; banned from elections,
  22; barred from airwaves, 219; campaign
  for GA's release, 288; coalition issue, 314;
  Connolly House, 174, 219; dialogue with
  SDLP, 196–7; Divis Street office shooting,
  213; Dublin peace rally, 220; election
  campaigns, 170, 197, 203; election results
  (2017), 324; endorsement of policing,
  252, 269, 303; established, 170; GA's role,
  2, 45, 138, 170, 184, 185, 193, 197, 201, 288,
  312, 314–15, 325; growth, 226, 228–139,
  311, 314; IRA relations, 129, 169–72, 175,
  197–200, 226, 241–2, 314; Irish language,
  317–18; Irish unification possibility,
  311; leadership, 201, 314–15; left out of
  power-sharing settlement (1974), 113;
  peace process, 234; peace process effects,
  228; police spy in, 227, 295; policies on
  abolition of Seanad, 281; policy objectives,
  171–2, 197–200, 314–15; political machine,
  175–6; political units, 169–70; shooting
  at offices, 3; split, 199–200, 234; Stormont
  executive, 252; view of police, 288–9; view
  of violence, 238–9; youth movement, 293;
  see also Republican Sinn Féin
Smith, M. S., 326
Smith, William 'Plum', 109
South, Sean, 20
Special Branch, RUC, 181, 201, 205, 207–8,
  287, 328
Special Category Status, 135, 138, 139, 141,
  143, 150
Spence, Augustus (Gusty) Andrew, 25
Spotlight (BBC programme), 309
Stack, Austin, 276, 277–84, 322–3, pl.
Stack, Brian, 276–80, 282, 322
Stack, Oliver, 276, 277–83, 323
Steele, Frank, 74–6, 78–80, 139
Steele, Jimmy, 19–20
Stone, Michael, 210–11
Storey, Bobby, 93, 286, 288, 293, 308, 313–14
Stormont: ban on parades, 57; closure of
  pubs, 43; debate on Máiría Cahill affair,
  332; experimental assembly, 197; language
  issues, 317–18, 324; parliament building,
  13; Sinn Féin–DUP executive, 252, 324;
  Special Powers, 65, 66; suspension of
  parliament, 72; withdrawal of SDLP, 66
Sullivan, Jim, 61–2